T0304869

INTENT
TO
DESTROY

ALSO BY EUGENE FINKEL

Bread and Autocracy: Food, Politics, and Security in Putin's Russia
(as coauthor)
Reform and Rebellion in Weak States (as coauthor)
Ordinary Jews: Choice and Survival During the Holocaust
Coloured Revolutions and Authoritarian Reactions (as coeditor)

INTENT TO DESTROY

RUSSIA'S TWO-HUNDRED-YEAR QUEST TO DOMINATE UKRAINE

EUGENE FINKEL

LONDON

First published in Great Britain in 2024 by Basic Books UK
An imprint of John Murray Press

1

Copyright © Evgeny Finkel 2024

A CIP catalogue record for this title is available from the British Library

Hardback ISBN 9781399809719
Trade Paperback ISBN 9781399809726
ebook ISBN 9781399809740

Typeset in Minion Pro

Printed and bound in Great Britain by Clays Ltd, Elcograf S.p.A.

John Murray Press policy is to use papers that are natural, renewable and
recyclable products and made from wood grown in sustainable forests. The logging
and manufacturing processes are expected to conform to the environmental
regulations of the country of origin.

Carmelite House
50 Victoria Embankment
London EC4Y 0DZ

www.basicbooks.uk

John Murray Press, part of Hodder & Stoughton Limited
An Hachette UK company

The authorised representative in the EEA is Hachette Ireland, 8 Castlecourt
Centre, Dublin 15, D15 XTP3, Ireland (email: info@hbgi.ie)

To my grandmother, Lina Guler, born in Kyiv, 1931.
May she live long enough to see her hometown at peace again.

CONTENTS

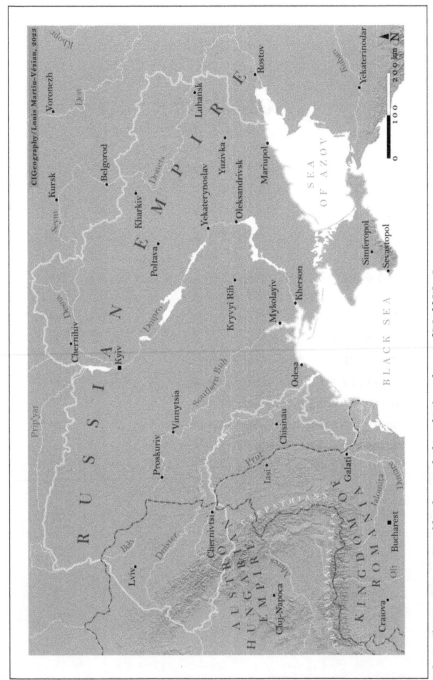

Ukraine (current international borders marked in white) on the eve of World War I

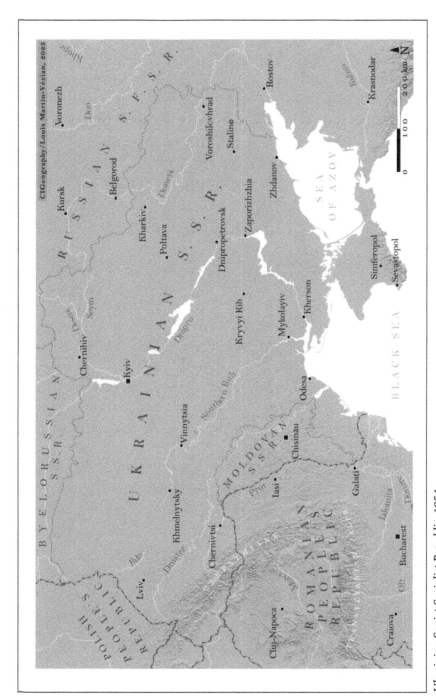

Ukrainian Soviet Socialist Republic, 1954

Ukraine on the eve of the Russian invasion, February 24, 2022

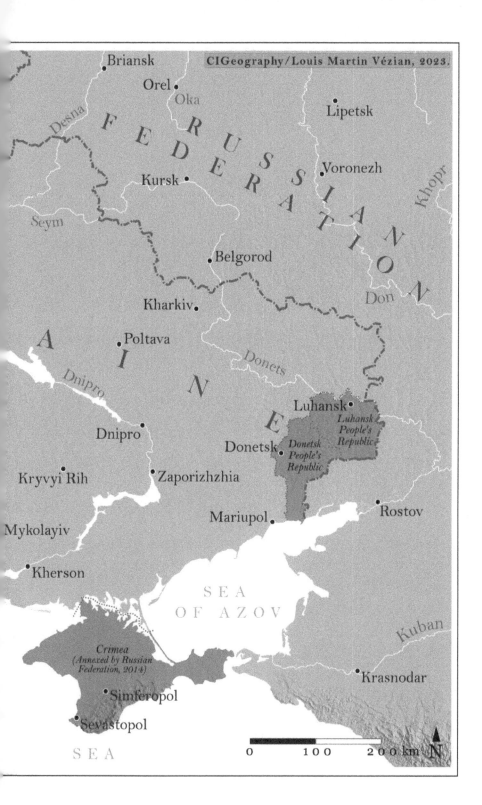

Briansk

Orel

Oka

Lipetsk

Desna

F E D E R A R U S S I A T I O N

Kursk

Voronezh

Khopr

Seym

Belgorod

Kharkiv

Don

Poltava

A I N E

Dnipro

Donets

Luhansk

Luhansk People's Republic

Dnipro

Donetsk

Donetsk People's Republic

Kryvyi Rih

Zaporizhzhia

Rostov

Mykolayiv

Mariupol

Kherson

S E A
O F   A Z O V

Kuban

Crimea
(Annexed by Russian Federation, 2014)

Krasnodar

Simferopol

Sevastopol

S E A

0   100   200 km   N

CIGeography/Louis Martin Vézian, 2023.

A NOTE ON PLACES
AND NAMES

Every place in Ukraine has multiple names and ways of spelling. The Ukrainian L'viv is L'vov to the Russians and Lwów to the Poles. Jews, until World War II the city's second largest community, called it Lemberik, and the Austro-Hungarian government that ruled it before 1918 knew it as Lemberg. For all places within the internationally recognized borders of Ukraine and for people who have lived there, I use the Ukrainian name and follow the Library of Congress transliteration rules unless there is an internationally recognized spelling or these people explicitly consider themselves Russians. Thus, Chernobyl Nuclear Plant even though it is Chornobyl in Ukrainian, and Nikita Khrushchev rather than Mykyta Khrushchov. Where possible, I also tried to eliminate apostrophes and other diacritical marks. Readers who know Ukrainian will easily recognize the place or the name even without these marks, and those who do not will not be affected by this decision. All translations from Ukrainian and Russian are mine unless indicated otherwise.

INTRODUCTION

"R ussians and Ukrainians [are] one people—a single whole," the leader of Russia proclaimed. Ukrainians are "Russian brothers who are being freed," declared the Russian commander in chief before going to war. Moscow was invading to protect "brothers of the same blood, Ukrainians," claimed the Kremlin. Each of these declarations could have been made by Russian president Vladimir Putin prior to the massive invasion of Ukraine on February 24, 2022. Yet only one was. The other two date to 1914 and 1939, and without deep historical knowledge, it is difficult to distinguish Putin's words from 2021 (the first statement) from those made by Russian imperial (second) and Soviet (third) officials at the beginning of the two world wars.

Russia's full-scale invasion of Ukraine is the single most important event in Europe since the collapse of the Soviet Union in 1991. It is also arguably the major global geopolitical development since 9/11. Putin's explicit goal is to dismantle the Western-dominated, post–Cold War global order and reestablish the Kremlin's domination over much of Eurasia. Russia cannot achieve this without controlling Ukraine, "the gates of Europe." The Russian invasion has reshaped relations between the world's great powers and redefined the nature of existing alliances

1

and international organizations, such as the North Atlantic Treaty Organization (NATO) and the European Union (EU). It also seems to be inescapable—on television, on social media, at sporting competitions, on theater stages, in dinnertime conversations. This is how 1939 might have looked, had the internet and cell phones existed eighty years ago. Russian violence against Ukraine will continue to shape European and global politics for decades to come.[1]

The Russian invasion has also brought mass murder back to Ukraine. It has already killed tens, likely hundreds, of thousands of soldiers and civilians, displaced millions, revived the threat of nuclear conflict between Russia and the West, and it might yet unleash a global famine. The Russian state targets civilian infrastructure, destroys Ukrainian identity and culture, and intentionally kills, tortures, and rapes civilians. More than seven hundred thousand Ukrainian children have been transferred from Russian-occupied territories in Ukraine to Russia proper. There, they will be reeducated and taught to be Russians. Russian propagandists and state officials openly talk about destroying Ukraine and Ukrainians, killing millions, drowning and burning children.

Genocide and crimes against humanity are, sadly, found frequently throughout Ukraine's history. Indeed, both concepts became enshrined in international law thanks to scholars from Lviv, a city in western Ukraine and my birthplace. Raphael Lemkin, a graduate of Lviv University when the city belonged to Poland, coined the term "genocide," a combination of the Greek word *genos* (a race) with the Latin *cide* (killing). For Lemkin, genocide was a coordinated effort to annihilate national groups by destroying the very foundations of their existence. The United Nations (UN) later defined the term as "acts committed with intent to destroy, in whole or in part, a national, ethnical, racial or religious group, as such." Sir Hersch Lauterpacht, a British legal scholar who grew up in Lviv, played the key role in developing the concept of crimes against humanity, which now encompass acts such as murder, rape, torture, or deportation "committed as part of a widespread or systematic attack directed against any civilian population."[2]

2

The Russian violence against Ukraine is neither sudden nor unprecedented. The ongoing aggression, the mass murder, and the ideas that undergird them did not spring into being in 2022. Rather, they are products of a two-hundred-year-old history. Since the mid-nineteenth century, dominating Ukraine and denying Ukrainians an independent identity, let alone a state, have been the cornerstone of imperial, Soviet, and, eventually, post-Soviet Russian policies. These policies rejected and suppressed the very existence of the Ukrainian language, history, and culture. Even during the brief periods in which Soviet and post-Soviet governments in Moscow tried to move away from these ideas, they persisted among large segments of Russian society and became policy once again when new leaders arose. Russian emperors, Joseph Stalin, and now Putin have been intent on destroying Ukraine as a state, as an identity, and as an idea. At times, the goal of the political destruction of Ukraine morphed into physical annihilation of Ukraine's residents. Massacres, deportations, famine, and torture are time-tested methods of Russian domination over Ukraine and its residents.

Russia's quest to dominate and, occasionally, physically destroy Ukraine has long been driven by two key factors: identity and security. The idea of the shared origin and fraternity of Russians and Ukrainians (and Belorussians) is a staple of Russian self-perception and historiography. Russian elites and intellectuals see their state as the sole heir of Kyivan Rus'—a medieval polity that encompassed most of contemporary Ukraine, Belarus, and western Russia—and thus as the rightful inheritors of Kyiv's geographic and spiritual legacy. Being Russian implies a special relationship with—and very often a sense of entitlement to—at least some parts of Ukraine and its past.

The second key factor is security, first and foremost the security of Russia's autocratic regime. Insurgencies, subversive ideals, and utopian philosophies threatening the stability of successive Russian and Soviet governments have found fertile ground in Ukraine from which to spread into Russia. Nothing scares a Russian autocrat more than a democratic and free Ukraine, because if Ukrainians can build a democracy, then the supposedly fraternal (from the Kremlin's perspective) Russians might too.

National security concerns have also played a role. The "gates of Europe" open both ways, and many a Western invader has passed through Ukraine to attack Russia. Finally, Ukraine's fertile soil was crucial to feeding and funding the Russian and Soviet empires, necessitating their control over Ukraine.

Combined, identity, security, and the interaction between them have driven Russia's policies toward Ukraine since the nineteenth century. During some periods, identity politics reigned supreme, in others security took precedence, but both were almost always present.

Identity and security concerns, however, do not automatically translate into actions. Notions of identity are a necessary foundation for Russia's quest for domination of Ukraine, but identity alone cannot explain specific policies and decisions. There is no straightforward, pre-determined path from believing that all Russians ought to live under Moscow's rule to mass murder. Nostalgia, nationalist resentment, and a sense that one's nation is unjustly divided by borders are not cultural trends unique to Russia, and these feelings do not necessarily lead to violence. National security concerns can also be addressed in multiple ways, and most do not involve invading neighboring states and annexing their territory.[3]

The story of Russia and Ukraine is therefore not merely a story of society-level factors and historical processes but also a story of the choices people make. That Russia and Russians would be deeply interested in Ukraine is natural considering history and geography; that they would, time and again, *decide* to destroy Ukraine is not.

The story of Ukraine is also the story of all the groups living there, not just ethnic Ukrainians. The defining feature of the lands lying between Western Europe and Russia is diversity. Ukraine, as a quintessential and literal borderland, historically did not just separate but also blended nations, languages, religions, cultures, and empires. Ukrainians, Poles, Russians, Jews, Greeks, Tatars, Germans, Bulgarians, Armenians, Hungarians, Romanians, Serbs, Swedes, Turks, Roma, Czechs, and other communities called the lands that now constitute Ukraine home. Stalinist repression,

World War II, and postwar violence shattered many of these communities, but Ukraine's diversity, though greatly diminished, remains.

Often this diversity was an advantage, but at times of crisis, ethnic, religious, and linguistic differences would tear the region apart in spasms of violence, turning Ukraine into what historian Timothy Snyder famously labeled "bloodlands." Appreciation of Ukraine's diversity is crucial to understanding the region and Russian-Ukrainian relations. Ukraine's diversity allowed Russian and Soviet governments to practice a "divide and repress" strategy that leveraged local cleavages to recruit supporters for Russian rule and ensured the acquiescence of large parts of the population. Control over Ukraine depended upon a ready pool of local supporters who sustained and promoted the Russian-dominated political order. Often these people were local elites, but, when needed, imperial, Soviet, and post-Soviet Russian governments would also rely on other groups.

Thus, the *Holodomor*, the man-made famine of 1932–1933, killed millions in the ethnically Ukrainian countryside but largely spared the Russian-speaking cities. The brutal Soviet counterinsurgency and mass deportations of the 1940s were limited to Ukraine's westernmost regions and Crimea. The oppression of Jews and the expulsion of Crimean Tatars did not threaten the Slavs, while the attacks on the Ukrainian national movement, language, and culture typically left minorities unmolested. At any given time, there were substantial parts of Ukraine's population that were safe, prioritized over their neighbors, and content with Moscow's or Saint Petersburg's dominance.

Russia and Ukraine both trace their origins to the Kyivan Rus', a medieval state centered on Kyiv, Ukraine's current capital. As much as anything, Russia's violence against Ukraine is about history and inheritance, both physical and symbolic. In the thirteenth century, a Mongol invasion destroyed the Kyivan state, and its western parts, including Kyiv, were soon swallowed by the Polish-Lithuanian Commonwealth. While Kyiv declined, Moscow, originally a tiny and unimportant principality, prospered and grew stronger. After breaking free of Mongol rule, Moscow elites started viewing themselves as the rightful (and sole) heirs of both the Kyivan Rus' and the Orthodox Christian Byzantium. Moscow's territorial expansion quickly turned it into a formidable Eurasian power. Meanwhile, in Ukraine, a mid-seventeenth-century Cossack uprising against Poland led to the creation of a semi-independent Ukrainian polity in parts of what is now eastern and central Ukraine. Too weak to protect their rule against the larger and stronger Poland, Cossack elites in 1654 swore allegiance to the Moscow tsar. Kyiv came under Russian rule, and the region eventually became officially known as "Little Russia" (whereas Moscow's original domain was referred to as "Great Russia").

Throughout the eighteenth century, Russia continued expanding. In several wars it defeated the Ottoman Empire and conquered today's southern Ukraine, annexed Crimea, and, together with Prussia and Habsburg Austria, partitioned Poland, thus bringing almost all of Ukraine under the Romanov empire's control. By the nineteenth century, the Russian Empire ruled all Kyivan Rus' lands apart from the Austrian-controlled Galicia, now western Ukraine. But repeated Polish uprisings, aimed at regaining lost independence and bringing large parts of Ukraine back under Warsaw's rule, threatened Russian control of the region. In response, the Russian government began promoting ideas that legitimized the Russian ownership of Ukraine. A historical narrative that emphasized the shared origins of the Great and Little Russians and positioned the Russian Empire as the successor of Kyivan Rus', and thus the rightful owner of its patrimony, became a staple of official Russian historiography and identity. Importantly, this narrative was not simply imported from Saint Petersburg and shoved down the throats of Little Russians; people hailing from or living in what is now Ukraine and whom we would now label as Ukrainians played an important role in articulating the ideas that undergirded Russian perceptions of itself and of Ukraine.

In several short decades during the nineteenth century, these perceptions of shared origin along with Russia's increasingly repressive nature and turn toward narrow, exclusionary nationalism transformed the celebration of historical unity of two fraternal yet distinct groups into a campaign of forced Russification. Starting in the 1860s, the publication of Ukrainian-language books was first significantly restricted and then virtually banned altogether. The Little Russian elites, intellectuals, and small but growing middle class had to either become Russians without adjectives or face persecution. Many chose the former option, but a small group of activists and intellectuals rebuffed the Russian identity and began promoting a distinct Ukrainian one that rejected the myth of the shared origin and fate of Russians and Ukrainians. In doing so, these activists joined and were assisted by the rapid development of Ukrainian culture, identity, and political life that was happening across the border in Austro-Hungarian Galicia. The stakes of this identity conflict were high for the Russian Empire; because of Ukraine's size, strategic location, and economic importance, the government in Saint Petersburg perceived the Russification of Ukraine as essential to the survival of both the Romanov empire and the Russian nation.

When World War I broke out in 1914, Ukraine became one of its main theaters. The Russian Empire viewed the war as an opportunity to solve the Ukrainian question once and for all by occupying and annexing the Ukrainian-majority Austrian regions of eastern Galicia and Bukovyna and destroying the Ukrainian culture, language, and political activism in these areas. The Great War was also a watershed moment, when Russian policies expanded beyond the persecution of individuals and targeting of Ukrainian language and culture to large-scale physical violence against entire communities. Mass expulsions, pogroms, and looting now went hand in hand with banning Ukrainian-language publications, targeting culture, and forcing Galician Ukrainians, most of whom were Greek Catholics, to convert to Orthodox Christianity.

The Great War destroyed the Russian Empire, and Ukraine became ground zero for the wars that followed the empire's collapse. Millions perished during the years of chaos and violence that included pogroms, famine, economic ruin, disease, warfare, and massacres by different armies, militias, and bands fighting it out in Ukraine. The disintegration of the Russian Empire also gave Ukraine a chance to establish an independent state, the Ukrainian People's Republic (UNR). Yet Ukrainian statehood did not last, in large part due to internal weakness and divisions. Decades of extensive Russification meant that the urban professional and working classes—the backbone of government administration and the modern economy—were mostly hostile to the idea of independent Ukraine, and pogroms perpetrated by the Ukrainian government forces alienated Ukraine's large and important Jewish community.

As if internal divisions were not enough, Ukraine was also facing multiple external enemies. In Galicia, an attempt to create a Ukrainian state failed after a bitter war against Poland. The two main adversaries in the Russian civil war, the Communist Reds and the anti-Communist Whites, were both determined to destroy the UNR. For Vladimir Lenin and his Communist regime, control over Ukraine was crucial for security reasons. The Reds needed Ukraine as the breadbasket to feed Russia's cities, as a buffer to protect Moscow from Western invasion, and as a springboard to export the Communist revolution to Warsaw, Berlin, and Paris. The Whites were committed to the idea of "one, indivisible Russia" and despised the Ukrainian national movement even more than they hated the Communists. For many Whites, a Communist Russia that controlled Ukraine was preferable to a White one that did not.

After the Reds' conquest of Ukraine and defeat of the Whites, the Soviet Union, as the new Communist state became known, sought to accommodate the supporters of Ukrainian identity by promoting Ukrainian language, education, and culture, as long as the content was compatible with Communist ideology. But Joseph Stalin, who replaced Lenin in 1924, was hostile to all things Ukrainian and viewed Ukrainian language and culture as inherently anti-Soviet. Ruthless and paranoid, Stalin set out to turn Ukraine into "a model republic" and the bastion of Moscow-based Soviet power. Forced Russification returned with gusto, and Soviet Ukrainian writers, artists, and scholars were mercilessly repressed. Stalin's collectivization of agriculture and food procurement policies, which were heavily biased against Ukrainian peasants, produced a massive famine, the Holodomor, in which up to five million people perished. For Stalin, famine, repression, and state terror were tools to eliminate any threats to Kremlin rule by destroying Ukraine's potentially unreliable social and ethnic groups one by one through the "divide and repress" strategy.

In 1939, Stalin teamed up with Adolf Hitler to invade and, once again, partition Poland. This invasion brought all Kyivan Rus' lands under Moscow's rule and united Polish-ruled western Ukraine with the Soviet one. World War II violence, the Holocaust, and the ethnic cleansing of the Polish minority—first by the Ukrainian nationalist forces and then by the Soviet government—reduced Ukraine's diversity even further. Postwar deportations and repression of Ukrainian nationalists in Galicia finally turned Ukraine into a reliable, loyal, and increasingly Russian-speaking part of the Russia-dominated Union of Soviet Socialist Republics (USSR).

After almost seventy years of Soviet rule, the built-in flaws of the Soviet economic model, mismanagement, corruption, and repression destroyed the USSR. As the Soviet Union barreled toward disintegration and Ukraine's independence became increasingly likely, Russian nationalism reared its head. The tsarist-era perceptions of historical unity and shared origin and fate of Russians and Ukrainians had become fully ingrained during the Soviet times; most Russians viewed themselves and Ukrainians as practically indistinguishable and Ukraine as an extension of Russia. The prospect of suddenly losing Ukraine was simply too painful for many Russians. This fear of loss was especially acute with regards to eastern Ukraine, which had a substantial number of ethnic Russians, and Crimea, a region that occupied pride of place in Russian and Soviet myths of martial glory.

When the USSR collapsed in 1991 and Russia and Ukraine went their separate ways, the return of Ukraine under Russian dominance became the dream of Russian Communists, nationalists, and conservatives. These groups despised democracy and sought to recreate the Russian Empire or the USSR, a resurrection that would be impossible without controlling, and, if needed, destroying Ukraine. Even among Russian liberals, many viewed Ukraine as an artificial state and some harbored neo-imperialist attitudes.

Yet Ukraine, while young, inexperienced, and struggling, was now an independent country, and with every passing day its distinct character, national identity, and differences from Russia became more entrenched. This attachment to Ukraine's statehood was especially pronounced among the younger generations who grew up in independent Ukraine, knew no other homeland, and did not feel nostalgic for the USSR. These people, and the growing Ukrainian middle class more broadly, wished to live in a prosperous, European, and democratic country rather than be junior partners in the Kremlin's autocratic and repressive Russian World. When Russia invaded, these "independence generations" would lead the fight to save Ukraine.[4]

Russia's first president, Boris Yeltsin, did not let imperial restoration and conquest become official policy, but when Vladimir Putin replaced Yeltsin in 2000, Russia's policies toward Ukraine gradually changed. Putin, a product of Soviet security services, was deeply nostalgic for the lost empire. Increasingly nationalist, he set out to restore Russia's greatness. Putin also dismantled what little remained of Russia's democratic institutions and, over time, transformed Russia into a full-blown autocracy. When, in 2004–2005, the citizens of Ukraine took to the streets to protest a stolen election and prevented Putin's preferred candidate, Viktor Yanukovych, from becoming president, the Kremlin began viewing Ukraine as a key threat to regime survival. The West, Putin believed, was using Ukraine as a base to undermine his rule, and if Ukrainians could defeat an autocratic takeover, then Russians might too. The anti-Ukrainian phobias of the Kremlin, the nationalists, and the Communists converged.

Yet, from the Kremlin's perspective, if Ukraine could be controlled it did not need to be destroyed. In 2010, Yanukovych came to power by winning a free and fair election. In 2013, his increasingly dictatorial tendencies, extreme corruption, and decision to eschew a pro-European path in favor of membership in a Moscow-led alliance sparked a revolt among Ukrainians who rejected this autocratic and Moscow-dominated future.

In February 2014, after the Euromaidan protests—or, as Ukrainians call it, the Revolution of Dignity—a violent standoff that left more than a hundred protesters dead, Yanukovych fled Ukraine.

For Putin, the ousting of Yanukovych was a watershed. Ukraine could no longer be controlled, and thus the Kremlin moved to dismantle it. While many histories of the Russian war on Ukraine begin with the February 2022 attack, in fact the invasion started in 2014. Immediately after the Euromaidan's triumph, Russian troops took over Crimea, and in March 2014 Russia annexed the peninsula. Russian nationalists, adventurers, and mercenaries with deep ties to the Russian government and security services then moved to eastern and southern Ukraine to join forces with local pro-Russian activists and foment violence in the hope of creating New Russia (*Novorossiya*). Pro-Russian sentiments did exist in these regions, but most Ukrainians did not wish to become Russians and the Novorossiya project faltered, with the exception of parts of the Donbas region that were captured by squads of armed Russians. When Ukraine moved to quash this armed insurrection, the Kremlin sent the Russian army to save Novorossiya from defeat while flatly denying any involvement. In the meantime, the Russian propaganda machine went into overdrive, depicting Ukraine as a fictional entity, its government as a NATO-controlled illegitimate junta, and its population as Russians who are oppressed by violent, neo-Nazi Ukrainian nationalists and who pine for a return to Moscow's fold.

The Russian annexation of Crimea and the war in the Donbas shook and mobilized Ukrainians. Over the two decades of independence, most citizens of Ukraine had developed a patriotic attachment to their country. Many of those previously sympathetic to Russia were offended by the invasion, Putin's blatant lies, and Kremlin propaganda. To better resist the Russian threat, the Ukrainian government that replaced Yanukovych introduced multiple reforms, strengthened governance, improved trust in institutions, and reduced corruption. Ukraine's diversity and cleavages did not disappear, but a broad civic national identity became dominant in response to the existential danger. Ukrainians also wanted peace and in 2019 elected

Volodymyr Zelensky—a Russian-speaking Jewish actor from the country's south who was popular in Russia and spent years working there—as president in the hope of negotiating a compromise with Putin. The Kremlin, however, did not want a compromise; it wanted Ukraine, and even Zelensky was not willing to give Putin de facto control over the country.

By 2021, a combination of a stalemate in the Donbas, Putin's slide toward extreme Russian nationalism, his detachment from alternative sources of information because of COVID-19-induced isolation, and growing concerns about the aging dictator's historical legacy all combined to convince him to solve the Ukrainian question once and for all.

On February 24, 2022, Russia launched a massive invasion of Ukraine. The Kremlin envisioned an easy victory, after which Ukraine's political and social elites would be either killed or repressed and a new puppet government would turn Ukraine into Russia's client state. High on their own supply of propaganda and oblivious to what Ukraine had become since 2014, the advancing Russian troops expected to be greeted as liberators and did not anticipate much resistance from the presumably weak and divided Ukrainian state. But instead of flowers and welcoming ceremonies, Russian forces were met with widespread, determined, and successful defiance from the overwhelming majority of Ukraine's population—Russian and Ukrainian speakers, Orthodox and Greek Catholics, Muslims and Jews.

Being Ukrainian in a civic, political sense is a deliberate choice. This choice means rejecting the Kremlin's deep-seated belief in its right to dominate Ukraine and its certitude about the unity of Russian and Ukrainian people. From the Russian perspective, Ukraine's defiance represented a rejection of the natural order of things and a betrayal that could not be tolerated. The punishment for this betrayal was violence. Unable to destroy Ukraine, Russian troops switched to killing Ukrainians. Unlike Jews during the Holocaust or the Tutsi in Rwanda, Ukrainians are being persecuted not because they were *born* different but because they *chose* to be different. The invasion became a genocide, deadly violence intended to destroy Ukraine as a state and Ukrainians as a national group because they dared to chart an independent path.

————

I grew up in Soviet Ukraine during the perestroika and then lived in Israel, so as a scholar I had always been interested in how societies and people respond to extreme situations: war, genocide, state collapse, and rapid change. As a professor of international affairs at Johns Hopkins University, I wrote and coauthored three books and multiple articles on past violence and genocide: the Holocaust, the legacies of World War II, and rebellions in the nineteenth-century Russian Empire. I've also written widely on contemporary politics—autocracy, national identity, political use of past tragedies, strategic thinking, and reforms—in post-Soviet Russia and Ukraine. Never did I imagine that my expertise in past mass murder and post-1991 Russia and Ukraine would eventually intersect, yet the Russian invasion did just that. When Russia invaded, my experience helped me to understand the nature of Russian violence early on. To the best of my knowledge, I was the first expert to argue, in an April 6, 2022, article in the *Washington Post*, that Russia's actions—a combination of eliminationist rhetoric on state media and mass murder conducted by the Russian troops in northern Ukraine—meet the legal definition of genocide.[5]

The idea that Russia seeks to destroy the Ukrainian nation as such is now generally accepted among scholars of genocide. But the genocidal violence that started in 2022 is only a snapshot of the much longer Russian effort to dominate Ukraine. Other books on the Russian invasion typically focus on the most recent events or present blow-by-blow reportage, but I believe that it is impossible to understand the invasion of 2022 and the ideas that drive Putin without going back decades, even centuries, to the origins of Russia's intent to destroy Ukraine. Even more crucially, without comprehending these ideas we cannot hope to prevent future violence once the current war is over. At the same time, nationalist visions and historical myths alone cannot explain when mass violence erupts, why people fight, and how humans turn into genocidal perpetrators. For that, we need to rely on social science research and evidence from other genocides, such as the Holocaust or Rwanda. In short, to understand Russian violence and Ukrainian resistance, we need to combine a historical narrative that goes back to the origins of the conflict with insights from political science, sociology, and research on genocide. This is exactly what I aim to do.[6]

This book is also how I fight back. On June 16, 2022, when I was spending most of my days reading, speaking, and writing about Russian violence against civilians in Ukraine, Dutch security services revealed that an undercover Russian military intelligence (GRU) officer had tried to infiltrate the International Criminal Court (ICC) and had even gotten a position at the institution. The ICC—which investigates Russia's crimes in Ukraine and which, in March 2023, issued an arrest warrant against Putin—is an important target for the GRU. The Russian spy, Sergei Cherkasov, spent years preparing for this task while living under a false identity as Brazilian citizen Victor Muller Ferreira. Victor Muller Ferreira was my student. He attended two of my small, research-intensive, master's level courses, including one on genocide. After graduation, Victor/Sergei asked me for a recommendation letter for a position at the ICC. I happily obliged. I helped a Russian spy in his task to infiltrate the ICC and potentially gain access to its investigations in Ukraine.

I have not done anything wrong; I have neither the tools nor the training to identify an extensively prepared intelligence officer. Still, the cruel irony of doing everything I could to raise awareness of Russia's violence while inadvertently helping a Russian agent tasked with harming an institution that investigates it almost broke me, physically and mentally. My job is not fighting Russian intelligence, it is research and teaching, but what's the point of being a scholar if the only nonacademics who benefit from my expertise are Russian spies?

I therefore neither claim nor wish to be a dispassionate and detached observer. My connection to Ukraine is personal. I was thirteen when I left the USSR, but Ukraine is and will always be an important part of who I am. Personal attachment might blur one's vision, but it also permits feeling things bone-deep that detached observers cannot. Major historical events are, after all, not just about abstract social processes but also about humans and the pain they inflict and suffer.

CHAPTER 1

DEEP STATES

In Ukraine, Bohdan Khmelnytsky is everywhere. "Khmelnytsky" is one of the most popular street names in the country, and a city and a region in central Ukraine are named after him. Khmelnytsky's face is on the five-hryvnia coin and note. A statue of him, sitting astride a stallion, is among the landmarks of downtown Kyiv. Such commemoration is well warranted, for Khmelnytsky led the uprising against the Polish-Lithuanian Commonwealth that created, in the mid-seventeenth century, the first recognizably Ukrainian polity. Khmelnytsky's distinguished military service to the Polish crown; his two-year stint as a captive in Ottoman Constantinople, during which he learned the Turkish language; his romance-driven conflict with a neighboring Polish landlord that triggered the chain of events that sparked the revolt; and his spectacular victories over large Polish armies quickly became the stuff of legend, in which myth is hard to clearly distinguish from historical fact. Even during his lifetime, Khmelnytsky was called "a modern-day Moses who had succeeded in leading his Rus' people" out of bondage, and for many Ukrainians, both in the past and now, Khmelnytsky is the embodiment of Ukraine's long, bloody struggle for independence.[1]

Yet Khmelnytsky is also a hero for the Russians. In 1654, unable to protect his domain from the larger and better-organized Polish-Lithuanian Commonwealth, Khmelnytsky accepted the sovereignty of Moscow's tsar, an act that paved the way for Russia's rule over the region. As the state he established melted away, Khmelnytsky gained pride of place in Russian imperial history and nationalist mythology as the leader who unified Ukraine with Russia. It was the tsarist government, not independent Ukraine, that in 1888 erected Khmelnytsky's monument in the center of Kyiv.

Communist rulers, who replaced the Romanov dynasty as Russia's overlords, were equally fond of Khmelnytsky. During World War II, the Order of Bogdan Khmelnitskii (the Russian spelling of the name) was established as a prestigious Red Army decoration, and it was the Soviet authorities who in 1954 renamed the city of Proskuriv as Khmelnytsky. The collapse of the USSR and the emergence of Ukraine as an independent state did not affect Khmelnytsky's standing among Russian nationalists. "A new unification is upon us. The spirit of Bogdan Khmelnitskii has awoken. Death to the enemies of the Russian people!" proclaimed Russian far-right ideologue Alexander Dugin in March 2014 as the Kremlin embarked on the annexation of Crimea and fomented the war in the Donbas.[2]

Khmelnytsky's legacy is just one of many examples of how Russian and Ukrainian history and identity are interwoven, forming a dense web of shared images, symbols, and personalities that are passionately claimed by both groups, states, and national histories. For each, these personalities and symbols have different meanings, send different signals, underscore often incompatible values, and prescribe conflicting policies. Russian violence in and against Ukraine is as much about the centuries-old past as it is about the present. This deep past sets the stage for the story of modern Russian-Ukrainian relations and is crucial for understanding the violence.

On February 22, 2022, less than forty-eight hours before the first columns of Russian tanks crossed Ukraine's borders, the Twitter account of the US embassy in Ukraine posted a picture that comprised two rows of images.

The top row showed a timeline of the construction of Kyiv's historical landmarks, such as Saint Sophia's Cathedral and Saint Michael's Monastery, in 996, 1011, 1070, and 1108 CE. The bottom row showed Moscow during the same years: a forest, as Russia's capital was not founded until 1147. Internet trolling might not be the most appropriate behavior for diplomats, especially if their own capital was only established in 1790, but the embassy's message was a pointed response to Putin's claim that Ukraine has never been a real state. It also underscored how crucial early history and the legacy of Kyivan Rus'—the East Slavs' medieval state—are for Russia's perception of Ukraine and of itself.[3]

The word *rus*, from which Rus' and Russia derive, is of Nordic origin and refers to "rowers": Vikings who used the rivers between the Baltic and the Black Seas to engage in commerce, plunder, and slave raids. The routes that these Vikings used in the southern parts of their journeys have been well-known since antiquity and traditionally carried grain, people, and pathogens from western Eurasia to Greece and the broader Mediterranean. To protect these trade routes, the traditional story goes, Vikings established trade posts that soon became permanent forts. These forts eventually grew into towns and chiefdoms ruled by the Scandian warrior elite, which subjugated the indigenous, predominantly Slavic population. A rival theory presents these princes as having been Slavs rather than Vikings, but whoever they were, Kyiv quickly emerged as the center of their power.[4]

Kyiv, the legend has it, was founded in 482 CE, but the first known written mention of the city is found in a tenth-century, Hebrew-language letter that eventually found its way to Cairo. Governed by Vikings, populated predominantly by Slavs, and written about by Jews, the area was already defined by diversity, contact, and conflict between different groups, religions, and cultures. Choosing between Islam, Judaism, Catholicism, and Orthodox Christianity as his new religion, Kyiv's Prince Volodymyr opted for the last, conveniently also the faith of the Byzantine Empire, the Kyivans' most powerful neighbor. According to legend, Volodymyr's baptism took place in 988 or 989 in Crimea, which gave the peninsula a special spiritual importance for Rus' Christians. But Byzantium was just one of many societies with which Kyivans interacted. The inhabitants of Kyivan Rus' traded, traveled, fought, and intermarried across western Eurasia, from contemporary Kazakhstan to the royal court of France, and from Palestine to Norway.[5]

Unfortunately, the Kyivan state perished without designating an heir, "leaving a will and putting its affairs in order," which inevitably led to long, contentious, and occasionally bloody inheritance struggles between potential successors. The reason for the sudden death of Kyivan Rus' in the mid-thirteenth century was an unstoppable force from the east: the Mongols. In 1223, a vanguard Mongol force defeated a coalition of Russian principalities and their steppe allies on the banks of the Kalka River. Several princes died in battle; the ruler of Kyiv was captured and executed. Shortly after this triumph, the Mongols left for home without completing the conquest. This brief respite ended in 1240–1241, when a new Mongol army sacked Kyiv and subjugated most of the Rus' lands. This time the Mongols stayed, establishing the Golden Horde—a powerful state centered on the Volga River. Devastated and half destroyed, Kyiv quickly declined and lost its political and economic significance for more than six hundred years.[6]

Kyiv's ruin and the Mongols' indirect and rather lenient rule—as long as the remaining Rus' princes paid their taxes and obeyed the Mongol khan's authority—created opportunities for new players in the region. Two previously minor principalities, Moscow and Tver', eventually emerged as the chief beneficiaries of the new Pax Mongolica and key rivals for Kyiv's legacy. After a series of skirmishes, rebellions, and court intrigues, the Muscovites secured the Mongols' support and prevailed over their Tver' rivals.

Rich (one prince was known primarily by the sobriquet "Moneybag"), determined, and shrewd, Muscovite rulers quickly expanded their realm. As Moscow grew, the old core of the Kyivan state declined. Never having fully recovered from the devastation wrought by the Mongols, Kyiv came under the domination of western and northern neighbors throughout the fourteenth century. Poland conquered parts of the Rus' kingdom of

Galicia-Volhynia, while the Grand Duchy of Lithuania took the rest and absorbed Kyiv and what is now central Ukraine. The transition of both political power and symbolic status from Kyiv to Moscow was completed when the seat of the metropolitan of the Orthodox Church, the highest religious authority in the Rus' lands, originally located in Kyiv, moved to Moscow in 1325.

In the late fifteenth century, the increasingly bullish Moscow challenged the Golden Horde, eventually breaking free from its dominance and replacing the Mongols as the overlords of Eurasia. Nationalist historiography and popular myths, both Russian and Soviet, depict Mongol rule as a "yoke," an era of oppressive subjugation, but the reality is different. Moscow's rise and expansion would have been impossible without the Mongols' destruction of Kyiv and the Golden Horde's support for Moscow's princes. Mongols also influenced many of Moscow's governmental and social practices, including its drive for territorial conquest and imperial outlook.[7]

This imperial self-perception was further enhanced by the fall of Constantinople, which was conquered by the Ottoman Empire in 1453. In the wake of Byzantium's demise, Moscow became the most powerful Orthodox state and, in the minds of its rulers, the Eastern Roman Empire's natural heir. For the Muscovites, the marriage between Moscow's Grand Prince Ivan III (reigned 1462–1505) and Sophia Palaeologus, the niece of the last Byzantine emperor, Constantine XI, cemented the passing of the imperial baton from Constantinople to Moscow. In 1497, the Grand Principality of Moscow, also known as Muscovy, even adopted the Byzantine double-headed eagle as its symbol.

Ivan and Sophia's grandson Ivan IV, better known as Ivan the Terrible, finally shed in 1547 the title of grand prince and crowned himself tsar. The term is a Russian variation of the Roman imperial title Caesar but also an epithet by which Russian princes previously referred to the Mongol khans. "Two Romes have fallen, the third [Moscow] stands and there will be no fourth," prophesied the Russian clergyman Philotheus in the sixteenth century. Muscovy, increasingly known as Russia, was now a rising power with a heritage that blended the Byzantine Empire, Kievan Rus', and the Golden Horde—a kingdom with a self-prescribed divine mission, confident in what it saw as a natural right to unite all Rus' lands under its rule.[8]

For Moscow's elites, expansion was destiny. But to the west and north of their realm lay two powerful neighbors: Sweden and the Polish-Lithuanian Commonwealth, which was created out of the merger between the Kingdom of Poland and the Grand Duchy of Lithuania and which controlled most of Ukraine's territory. Becoming the key Rus' principality did not automatically require immediate physical control over Kyiv, and thus Muscovy could direct its energy eastward rather than fight the powerful Poles over Ukraine. By the mid-seventeenth century, Muscovy had reached the Pacific Ocean, over 6,300 kilometers (almost 4,000 miles) east of Moscow, while Kyiv, a mere 755 kilometers (470 miles) to the southwest, was still under Polish rule. This would shortly change, because Ukraine, as Poland's eastern borderland region became unofficially known, was in turmoil.

The sixteenth and early seventeenth centuries were a period of escalating tensions and intermittent violence in Ukraine. After most of the remaining Rus' elites converted to Catholicism and adopted Polish language and culture, the commonwealth authorities gradually abandoned their initial religious tolerance and sought to convert the entire Orthodox population. The Union of Brest (1596) was a compromise, establishing the Greek Catholic (Uniate) Church, which preserved most of the Orthodox rite but recognized the authority of the pope; this failed to satisfy either side. As Catholic pressure increased, Orthodox clergy fought tooth and nail to preserve their role, identity, and privileges and increasingly looked to the coreligionist state of Muscovy for support.

Oppressive serfdom forced many Orthodox peasants to escape agricultural estates for the freedom of southern Ukraine, a vast and mostly ungoverned steppe borderland lying between the Polish-Lithuanian Commonwealth and the powerful Muslim Crimean Khanate, ruled by the Tatar descendants of Genghis Khan. There, beyond the Dnipro River rapids, outlaws, adventurers, and runaways of various backgrounds mingled to create the Cossacks: a fiercely independent, Orthodox society of professional warriors who engaged in bloody but profitable raids against neighboring powers, first and foremost the Ottoman Empire. The name "Cossack" likely derives from the Turkic *kazak*, referring to a free man or a nomad.

The Polish response to the emergence of the Cossacks was a mix of regulation, accommodation, and repression. Cossack uprisings were brutally put down, but in exchange for military service to the crown and protecting the borders against Tatar raids, Cossacks received a degree of self-governance, as well as pay and privileges. However, the number of so-called registered Cossacks covered by this arrangement was substantially lower than the overall size of the Cossack community. The size of the registry and the government's efforts to reduce it thus became a constant source of Cossack resentment and a flash point for conflict.[9]

Climate change also shaped Ukrainian politics of the era. The Little Ice Age, which reached its peak in the seventeenth century, negatively affected agricultural yields and pushed many a farmer into destitution. Dues and taxes, onerous even in good times, became unbearable as climatic conditions worsened. Religious conflict, economic resentment, and climate change were long-term sources of tension, building up and simmering underneath the surface, ready to erupt at the right provocation. It took the personal vendetta of one aggrieved Cossack officer to make them burst in 1648, unleashing an orgy of violence that also produced the first distinctively Ukrainian polity.[10]

That officer was Bohdan Khmelnytsky. Born in 1595, Khmelnytsky was an Orthodox Christian and hailed from the minor gentry. After graduating from a Jesuit school, Khmelnytsky faithfully served the Polish crown as a prominent "registered Cossack" officer and administrator. After a Polish official married Khmelnytsky's love interest, appropriated his estate, and flogged his son, who died from the wounds, Khmelnytsky turned to the Polish courts and the king for help but could not secure the return of his property. Adding insult to injury, Khmelnytsky's adversaries retaliated by arranging his imprisonment. Outraged and eager for revenge, Khmelnytsky escaped to the Cossack lands, where he was welcomed and elected as Cossack *hetman* (leader). The great Cossack uprising had begun.[11]

The Cossacks, who allied with the Crimean Khanate and drew many destitute Orthodox peasants to their ranks, quickly crushed the Polish-Lithuanian armies in two major battles at Zhovti Vody and Korsun. By the end of 1648, Cossack troops had marched across most of central Ukraine and were busy devastating Galicia and threatening Lviv in the west. Another Cossack victory in 1649 led to an agreement that established a de facto independent Ukrainian Cossack polity, which later became known as the Hetmanate. But soon the cease-fire was over, and the war continued. The revolt, in addition to large-scale regular warfare, unleashed a wave of violence against civilians.

Though the Cossacks' main grievances were directed at the Polish state and nobility, other groups were killed or plundered as well, including their Orthodox coreligionists and clergy living in the region's towns. But the main civilian victims of Cossack violence were the Jews. There were few Jews in Ukraine during the Kyivan Rus', but the Jewish population swelled when the region was incorporated into the Polish-Lithuanian Commonwealth. At a time when west European rulers were busy banishing Jews from their realms, Polish magnates offered Jews employment on their estates as tax collectors, stewards, leaseholders, and tavern keepers. Though handsomely lucrative, these lines of work inevitably pitted Jews against Orthodox peasants, for whom Jewish officials and middlemen—rather than the distant, often absentee landlords—became the embodiment of oppression. The Jews' privileged position in the local social hierarchy also reversed the traditional order of things, in which Christians were, by definition, held to be superior to members of other religions. This mix of religious prejudice and economic conflict produced passionate resentment that led to anti-Jewish violence.[12]

Rabbi Nathan Hanover of Izyaslav in Volhynia graphically described the many horrors suffered by Ukraine's Jews at the hands of the Cossacks and the peasants who joined their revolt:

Some [Jews] were skinned alive and their flesh was thrown to the dogs; some had their hands and limbs chopped off, and their bodies thrown on the highway. . . . The enemy slaughtered infants in the laps of their mothers. They were sliced into pieces like fish. They slashed the bellies of pregnant women, removed their infants and tossed them in their faces. Some women had their bellies torn open and live cats placed in them. The bellies were then sewed up. . . . Some children were pierced with spears, roasted on the fire and then brought to their mothers to be eaten. . . . Women and virgins were ravished. They lay with the women in the presence of their husbands. They seized comely women as handmaids and housekeepers, some as wives and concubines.[13]

Hanover's dramatic account likely exaggerates the graphic nature of the violence, but its scale and overall brutality are undeniable. The uprising devastated the forty-thousand-strong Ukrainian Jewish community; exact numbers of victims are unavailable, but scholars believe that eighteen thousand to twenty thousand died because of the uprising and at least six thousand left Ukraine. Thousands more became internally displaced, and many Jews were taken captive by Khmelnytsky's Crimean Tatar allies and sold into slavery. So powerful was the impact of the violence that Jewish communities throughout Europe introduced a special prayer and a dedicated day of mourning to commemorate those killed in Ukraine. A decade later, Jewish captives were still ransomed at slave markets in Istanbul and Cairo and refugees from Ukraine were turning up all over Europe, from Belgrade to Malta to Amsterdam.[14]

Hanover, who was lucky enough to survive the carnage, lost his father and became a refugee. From Ukraine, he escaped to Prague, later moved to Germany and Holland, then continued to Venice. There he published his account before moving to Livorno. Eventually Hanover made his way back east, first to what is now Romania and finally to Uherský Brod in what is now the Czech Republic; he never returned to Ukraine. Ukraine's Jewish community eventually rebounded; a century and a half later, Russian travelers would comment with a mixture of amazement and disgust on Ukraine's ethnic and religious diversity. "Greeks, Italians, Germans, French, yids (there are a lot of them here), Armenians, and a mass of Ukrainians," observed one. Yet even as the number of Jews swelled, the trauma of 1648 still shaped Jewish (and to a lesser degree, Polish) communal experience and their attitudes toward Khmelnytsky, Cossacks, and Ukraine's statehood writ large.[15]

Cossack statehood did not last long. The Crimean khans had their own geopolitical goals, and the alliance unraveled. The war continued, and in 1651 a new Polish army trounced Khmelnytsky's force at Volhynia. Over the next few years neither side was able to secure a decisive victory, but in the long run, the Poles' superior numbers and equipment began to show. In 1654, desperate for military support, Khmelnytsky made the fateful decision to accept the protection of the ruler of Muscovy, his Orthodox coreligionist.[16]

The arrangement, which took several years to negotiate, was a boon to the tsar's government; it, like the Cossacks, had been locked in a long-standing conflict against the Polish-Lithuanian Commonwealth. Only forty years prior, Polish armies—which included Cossack units—had occupied Moscow. From 1632 to 1634, the two states fought a bitter but inconclusive war over Smolensk and were now actively preparing for a new round. Cossack armies and the Hetmanate's territory would play an important role. Beyond providing resources, the agreement positioned Moscow as the protector and overlord of Orthodox Slavs at the very heart of the ancient Kyivan domain, including the historic capital itself.

On January 18, 1654, in the town of Pereiaslav, Cossack elites swore allegiance to the Russian tsar Alexei, thus cutting off any remaining ties to the Polish-Lithuanian state and placing the Cossack polity and Kyiv under Moscow's sovereignty. In exchange for their acceptance of the tsar's authority, the Cossacks expected to receive military support, self-governance, and affirmation of their traditional privileges. Yet when they asked Moscow's representative Vasilii Buturlin to also swear by the treaty's terms, he steadfastly declined. This refusal was not the wily maneuver of a clever courtier but Buturlin's recognition of the lack of constraints on the tsar in relation to his subjects. In Muscovy, the status of the monarch was such that when Tsar Alexei dispatched an ambassador to Spain, the Russian "demanded that the Spanish King uncover his head each time the Tsar's name was mentioned." The hetman was not even a king. Clearly, the Muscovites and the Cossacks (who required translators to communicate with each other) viewed their agreement, its implications, and the two sides' future relations rather differently. The long-awaited reunification of two forcibly separated branches of the same people the Pereiaslav treaty was patently not.[17]

Faced with such an unequal and uncertain arrangement, Khmelnytsky attempted to back out. Eventually, however, military concerns prevailed, and the Cossack domain and Kyiv came under Moscow's rule. Initially the Hetmanate, which eventually spanned most of the Left-Bank Ukraine (east of the Dnipro River) enjoyed a largely autonomous existence, but the long-term visions of the Russian and Cossack elites diverged. Whereas the Hetmanate leadership wished to preserve the status quo, Moscow increasingly came to consider the arrangement as merely the first step toward the Hetmanate's full incorporation into Russia. The pressure to deepen ties, however, came not just from Moscow; Hetmanate intellectual and religious elites played a crucial role in promoting the idea of Russian-Ukrainian unity.[18]

In the wake of the Pereiaslav agreement, Moscow viewed their new Hetmanate subjects with suspicion and occasionally outright hostility. Products of the unruly steppe, Cossacks were perceived as potential rebels and traitors. Derisively called "Lithuanians," many were even forced to undergo reconversion to Orthodox Christianity, as the purity of their faith was doubted by Muscovy's religious establishment. This negative attitude eased over time, mostly under the influence of Hetmanate-based scholars and clerics. It was "Ukrainian clergymen who began linking Ukraine with Russia through a combination of history (Kyivan Rus') . . . religion (Orthodoxy), and even a vague sense of ethnicity."[19]

By far the most influential example of this trend was the *Synopsis*: the first Russian history textbook, published by a Kyiv-based theologian, Innokentiy Gisel, in 1674. Meant to provide intellectual justification for Muscovy's control over the Hetmanate, the book presented both entities as offspring of the Kyivan Rus' and Kyiv as the original birthplace of the tsar's state and religion. Astonishingly successful, the *Synopsis* was republished approximately thirty times and remained popular until the mid-nineteenth century.[20]

Gisel and Kyiv's wider Orthodox clergy wished to achieve two key aims: first, against the background of a struggle over Ukraine between the Polish-Lithuanian Commonwealth and Muscovy, they strongly preferred their Russian coreligionists and sought to provide historical arguments for a separation from Poland. Second, after Moscow's rule over the Hetmanate was secured, they wished to be accepted as equals by Moscow's establishment, a task at which they ultimately succeeded. Yet as natives of the Hetmanate became increasingly prominent in Russia's culture, this intellectual campaign also undermined the justification for the Hetmanate's semi-independent status.

Subsequently, though much later than Gisel hoped for, the idea of a shared origin and common (though not necessarily indistinguishable) identity was picked up by Russian writers and became a staple of Russian historical thinking. As a result, even in modern-day Russia, the origins of the Russian state and nation and the most important events of early Russian political and religious history are all viewed as having taken place in Ukraine.[21]

Against the background of growing integrationist pressure from Moscow, Russia's 1700–1721 war against Sweden gave the Hetmanate leadership an opportunity to try to break free. In 1709, the hetman, Ivan Mazepa, reneged on his allegiance to Tsar Peter I and sided with the Swedes. Russia and Russians never forgave Mazepa for what they saw as devious and unjustified treason. In Alexander Pushkin's poem "Poltava," which describes the war's crucial battle, Mazepa is referred to as "Judas" and "snake"; during the Russian Empire's final years, *mazepist* became the standard pejorative term for promoters of Ukraine's identity and political rights.

At Poltava, a medium-size town in eastern Ukraine, the Russian army decisively defeated the Swedes and their Cossack allies on July 8, 1709. Peter's retribution was swift and bloody. Even though many Cossacks remained loyal to Moscow and Mazepa himself died in exile shortly after the battle, Baturyn, the Hetmanate capital, was sacked by Russian troops and its inhabitants slaughtered. The Cossack leadership, shaken and subdued, then went out of their way to signal loyalty to the tsar and gave up on any desire to recoup lost freedom. The region's governance was transferred from the hetman's administration to Russian officials. Gradually, not just the Hetmanate's official name but also its identity became Little Russia (*Malorossiya*), a designation that first appeared before Pereiaslav but now explicitly bound the region to Moscow's Great Russia. Later, the label expanded to other parts of Polish-ruled Ukraine as they came under the empire's control. Even though, originally, Great and Little Russia were simply geographic terms, their eventual evolution into a hierarchical relationship was inevitable.

The Hetmanate was gradually dismantled and became fully incorporated into the Russian Empire, its territory given the same status as other provinces. The last formal remnants were abolished in 1783. Though a tragedy for the previously free but now enserfed peasants—as Russian serfdom differed little from slavery—the end of the Hetmanate benefited many of the Cossack elites. Some grew fabulously wealthy from peasants' forced labor, while others become key partners in Russia's imperial projects by embarking on careers in the military and civil service. As long as they considered themselves Little Russians and did not challenge the system, Left-Bank nobles faced no discrimination; all positions and careers were open to them.

The demise of the Hetmanate was also part of the broader process of the Russian Empire's territorial growth and administrative consolidation. In 1772, 1793, and 1795, Russia portioned Poland with the Habsburgs' Austria and Prussia, thus bringing Right-Bank Ukraine—including its large and vibrant Polish and Jewish communities—under the rule of the empire's Romanov dynasty. Galicia, which went to the Austrian Habsburgs, was the only part of the former Kyivan Rus' that remained outside of the Russian Empire. Meanwhile, an even more important expansion was happening to the south of the Hetmanate, on the shores of the Black and Azov Seas.

The conquest of the Black Sea coast had long been a goal of Russia. Strategically, it provided the empire with permanently ice-free ports, which it lacked in the Baltic Sea, and allowed relatively easy access to the Mediterranean. Control of this territory also protected Russia from economically painful and humiliating slave raids from the Crimean Khanate (the last of which happened as late as 1768), and threatened the Ottoman Empire, Russia's key adversary. Ideologically, Crimea was the place of Prince Volodymyr's conversion to Christianity and therefore symbolically important. Even more crucially, controlling the Black Sea coast would be a major step toward realizing the dream of liberating Constantinople—Orthodoxy's spiritual center and the source of Moscow's self-perception as "the Third Rome"—from Muslim rule.[22]

Russia's southward expansion was a decades-long joint project of Empress Catherine the Great and her general, statesman, and lover Prince Grigorii Potemkin. The region Catherine and Potemkin brought under the rule of Saint Petersburg, the empire's new capital, became known as New Russia (Novorossiya). Like New England or New Spain, New Russia was an unabashedly colonial endeavor. The Romanovs' "southern empire" would see new rules introduced, natives subjugated and displaced, and new settlers welcomed, all to the benefit the imperial core. Much like other colonies, it also became a dumping ground for the metropolis's troublemakers and a breeding ground for revolutionaries and other radicals.[23]

Thanks to the efforts of Potemkin, cities—Odesa, Kherson, Yekaterynoslav (now Dnipro)—and multiple smaller settlements, some functional and viable, others not so much, popped up. Vast tracts of land were distributed among imperial elites, both Russians and those hailing from the Hetmanate. New settlers, considered more reliable than the indigenous Muslim Tatars, were invited to settle and establish colonies. Many came from within and without the empire: some in search of a better life and economic opportunities; others, like the German Mennonites, to escape religious intolerance, though tax benefits and exemption from conscription were also important factors. Among the newcomers were Russians from the imperial hinterland, as well as Greeks, Bulgarians, Albanians, Moldovans, Jews, Poles, Italians, and even Swedes. A plan to ship British convicts (who because of the American Revolution could no longer be sent to North America) to Crimea was also on the table but ultimately fell through. The region, diverse even prior to this mass migration, was soon characterized by a patchwork of identities. Yet when these communities put down roots and began abandoning their original languages and cultures, they switched to Russian, not Ukrainian.[24]

The effects of Russian colonialism were especially acute in Crimea. When the empire annexed Crimea in 1783, the same year it abolished the Hetmanate, Muslim Tatars were 84 percent of the peninsula's population. By the 1860s, their share had dropped by half. Many fled to escape religious repression and economic hardship, though some Tatar elites were also incorporated into the imperial military and administration and benefited from the new order.[25]

Another wave of migration into Ukraine took place in the late nineteenth and early twentieth centuries, centered on the coal mines and booming industrial towns of eastern Ukraine and the Donbas, an area that now describes the Donetsk and Luhansk regions. This previously rural and sparsely inhabited region underwent rapid development following Russia's humiliating defeat in the Crimean War (1853–1856). The war, which the Russian Empire fought against a coalition of Great Britain, France, the Ottomans, and Piedmont-Sardinia, prompted a wave of popular mobilization across Russia. Driven by patriotic fervor and rumors of potential emancipation, tens of thousands of serf peasants abandoned their estates and trekked to Crimea to join the fight. The writings of officers who served in the war, chief among them Leo Tolstoy, solidified the peninsula's special place in the Russian nationalist imagination. The Black Sea Fleet base at Sevastopol, besieged for almost eleven months, became a symbol of Russian heroism and tenacity despite—or possibly because of—the city's eventual surrender.[26]

In Crimea, war and state repression caused a new wave of Tatar exodus, reducing the indigenous population even further. In 1857, Tsar Alexander II spoke of cleansing Crimea of Tatars and replacing them with Russian peasants. For Saint Petersburg, the defeat was also a painful wake-up call that ushered in an era of major reforms. In 1861, serfdom was abolished, and new hands became increasingly available for employment in manufacturing. To remain a great power, the still mostly agrarian Russian Empire had to modernize, and fast.[27]

The steppes of eastern Ukraine—rich in coal, close to the Black Sea, and connected to rivers and railroads—became the new center of Russian industry. The necessary capital and managerial expertise often came from the West (Donetsk was originally named Yuzivka after its founder, the Welsh entrepreneur John Hughes), but the laborers who mined coal and worked the factory floors were predominantly impoverished ethnic Russian peasants, attracted by abundant jobs and relatively high wages. Quite typical was the family of the future Soviet leader Nikita Khrushchev, whose parents moved to Yuzivka to earn enough to buy "a little house, a horse, and a piece of land" back home in the Kursk region of Russia. The father of Leonid Brezhnev, who replaced Khrushchev, also migrated to eastern Ukraine from a village near Kursk.[28]

Members of other ethnic groups such as Ukrainians, Tatars, Poles, Jews, and even Serbs also joined the emerging proletariat or provided essential services to the new settlements, though in much smaller numbers than Russians. The rates of population growth were unprecedented in the Russian Empire. Yuzivka, founded in 1869, was a boomtown of forty thousand less than forty years later. Life in factory and mining towns was harsh and often short. Violence and crime were common, public services and cultural institutions almost nonexistent. In 1892, the region had a school for every 2,040 residents but a pub for every 570.[29]

The Donbas had always prided itself on its unique identity, independent streak, and penchant for unruliness, but the language spoken in the region's towns was Russian, the lingua franca of imperial governance, technological education, and commerce. Though xenophobia and ethnic violence were common, non-Russians who migrated to the mining and factory towns of the Donbas quickly Russified; many Ukrainian workers did so to the point of abandoning their native language altogether. But the ethnically Russian working class also adopted some Ukrainian words and customs, thus creating a distinct regional blend of language and culture. Ukrainian activists and even some outside observers, such as the Zionist ideologue Vladimir (Zeev) Jabotinsky, decried this growing Russification but were powerless to stop it.[30]

Russification was not just a bottom-up process but also a key ideological priority of the state, and Ukrainian institutions therefore had very limited presence in Novorossiya and the Donbas. Yet identities were fluid in the region and could split families down the middle. The Dontsovs of Melitopol, a town midway between Kherson and Mariupol, are an extreme but hardly unique example of this dynamic. The family spoke Russian at home but also read Ukrainian books. Of the three Dontsov brothers, two chose Russian identity: one enjoyed a successful career as a senior tsarist bureaucrat in Saint Petersburg, the other became a militant Marxist. But the youngest, Dmytro, opted for a Ukrainian one and eventually became the chief ideologue of Ukrainian "integral nationalism": an extreme, xenophobic, and virulently anti-Russian worldview.[31]

By the late nineteenth century, such identity choices—Russian, Little Russian, Ukrainian, or something else entirely—affected the literate and politically conscious residents of Ukraine, including minorities who became witnesses of and occasionally collateral damage in intra-Slavic struggles. In these conflicts, the empire's government was not an impartial umpire; instead, it acted as a committed and increasingly repressive guardian of a narrowly defined, anxious, and xenophobic Russian nationalism that saw Ukrainian identity as its key challenger.

CHAPTER 2

OF BROTHERS AND EMPIRES

O n May 26, 2019, Russian media was especially upset with Ukraine's president Volodymyr Zelensky. The reason was neither the conflict over Crimea, which Russia annexed in 2014, nor the ongoing war in the Donbas, but a post Zelensky had published on Facebook a day earlier. In this post, Zelensky described Igor Sikorsky (1889–1972), a renowned aircraft designer who developed the first practical helicopter, as a "famous Ukrainian." Russians, who viewed Sikorsky as their own, were outraged, even though Zelensky had a point; Sikorsky was born in Kyiv and his family hailed from a nearby village. But if Igor Sikorsky was a famous Ukrainian, so, too, was his father Ivan, one of world's leading psychiatrists in his day. The problem is that the elder Sikorsky would have surely hated the designation, for he was a leading member of Kyiv's Club of Russian Nationalists and believed that the Ukrainian nation was a fiction.

The argument about the Sikorsky family goes to the very heart of the conflict between Russia and Ukraine: Who is a Ukrainian and do Ukrainians even exist as a distinct group, separate from the Russians? As the Romanov empire transitioned during the nineteenth and early twentieth centuries from a rule based on traditional, divinely ordained monarchical authority to one based on nationalism, popular support, and public mobilization, the very existence of the Russian state and nation hinged on the self-identification and allegiance of Ukraine's Orthodox population. The stakes were high: if these people were Russians, the multiethnic Romanov empire would also be a Russian nation-state with a solid Russian majority. But if those in Ukraine were to reject Russianness and choose a fully separate, Ukrainian identity, Russians would become a minority in their own continental empire.

Faced with the threat of minority nationalisms, first Polish and then others, in the first half of the nineteenth century, Russia's political and intellectual elites responded by cultivating the idea of a shared origin and destiny of Great and Little Russians. By the 1860s, however, efforts to construct unity gave way to a campaign to stamp out alternative visions and identities by force. Under the combined pressures of economic backwardness, growing demands for political rights, and lost wars, the imperial government increasingly turned to narrow and exclusionary Russian nationalism as the backbone of its rule. For the champions of the Russian nationalist project, the existence of a distinct Ukrainian identity and language was a mortal threat that endangered the very foundations of the empire. The increasingly paranoid and repressive imperial government effectively banned Ukrainian-language publications and persecuted those who challenged the unity of the Russian and Ukrainian people. Many Little Russian elites and intellectuals, such as the Sikorsky family, became fully and proudly Russian, quite a few of them to the point of embracing xenophobic, radical nationalism. The minority defied persecution and rejected the Russian identity altogether in favor of the Ukrainian one.

This conflict over identity choices—Russian, Little Russian, Ukrainian—cut across class and party lines, created improbable alliances, and spilled over to seemingly unrelated issues such as urban planning and whether Jews practice ritual murder and use Christian blood to prepare Passover matzo. And it is still relevant today, as identity concerns lead Russian authorities to reject the very existence of Ukrainians as a distinct group rather than an appendage of Russia and use violence in an attempt to destroy Ukrainian language, identity, and culture.

On July 12, 2021, Vladimir Putin published his views on Russian-Ukrainian relations. The article, titled "On the Historical Unity of Russians and Ukrainians," was written by the Russian president himself. During his self-imposed COVID-19 isolation, Putin became an avid consumer of history books. The history Putin read informed his writing and shaped his views, and it contributed to the decision to invade Ukraine six months after the article was published. Yet beyond the identity of the author, the most remarkable thing about this article is how sloppy and amateurish the text is. A collection of myths and clichés (quite a few of which are empirically wrong), the article repeats almost verbatim the staple Russian historical narrative. Putin's text starts with the ancient Rus', a joint state of East Slavs (Russians, Ukrainians, and Belorussians); proceeds to the Mongol invasion; draws a direct line from Kyiv to Moscow; and finally presents Russia as the driving force behind the "reunification" of people who share a common origin, language, and faith—Russians and Ukrainians.[1]

This narrative of a unified, ancient Russian nation that dates to the Kyivan Rus' and comprises three branches of East Slavs is widespread but also surprisingly recent; it is a product of nineteenth-century historiography. Though Innokentiy Gisel had underscored the shared heritage of Muscovy and the Hetmanate as early as the seventeenth century, and though many early proponents of Russian nationalism had hailed from Ukraine, Russian elites in Gisel's time knew all too well that the two territories were distinct. For the Russians, the Hetmanate was a provincial backwater, and the few of them who did visit Ukraine at the time invariably commented on how different it was from Russia in language, ethnic composition, landscape, and the appearance and behavior of the people.[2]

Up until the late eighteenth to early nineteenth centuries, Russian intellectuals rarely considered Ukraine part of *their* history and identity; the region was increasingly referred to as Little Russia, but the "historical unity" narrative later promoted by Putin simply did not exist. The change came when, because of the Napoleonic Wars, young Russian aristocrats could no longer go on previously mandatory "grand tours" of classical Europe and instead switched to visiting the much closer but still unknown Ukraine. As a result, Russian elites finally "discovered" Ukraine, both the Hetmanate and the Right Bank, which the Russian Empire had gained only in the late eighteenth century after the partitions of Poland. With exposure came interest and a sense of ownership. In Russian travelogues of the era, Ukraine is often described as "Russian Italy," a land of antiquity and the cradle of Russia's own civilization, while Kyiv became the site of cultural and spiritual pilgrimage. The land's beauty, vastness, and distance from the empire's capital fueled dreams of glory, conquest, and martial and sexual exploits, while the presence of minorities, especially Jews and Muslims, signaled the need to protect the newly discovered heirloom from despised "others."

The Russian elites' growing sense of ownership was shaken by the massive Polish uprising of 1830–1831. The Romanov empire had gained most of Poland's territory as a result of the country's partitions in the late eighteenth century, but the so-called Congress Poland, centered on Warsaw, originally enjoyed a semiautonomous existence. In November 1830, the Russian government's efforts to undermine Poland's rights sparked a revolt, led by a group of junior officers who sought to reestablish a state that included territories that many Russians had come to consider theirs. The uprising also quickly spread beyond Congress Poland to Lithuania, Belorussia, and Right-Bank Ukraine, which had large Polish communities and were dominated by Polish nobility. The war continued until October 1831, and it took the empire substantial effort and tens of thousands of casualties to subdue the revolt. Even though the rebels were crushed, anti-Polish xenophobia and insecurity never fully disappeared from Saint Petersburg. The Poles' armed struggle threatened the empire's security, but their claims on Ukraine as a part of a Polish state were even more alarming, for they challenged the emerging Russian national identity, which viewed Ukraine as a key component of Russia's own history and statehood. Once the Russian elites began viewing Ukraine not just as a territorial possession but as the very cradle of Russia's civilization and statehood, losing Ukraine became unthinkable. To remove any further risk, the Poles' claims on Ukraine had to be countered not just militarily but also intellectually.[3]

The Polish uprising thus prompted the empire's government and intellectuals, many of them based in Ukraine, to work intensely to uncover the region's supposed original Russianness through cultural preservation, archaeological research, ethnography, and historical writing. The leading Russian nationalist historian Mikhail Pogodin argued that "Russia took back from Poland only what had belonged to it in medieval times." Aleksei Khomiakov, another prominent Russian writer, described Kyiv in 1839 as "the cradle of Russian glory" and a gathering place for pilgrims from all over the empire, from Pskov in the northwest to the Yenisei River in Siberia. The Orthodox residents of the region were for him "an organic and inseparable part of a single . . . Russian nation, with perhaps some dialectical differences in conversational language." Even as staunch a liberal as the writer and critic Vissarion Belinskii viewed Ukrainians as just a tribe, their history simply one episode of broader Russian history and the Ukrainian language only a regional dialect of Russian. Russian intellectuals of the mid-nineteenth century were a fractious lot, but on the question of the Russian origins of Ukraine's Orthodox population, there was soon little disagreement.[4]

To bolster the effort to demonstrate the region's Russian identity, the empire created multiple institutions and committees, invested in education, and even transferred a previously Polish-language (and thus suspicious) university from Wilno (now Vilnius, the capital of Lithuania) to Kyiv. Reestablished in 1834 as the Russian-language Saint Vladimir Imperial University, the institution became the government's intellectual heavy weapon in the fight for Russia's historical rights to and ownership of Ukraine. These policies, however, did not aim to make Little Russians a carbon copy of their Moscow siblings or to erase the region's folklore and traditions, which local Orthodox scholars, intellectuals, and activists so cherished. In fact, this focus on the local Little Russian character was even welcomed as evidence of the region's Russian (broadly defined) identity and history.

In parallel with integrating Ukraine into the broader Russian narrative, the government set out to define what the empire itself was. On April
2, 1833, the minister of education, Count Sergey Uvarov, suggested "the
triad": Orthodox Christianity, autocracy, and *narodnost'*—a term that
does not have a perfect English equivalent but is traditionally translated
as "nationality"—as the empire's doctrine of "official nationality." Yet
despite the overtly nationalist and exclusionary overtones, the chief aim of
the "official nationality" doctrine was to strengthen the monarchy, rather
than to elevate ethnic Russians as a whole. In the first half of the nineteenth century, the idea of the Russian nation was still broad and porous
enough to accommodate different visions and identities within it. As far
as Saint Petersburg was concerned, the Little Russian identity—many proponents and practitioners of which came from the nobility—was neither a
threat nor a politically meaningful marker of difference.[5]

The Little Russian elites never suffered personal discrimination; they
became junior partners in the empire-building project, and all positions
were open to them in Russian society and government. Still, the distinct
identity, the memory of Cossack self-rule, and the subordinate position
that was implied (even unintentionally) by the term "Little Russia" were
bound to eventually raise questions about Ukraine's status within the
empire. Mykola Kostomarov, a history professor at Kyiv's Saint Vladimir
University, accepted the shared origins of the Russian and Ukrainian people but also resented the Russian dominance over Ukraine. Kostomarov
wished to rectify this injustice by establishing a confederation of fourteen Slavic polities with a capital in Kyiv, in which units had equal rights,
leaders were elected, and no unit—not even the Great Russians—could
dominate the others.[6]

To promote these pan-Slavic and semi-democratic ideals, Kostomarov
teamed up in 1845 with other scholars, students, and activists to establish
a secret society: the Brotherhood of Saints Cyril and Methodius. Other key
brotherhood members (or, according to other accounts, nonmember asso-
ciates) included the writer Panteleimon Kulish and Taras Shevchenko, an
exceptionally talented poet and painter who was born in 1814 as a serf and

gained freedom only in 1838. Shevchenko's Ukrainian-language poetry soon made him a prominent symbol of Ukrainian identity and Ukraine's national bard (*kobzar*).

The brotherhood members were gifted artists and intellectuals but not at all capable conspirators. In 1847, the tsarist political police uncovered the organization and arrested its members. It is unclear which aspect of the brotherhood's ideology—its Ukrainian proto-nationalism or the rejection of autocracy—the authorities found most troubling, but neither could go unpunished. Still, whereas Polish secret societies were mercilessly repressed, the government was more lenient toward the Orthodox dissenters of the brotherhood. Unlike the Polish national movement, which had a track record of armed resistance, the utopian projects of Kyiv's intellectuals did little to threaten the monarchy. Shevchenko, who possessed the unlucky combination of radical views and low social status, received the harshest punishment: ten years' service as a private in a remote military garrison and a ban on writing and painting. Kulish was briefly exiled to Tula, south of Moscow, where he worked in the governor's office. Kostomarov was imprisoned for a year and then exiled to Saratov on the Volga. There, he soon resumed academic research, and in 1859 the former conspirator was appointed the chair of Russian history at Saint Petersburg University.

The brotherhood was not the only intellectual group active in nineteenth-century Ukraine. Young, educated activists, often the sons of village priests, sought to elevate the Little Russian language and traditions from their status as ethnographic and antiquarian curiosities. Derisively labeled *khlopomany* (admirers of peasants), these people, in addition to their devotion to the Little Russian identity, sought to improve the social and political standing of the peasantry. The authorities and the older, more politically conservative Little Russian intellectuals approved of the khlopomany's cultural zeal but were apprehensive of the reformist socioeconomic program these activists espoused.

It took yet another Polish uprising in 1863–1864 for the Romanov empire to fully embrace Russian nationalism as state policy. Even though the center of the uprising was in Lithuania and the Kingdom of Poland, western and central Ukraine also experienced violence. By then, Russia well understood the power of bottom-up nationalist mobilization. In 1848–1849, Russian military intervention helped save the Austrian Empire from defeat at the hands of a popular revolution in Hungary; during the Crimean War, nationalism on both sides was a major factor in starting and sustaining the conflict.

By the mid-nineteenth century, the traditional ideas, beliefs, and social arrangements that had previously sustained the monarchy had lost much of their appeal among the rapidly growing urban bourgeoisie and working class. Peasants—the majority of the empire's population—were still mostly loyal to the regime. Yet even the peasants wanted change. In the 1850s and early 1860s, a massive wave of peasant unrest shook the empire. Ukraine was one of the centers of peasant action. To strengthen rural support for the monarchy in this strategically important region affected by the Polish revolt, the government introduced better terms of serf emancipation in Ukraine compared to the rest of the empire. But tsarist authorities also realized the limits of such gestures; a fresh approach was required to keep the populace in the tsar's corner. Nationalism offered an answer. Peasants were to be turned into Russians.

In Ukraine, the tipping point came in early 1863, with a plan to publish the Ukrainian translation of the New Testament. Already alarmed by the presumably subversive and potentially even separatist activities of younger, more radical activists, government officials and conservative intellectuals in Ukraine began lobbying Saint Petersburg to take action. The Ukrainian-language gospel was perceived as a political statement; having the holy book in Ukrainian effectively settled the debate on whether it was a mere dialect of Russian or a separate language in favor of the latter. Against the background of the latest Polish uprising and the Poles' attempts to incite Ukrainians to join their revolt, officials came to see the proposal as a product of insidious Polish intrigues and as a clear and present danger to state security. This was a challenge, and the empire had to strike back.

In response, the minister of internal affairs Petr Valuev published on July 8, 1863, an instruction to censors that later became known as the Valuev Circular. The circular unequivocally stated that "a separate Little Russian language has never existed, does not exist and cannot exist, and that their dialect, used by commoners, is just the Russian Language, only corrupted by the influence of Poland." The circular declared that all instruction in schools should be conducted in Russian and forbade the publication of Ukrainian-language books. Only fiction books were exempt.[7]

Officially the circular was a temporary measure, though Valuev likely wished to maintain the restrictions in the long term. In 1876, an even more restrictive decree (*ukase*), signed by Tsar Alexander II during a vacation in the German spa town of Ems, made the ban permanent. Now even the publication of Ukrainian-language fiction required a special permit, and only the reprinting of historical documents originally written in Ukrainian was exempt. The target of the repression was the Ukrainian language as such; while the Bible could not be published in Ukrainian, tsarist censors approved the Russian translation of Karl Marx and Friedrich Engels's *The Communist Manifesto*.[8]

But even Russian-language publications about Ukraine were not safe. The authorities typically banned everything that strayed from the official narrative, even children's tales that reminded people of the Cossacks' past self-governance and rights. Censors were especially vigilant about writings that could be construed as calling for Ukrainian self-government, and even replaced the term "Ukraine" with "Little Russia" or "South-West Region." At the same time, popular, often humorous tales depicting Little Russians living a simple, cheerful life made it through censorship without a hitch.[9]

The Valuev Circular and the Ems Ukase marked a watershed moment in relations between the empire and its Ukrainian subjects. The circular was the first instance of Russian authorities attempting to destroy Ukraine: as an idea, an identity project, and a literary language. The scope of the repression of Ukrainian culture and language was unprecedented in the empire. Neither the feared Poles nor the despised Jews faced such an all-out assault on their collective identity and language.

By enacting these restrictions, the government also presented the Little Russian movement—whose key components, the language and the culture built upon it, were now under attack—with a stark choice. One option was to gradually abandon the "Little" adjective and become fully Russian, at least in a political and national sense. The other was to give up on the idea of being a part of the broader Russian project altogether and instead adopt a totally separate Ukrainian identity.

Against the backdrop of the government's crackdown, being consciously Ukrainian often required breaking the law. The Ukrainophile movement was also becoming increasingly socialist, which only strengthened the government's zeal to repress. Thus, for Ukrainian activists, the choice became to either face persecution or leave the empire altogether—typically to Austro-Hungarian Galicia. There, and further afield in Western Europe, Ukrainian scholars and activists could and did continue developing their vision of national identity, without being subject to the threat of imprisonment or exile to Siberia. The most prominent representative of this group was the historian and political activist Mykhailo Hrushevsky. Hrushevsky moved to Austria-Hungary in 1894 to become a professor of history at Lviv University in Galicia. More than anyone else, he contributed to the creation of a Ukrainian historical narrative that did not center on unity with Russia. The Ukrainians that took shape in his multivolume history were a distinct culture, identity, and ethnicity, not a regional component of something larger.[10]

As the relations between the Romanov and Habsburg states worsened and the empires found themselves on opposing sides of the pre–World War I alliances, the more paranoid segments of the Russian government and nationalist movement began to view the Ukrainian identity as an invention of Austrian intelligence services and the "avant-garde of the [German] *Drang nach Osten* [push to the east]" project. The struggle over Ukrainian identity, therefore, became both external—a matter of Saint Petersburg versus Ukraine—and internal, pitting Ukraine's post–Valuev Circular identity projects—Ukrainian and Little Russian—against each other.[11]

In this conflict, the political stakes were high, and the ramifications extended far beyond Ukraine. The differences between Little Russian and Ukrainian identities were not semantic but fundamental. The Little Russian identity focused on and cherished regional particularities that, while unique, were also an integral part of the broader Russian identity. The Ukrainian identity rejected this unity and positioned the region and its population as a separate people and culture completely outside of the Russian nation and history. Creating a new Ukrainian nation required the "unmaking" of the existing Russian one. If fully realized, this Ukrainian nation threatened to deprive Russians, not just in Ukraine but everywhere, of what they perceived as their mythical origins, sacred places, and patrimony. For the Russian government and Russian nationalists, Polish, Jewish, Baltic, and other national projects were external challenges: threatening, but expected and natural. The fight against them was a fight to preserve the empire. Ukrainian nationalism, on the other hand, was nothing less than treason from within; it required a harsh, uncompromising response and had to be rooted out. The fight against Ukrainian nationalism was thus a fight for the existence of not just the Russian Empire but the very Russian nation.[12]

Many Little Russian activists and intellectuals chose the Russian path. Their most important publication, the newspaper *Kievlianin* (Kyivite)—the city's first daily paper, established in 1864—could not have been more explicit about its political position: "This region is Russian, Russian, Russian," proclaimed the paper's motto. Inadvertently, the slogan's emotional zeal betrayed the fact that the region's Russianness was much more aspiration than reality.[13]

Russian activists also grasped the importance of wooing the masses, building cross-class coalitions, and investing in symbolism. One such symbol the Russian activists pursued eagerly was a statute of Khmelnytsky they sought to erect in Kyiv. The first prototype of the monument, designed in 1869, envisioned the hetman sitting astride a stallion who trampled on defeated enemies: the Jesuit priest, the Polish landlord, and the Jewish moneylender. The pedestal was to be adorned with the words of a seventeenth-century folk song: "Oh, it will be better / Oh, it will be more beautiful / When in our Ukraine / There are no Jews, no

Poles / And no [Uniate Church]," as well as the dedication, "A united, indivisible Russia—to Hetman Bohdan Khmelnytsky." Even though Alexander II approved the prototype, its violent and provocative nature was over-the-top even for Russia's xenophobic government; the final, currently standing version of the monument, unveiled in 1888, featured only Khmelnytsky atop his steed.[14]

The Russo-Japanese War (1904–1905), in which the empire was humiliatingly defeated by a non-European power, triggered an unprecedented wave of internal unrest. Throughout 1905, a combination of violent workers' protests, strikes, assassinations of state officials, and open urban warfare threatened to topple the monarchy. Pushed to the brink, the government was forced to institute political reforms. On October 17, 1905, Tsar Nicholas II published a manifesto establishing a national parliament, the Duma, and introducing civil liberties such as freedom of speech and assembly. These concessions, rightly seen as a sign of the government's extreme weakness, just energized the opposition further. In response, violent Russian nationalists, sometimes with the active support of local authorities, unleashed a wave of pogroms against Jews, whom they considered the regime's chief enemies. The pogroms in Kyiv (October 18–20) and Odesa (October 18–22) were especially bloody. In Kyiv, according to one eyewitness, "not a single [Jewish] store, warehouse, or office remained untouched." About four hundred lost their lives during the violence in Odesa. Responsibility for the pogroms should not be placed on the Russian nationalists alone; anti-Semitism was widespread in Ukraine and cut across ethnic and ideological lines. Economic factors and opportunity to plunder were also important motivations. Yet Russian nationalist agitators and mobs, already very active in Ukraine at the time, played a critical role in instigating the violence.[15]

After the violence of the 1905 revolution and the pogroms subsided, restrictions on publishing were softened. Ukrainian-language newspapers and books could be published in the empire instead of needing to be smuggled from Austro-Hungarian Galicia. Elections (albeit with limited suffrage), parliamentary politics, and representation for non-Russian minorities and opponents of autocracy (two agendas that often—but not always—overlapped) challenged the very foundations of the Russian monarchy. Under threat, the tsar and Russian nationalists became even more united, radical, and activist. Ukraine, with its large population and competing identity projects, became the key battleground.

The post-1905 Ukrainian national movement threatened Russian nationalism and the government that was increasingly becoming the nationalists' tool. This was not because it challenged the empire's territorial integrity; most Ukrainian activists wanted collective cultural and political rights, not independence. Rather, Ukrainian identity was threatening because it implied a need for a different type of state. Ukrainians were simply too large a group for the Russians to lose. The main justification for the empire being a *Russian* state—something that Russian nationalists (and many liberals) took for granted—was that in the early twentieth century, Great, Little, and White Russians (Belorussians), collectively made up more than two-thirds of the population. But if Little Russians were to become Ukrainians, the Russian share would immediately drop to a mere 44 percent. Of course, these numbers were known even before 1905, but in earlier periods the monarchy was less dependent on popular legitimacy; in the new era of parliaments and elections, this simple math had potentially devastating implications. The very nature of the empire and Russians' role within it thus hinged on identity choices made in Ukraine and the government's ability to prevent the emergence of a Ukrainian nation.[16]

Though no longer able to fully ban Ukrainian-language publications, the state nonetheless did its best to limit everyday use of Ukrainian. The government also began subsidizing Kyiv-based Russian nationalist newspapers. Extreme Russian nationalist organizations and societies, collectively known as the Black Hundreds, popped up throughout Ukraine and beyond. The most prominent of these groups, the Union of the Russian People, enjoyed the personal support of the tsar. The union's definition of Russian was a purely ethnic one, and it welcomed all Orthodox Slavs who shared its politics. Members of other ethnicities could be admitted under special circumstances, but ethnic Jews, even those who converted to

Christianity, were absolutely forbidden. The movement was exceptionally active in Ukraine, and most of its membership lived in the region despite it being an empire-wide organization. Many officials, including the governor of Kyiv, were also members, even though state officials were supposedly banned from joining political organizations.[17]

The smaller, more cerebral and elitist Club of Russian Nationalists was established in Kyiv in 1908. Whereas the Union of the Russian People fought against the enemies of the monarchy and nation in the streets, members of the club rhetorically battled them in papers and lecture halls. Among the many enemies of Russia and Russians that the club targeted, the Ukrainian national movement was first and foremost. One member of the club, a Kyiv-based government censor named Sergei Shchegolev, argued in his 1912 treatise *Ukrainian Movement as the Contemporary Stage of South-Russian Separatism* that Ukrainian national ideology was a heresy originating from Polish intrigues and lamented that the restrictions on the use of the Ukrainian language did not go far enough. In 2004, a Russian ultranationalist think tank, the Orthodox Center of Imperial Political Research, republished Shchegolev's book. The preface to this new edition, written by nationalist historian Mikhail Smolin, introduced for the first time the concept of an independent Ukraine being inherently "anti-Russia," a deliberate and insidious Western geopolitical weapon.* This term quickly became key to Russian nationalist discourse. When Putin announced Russia's invasion on February 24, 2022, Ukraine being an externally controlled "anti-Russia" was among his key justifications.[18]

Shchegolev's anti-Ukrainian views were standard among the Club of Russian Nationalists' members. In a lecture delivered at the club in 1913, the aging but still globally renowned psychiatrist Ivan Sikorsky relied on the racial theories of the day to argue that a single Russian ethnic group inhabits all the territory from Arkhangelsk in the north to the Azov Sea in the south, and from Poland in the west to the Volga in the east. Ukrainians, according to Sikorsky, simply do not exist: "Neither among the living

---

* I thank Dr. Oleksandr Polianichev for making this observation.

nor in the cemeteries, neither above nor under the ground." From this, Sikorsky maintained, it naturally followed that the very term "Ukrainians" should not be used, and "Ukraine" was simply an old geographic and administrative designation, an artifact that had lost any utility or meaning. Yet another Kyiv-based Russian nationalist writer accused those who promoted Ukrainian national autonomy within the Russian Empire of following "Jewish, Polish and mongrel elements" that sought to destroy the Russian people. Andrey Strozhenko, also a prominent member of the club, maintained that Mykhailo Hrushevsky, the leading proponent of the Ukrainian identity, collaborated with and promoted the interests of the "militant revolutionary Jewry." Some other Kyiv-based Russian nationalists even went as far as accusing the central government in Saint Petersburg of being suspiciously soft in battling the Ukrainian identity and argued that harsher measures were needed.[19]

The Russian nationalists' activism, fear, and feverish, violent rhetoric were not directed only at the Ukrainian national movement; the Russian people, these nationalists believed, were under mortal threat from multiple enemies. This intense and constantly growing insecurity drove paranoid Russian activists in Ukraine to adopt ever more radical measures and ideas. And because the central government heavily relied on its nationalist allies in Ukraine for political support, it had to accommodate these initiatives from below, even when they crossed into the nonsensical and the occult.

On March 12, 1911, the body of thirteen-year-old Andrii Yushchinsky was discovered in a cave on the outskirts of Kyiv. The child had been murdered, stabbed multiple times by a sharp object—likely an awl. Police investigators initially suspected that Yushchinsky, who came from an impoverished and troubled family, had been murdered by one of his relatives. But all key suspects had alibis, and as police struggled to crack the case, rumors began swirling around Kyiv that Yushchinsky was murdered by Jews who used his blood to bake Passover matzos. "The Yids have tortured Andryusha Yushchinsky to death!" proclaimed a leaflet distributed on the day of the funeral. "Russians! If your children are dear to you, beat the Yids. Beat them up until there is not a single Yid left in Russia. Have pity on your children! Avenge the unfortunate martyr. It is time! It is time!" implored another proclamation.[20]

Behind the blood libel campaign were Kyiv's radical Russian nationalists, led by the student Vladimir Golubev, son of Professor Stefan Golubev, a key member of the Club of Russian Nationalists. Grigorii Chaplinskii, Kyiv's chief prosecutor and yet another club member, soon ordered the police to investigate the case as a ritual murder. Ivan Sikorsky provided the intellectual justification for targeting Jews; the murder, he stated in a psychological profile commissioned by the police, was a "vendetta of sons of Jacob." Even more ominously, the Saint Petersburg government—including Nicholas II himself—became intimately involved in the investigation.[21]

In July 1911, Menachem Mendel Beilis, a Jewish clerk at a brick factory near which the body was found, was arrested and charged with Yushchinsky's murder. When the trial finally commenced in September 1913, the weakness of the prosecution's case was so glaring that the police themselves quietly accepted that Beilis was innocent and the actual murderer was Vera Cheberyak—a professional criminal whose son was Yushchinsky's best friend. Even some Russian nationalists thought the trial was beyond the pale. Vasily Shul'gin, editor of *Kievlianin*, publicly dismissed the ritual murder charge as "shameful superstition," a distraction from the "healthy and sensible anti-Semitism" that his paper promoted.[22]

Yet the stakes were so high for the Russian nationalists that the government in Saint Petersburg mobilized all its resources—and consciously broke multiple laws—to secure a conviction. Jurors were put under surveillance, the judge presiding over the case was promised a top job in exchange for steering the trial in the prosecution's favor, and the Ministry of Foreign Affairs was enlisted to prevent the timely transfer of an important document from the Vatican to the defense's lawyers. Nothing helped; so clumsy was the state's case that even a carefully handpicked jury—the majority of whom were Orthodox peasants, presumably susceptible to anti-Semitic superstition—acquitted Beilis. The trial became an international sensation, and the humiliating defeat only highlighted the empire's xenophobic foundations and incompetent governance.[23]

The absurdity of the ritual murder charge and the openly prejudiced way in which the case was handled weakened Russian nationalists in Ukraine and, for many Jews, demonstrated the impossibility of achieving equality in Russia. Six short years after the trial, Arnold Margolin, the most activist and outspoken of Beilis's lawyers, would join the government of newly independent Ukraine as a justice of the Supreme Court and later as deputy minister of foreign affairs.

Historians typically view the Beilis case as stemming from Russia's widespread and extreme anti-Semitism, the tsar's penchant for the mystical, and the government's desire to strengthen the bond between the monarchy and the people by scapegoating Jews. These arguments are correct but also too narrow; they overlook the broader Russian nationalist ecosystem in Kyiv and Ukraine more broadly. There, the perceived threat of different non-Russian identities—above all, Ukrainian and Jewish—formed a toxic brew that made a blood libel a top priority for the imperial government and forced the authorities to follow the lead of radical youths and retired racial scientists.

In calmer times and in more secure places, the Russian government could keep xenophobic zeal in check. Indeed, when Mykola Kostomarov—exiled to Saratov for his role in the Brotherhood of Saints Cyril and Methodius—had raised ritual murder allegations after two boys were killed in that city, the authorities immediately intervened to stop his inquiries. But early twentieth-century Ukraine was neither calm nor secure. It was a battleground, ideological and occasionally physical. Desperate measures were a sign of desperate times for Russian nationalism. Since the mid-nineteenth century, the empire had repressed the Ukrainian national movement and the non-Orthodox minorities in Ukraine in different ways, but the two campaigns were intertwined and originated from the same source. The same Russian nationalists who fought to eradicate an independent Ukrainian identity also framed Beilis.[24]

Ukraine had not yet fully recovered from the Beilis trail when another crisis erupted. At its center was not a poor Jewish clerk but the national bard himself. Nineteen fourteen marked the centennial of Taras

Shevchenko's birth, and Ukrainian activists wished to commemorate the occasion by erecting a monument of the kobzar in Kyiv. The planning and bureaucratic groundwork started several years in advance, and initially the government and even moderate Russian nationalists were open to the idea. But the more radical wing vociferously objected. They denounced Shevchenko as an "uneducated and uncultured" atheist, an alcoholic, a "complete nihilist," a revolutionary, and a Jewish agent who "cursed the Christian religion in the spirit of the Yids." In 1912, the Ministry of Internal Affairs in Saint Petersburg came out against the monument, which it believed to be a conspiracy to spread "separatist ideas" among the population. By 1914, the opposition to the monument had grown and became almost unanimous among Russian nationalists, who forced the government to halt the project. In the meantime, church authorities went a step further and banned the holding of religious events in Shevchenko's honor. Eventually, the imperial government banned any Shevchenko-related celebrations. The decision triggered protests, strikes, and riots throughout Ukraine, all of which were violently suppressed by the police.[25]

Russian nationalists and monarchists rejected the possibility of a Ukrainian identity out of hand, but Russian liberals were also suspicious of and eventually openly hostile to the Ukrainian national project. Whereas nationalists co-opted Kyivan history for themselves, Russian Westernizers typically viewed Ukrainian traditions, customs, and language with contempt and saw them as barbaric, parochial, and inferior to those of Russia's high culture. Even those who did not object to Ukrainian culture and language still feared the political implications of a separate Ukrainian identity.[26]

The Constitutional Democrats (*Kadets*), post-1905 Russia's leading liberal party, abhorred tsarist repressions and mostly (though not universally) accepted the existence of a unique Ukrainian culture and language, but they strenuously objected to granting Ukrainians collective political rights. Liberals though they were, the Kadets were above all else a *Russian* party and, like most Russian politicians and intellectuals, perceived the empire as a fundamentally Russian nation-state. For them, the entire Romanov domain, with the exceptions of Finland and Poland, was Russian land, and thus preserving the empire's territorial integrity was an immutable goal. The Kadets wished to transform the empire into a democracy, but this democracy had to be Russian. All minority nationalisms undermined this vision, but the Ukrainian one was particularly threatening.

In part, this attitude was born of pure, chauvinist prejudice. Petr Struve, one of the Kadets' founders and a key member of the party's central committee, praised Shchegolev's anti-Ukrainian book and declared that, above the elementary school level, education in the "[Little Russian language] would be an artificial and unjustified waste of psychic powers." A Little Russian who did not know the Russian language, he maintained, was "simply illiterate in the national and civic sense."[27]

A feeling of cultural superiority was not the only motive, however. Like the Russian nationalists, Struve was deeply alarmed by the potential impact of Ukrainian identity on the Russian national project as a whole. The transformation of Little Russian culture from a regional version of the all-Russian identity to a separate Ukrainian one could be achieved "only by the total destruction not just the historically developed form of Russian statehood but also of the Russian society."[28]

The Kadets' leader Pavel Milyukov was more accommodating toward Ukrainian culture and criticized the government's repression, though in his diary he typically put the words "Ukraine" and "Ukrainians" in parentheses. Yet even for Milyukov, collective political rights and any self-governance for Ukrainians would be a step too far. Fully committed to the idea of a unitary Russian state, "one and indivisible," Milyukov viewed any suggestion to transform the empire into a federation as utopian and outright dangerous. When asked directly about who Russian liberals would support if minorities rebelled against the imperial government, Milyukov deflected and replied that, in such an eventuality, liberals would also be among the "harmed ones." Any arguments for autonomy and collective self-governance put forward by representatives of the empire's many minority groups were for Milyukov an unnecessary distraction from the larger and much more important struggle for individual democratic rights. The only Russian political movement open to Ukrainian national demands were the socialists, who sought to transform the empire into a federation.[29]

The idea of the "historical unity" of Russians and Ukrainians, now a cornerstone of Russian national identity and history, was not inevitable but the outcome of a relatively recent process of imagining, creative thinking, historical writing, and intellectual activism. It was also a process that relied on government repression of Ukrainian activists and artists, restrictions on language, and heavy censorship, all in the service of Russia's own identity project. Driven by a combination of security concerns, emerging nationalism, and sense of ownership over historical Kyivan Rus' land, the imperial government was, by the early twentieth century, determined to prevent the emergence of a separate Ukrainian identity. In the process, Saint Petersburg became hostage to increasingly radical, occasionally delusional voices within the Russian nationalist movement. These dynamics and ideas, however, were not simply imported into Ukraine from Moscow and Saint Petersburg by transplant imperial officials and intellectuals; they were also to a significant degree a product of the beliefs and desires of many of those who can be now labeled Ukrainians—even if these people would certainly have rejected such a categorization.

Genuine support for the empire and Russian identity among sections of Ukraine's elites and the small but rapidly growing middle and working classes raised the stakes in the struggle between Russian and Ukrainian identities and political visions for the region. The top prize in this struggle was the peasantry. This group spoke Ukrainian and was acutely aware of their distinct culture and how they differed from Great Russians, but they also largely supported the monarchy and had little notion of any national political identity. In 1914, this great struggle over Ukraine and the allegiances, identity, and language of its inhabitants took a new and unexpected turn and spread out of the Russian Empire and into a different one: Austria-Hungary.

CHAPTER 3

LIBERATION
FROM FREEDOM

On August 2, 1914, just five days after the outbreak of World War I, Vladimir Grabar', a mild-mannered international law professor at Iur'ev University (now the University of Tartu in Estonia), received an urgent telegram from a friend, a senior Russian government official in Saint Petersburg. Would Grabar' be willing to join the Russian army as a legal advisor? After brief consideration, Grabar' accepted and soon was at the *Stavka*, the Russian army's Supreme Command, living and working out of a train compartment and rubbing shoulders with diplomats and generals.

Grabar'—or as he was known in Ukrainian, Volodymyr Hrabar—was born in Vienna in 1865 to a prominent Ukrainian family that supported the unification of Austria-Hungary's Ukrainian regions and people with Russia. In 1876, the family moved to the Russian Empire. After studying law in Moscow, Grabar' became a direct beneficiary of the empire's drive for Russification. When Dorpat University, a venerable German-language institution, was Russified and renamed Iur'ev University, most professors were forced to leave because they were unable to teach in Russian. As a result, in 1893, an international law professorship opened up, and Grabar' joined the faculty.

A great believer in international law and its ability to restrain the barbarity of war, Grabar' was tasked with ensuring the legality of the Russian military's conduct, including in the occupation of the Ukrainian regions of his native Austria-Hungary. But after spending just a few days at the Stavka, the lawyer's mood had soured. "The situation is not very favorable for international law," Grabar' noted in his diary on August 13. This would turn out to be a gross understatement. The professor's humanistic concerns for legality irritated the Russian high command, and in May 1915 he was forced out, ostensibly for health reasons.

The Russian occupation of majority-Ukrainian Galicia and Bukovyna, a largely overlooked but important chapter of the Great War, brought together the different strands of Russian nationalists' dreams and xenophobia: a desire to unify all Kyivan Rus' lands under the Romanovs, anti-Jewish violence, and unwavering determination to destroy Ukrainian identity, culture, and political activism. Russian rule was bloody and repressive. It was also a template for future and larger Russian violence in and against Ukraine. A century later, in 2022, policies remarkably similar to those the Russian Empire adopted in 1914–1915—looting, targeting Ukrainian political and cultural leaders, changing public signs and street names, and banning Ukrainian-language publications and education and forcibly replacing them with Russian—would become hallmarks of the Kremlin's actions in occupied Ukraine. Not just the goals but also the methods of Russian subjugation of Ukrainian territories have turned out to be remarkably consistent over time.

The standard story of the origins of World War I (1914–1918) starts with the rise of the German Empire and its implacable conflict with France over Alsace-Lorraine, a region that Prussia, which united the German lands, took from France after defeating it in 1870–1871. This animosity eventually led to the emergence of two hostile military blocs: Germany and the Austro-Hungarian Empire on one side and France and Russia on the other. Germany's ambition, industrial potential, military might, and desire to secure overseas colonies also alarmed the British Empire and eventually led it to join the Franco-Russian camp. The competition between the Habsburgs and the Romanovs over the Balkans added extra fuel to the already combustible situation, and other states joined opposing sides. When Serbian nationalist Gavrilo Princip assassinated the Habsburg Archduke Franz Ferdinand in Sarajevo on June 28, 1914, Austria-Hungary jumped on an opportunity to crush its increasingly assertive neighbor Serbia, which was also Russia's close Orthodox Christian, Slavic ally. Unwittingly, Europeans "sleepwalked" into a world war that would destroy empires and kill millions.[1]

Military histories of the Great War predominantly focus on the Western Front, trench warfare, and the great battles of the Somme, Ypres, Marne, and Verdun. Popular perception of the Great War is shaped by the classic works of German, British, French, and American writers and poets, such as Erich Maria Remarque's *All Quiet on the Western Front* or Ernest Hemingway's *A Farewell to Arms*. The memory of wartime violence against civilians is dominated by the Armenian genocide in the Ottoman Empire.

Although overlooked by the Western-oriented histories of the conflict, Ukraine was crucial for the course of the Great War. Between 1914 and 1916, Austro-Hungarian Galicia became a major battlefield that involved millions of troops. The need to prop up its failing Habsburg ally forced Germany to transfer units, badly needed on the Western Front, to the east. In parallel with conventional warfare, Ukraine became the site of large-scale violence against civilians, second only to the Ottoman mass-murder campaign.

Without Ukraine, the Russian Empire would simply have been too weak to oppose Germany. The Donbas was a key industrial center, and Ukraine was a crucial source of personnel for the army. Central and southern Ukraine were the Russian Empire's breadbasket and main source of sugar. When, because of wartime devastation, food ceased to reach the empire's cities, Russians rebelled, and the empire collapsed.[2]

Ukraine was even more central to the outbreak of the Great War. The Russian Empire's struggle against Ukrainian identity was the key driver of the Romanov-Habsburg conflict, arguably an even more salient one than the competition over the Balkans. A crucial obstacle to Russian domination of Ukraine and its ability to turn the region's Orthodox residents into Russians—the imperial government's key objective—was that the empire did not control all the territories in which people spoke Ukrainian and shared the Ukrainian identity. Most Ukrainians lived under the Romanovs' rule, but about four million resided across the border in the more tolerant Austro-Hungarian regions of Galicia, Bukovyna, and Carpatho-Rus. There, Ukrainian—or, as it was called, Ruthenian or Rusyn—culture, language, identity, and political activism were free to flourish, and Ukrainian activists from the Russian Empire could find refuge from persecution and challenge Saint Petersburg. As long as these islands of Ukrainian identity and activism existed, Russian control of Ukraine, which Saint Petersburg saw as paramount for the empire's survival, could not be secured. The prominent Russian nationalist Mikhail Menshikov, who was uninterested in the Balkan Slavs and recognized the grave dangers of a major European war, was nevertheless "willing to fight to the death" to prevent the danger of Ukrainian independence, which emanated from Austro-Hungarian Galicia.[3]

Of the Ukrainian regions in the Habsburg empire, Galicia (also known as Red Rus') was the largest and most important. The Kyivan Rus' principality of Galicia emerged out of the Mongol devastation in the thirteenth century as an independent kingdom, but it quickly declined and had been conquered by Poland by 1349. After the first partition of Poland in 1772, the region became part of the Habsburg domain. By 1914, Galicia was the only former Kyivan Rus' land not yet incorporated into Russia. Densely populated but underdeveloped, it was one of the poorest regions in Europe and a source of many thousands of working hands for the sweatshops of New York, coal mines of Pennsylvania, and farms of the Canadian prairies. Mostly rural, the region had by the early twentieth century also developed a growing working class, centered on the oil fields of Boryslav, as well as a multiethnic, multilingual urban bourgeoisie.

Western Galicia, the region around Kraków, was a distinctly Polish area. Eastern Galicia, with a population of about 5.3 million in 1910, was about 60 percent ethnic Ukrainian, with Poles and Jews (25 and 12 percent, respectively) being the two other major groups. Ukrainians, the vast majority of whom belonged to the Greek Catholic Church, were mostly peasants. Poles and Jews dominated the towns, including Lviv, the regional capital. At the provincial level, Poles were historically the dominant force in politics, governance, and education; though, as time went on, the government in Vienna increasingly invested in promoting Ukrainian organizations and culture as a counterweight to Polish dominance. Bukovyna was a much smaller region, in which Ukrainians were largely Orthodox and the other major groups were Romanians and Jews.[4]

Tolerance was the Habsburgs' guiding principle in governing the vast array of ethnicities residing in their lands, and in Austria-Hungary Ukrainians and Jews enjoyed collective and individual liberties of which their counterparts in the Russian Empire were deprived. In the second half of the nineteenth century, the combined effects of the abolition of serfdom, economic modernization, and political liberalization began to transform the Ukrainian-speaking peasantry in Austria-Hungary. Compulsory elementary education was introduced in 1873, literacy grew, reading rooms appeared in many villages—there were over two thousand Ukrainian-language reading rooms in Galicia by 1908—and Ukrainian activists began establishing cultural societies and political clubs. Ukrainian-language publishing houses thrived, and there was a busy smuggling route carrying books and newspapers into Russian Ukraine.[5]

Ukrainian-language education was also allowed by the Habsburg government, though discriminated against by the region's Polish leadership. Lviv University had Ukrainian-language chairs and departments (one of which was occupied by Mykhailo Hrushevsky) and offered classes in Ukrainian. There was even a plan to establish a separate Ukrainian-language university, but it was derailed by the war's outbreak. Even though the Ukrainian national movement in Galicia was not immune to xenophobia and anti-Semitism, these never reached the Russian Empire's levels. Ukrainians and Jews occasionally forged electoral alliances to defeat Polish groupings in elections to the regional diet (*Sejm*) in Lviv and the national parliament (*Reichsrat*) in Vienna. Pogroms did happen in the region but mostly in Polish-majority western Galicia. Unsurprisingly, rights, liberties, and physical safety translated into allegiance, and Ruthenians and Jews were among the Austro-Hungarian Empire's most loyal ethnic groups.[6]

Yet this support for the Habsburgs was not uniform. A minority—though a vocal one—of Ruthenians belonged to the "Russophile," also often called "Moskvophile," camp. These people considered themselves a part of the broader Russian nation, and quite a few of them dreamed of the Habsburg Ruthenian lands someday joining Russia. Some, like the Grabar' family, even immigrated there. Such pro-Russian orientation was not uncommon in the early and mid-nineteenth century, but it sharply declined in the wake of the Valuev Circular. Still, such people continued to exist and were actively supported and funded by prominent Russian nationalists such as Duma member Count Vladimir Bobrinsky. Indeed, a portion of the Ems Ukase, which finalized the restrictions on the Ukrainian language in the Russian Empire, focused on subsidizing a pro-Russian Galician newspaper named *Slovo* (Word).[7]

As the relations between the two empires soured, this pro-Russian orientation inevitably—and, according to the existing evidence, justifiably—began to arouse suspicion. Russian intelligence likely recruited spies among the Russophiles in Galicia. In 1882, eleven prominent Russophiles were accused of treason and put on trial in Lviv. Even though the defendants were acquitted, the popular perception of Russophiles as being Russian agents of influence, and potentially even spies, remained. Additional trials took place in Lviv and in Marmaros-Sziget in the Hungarian half of the empire in 1912 and 1914, and yet another was being prepared in

Chernivtsi when the war started. For the Ukrainians of Austria-Hungary, Russia's support for the Russophiles represented a mortal threat. George Raffalovich, a British Jew who wrote under the pen name Bedwin Sands and was a close ally of the Ukrainian national movement, expressed the common fear that:

> Russia, through her semi-official agents, was doing systematic work in Galicia. Day by day her emissaries—priests and students, journalists, and even army officers—sought to attract sympathizers in Austria-Galicia so that when the occasion offered Russia might declare war on the pretense of defending her alleged coreligionists, invade the province, and annex it. Then Russia might be able once more to crush the Ukrainian revival on her own soil by suppressing the "irredentism" of Galicia.[8]

The Russian view of the situation was a mirror image of these fears. Politically vibrant and proudly Ukrainian, Galicia was crucial to the development of Ukrainian national identity and political consciousness within both empires and was often called "the Ukrainian Piedmont"— an explicit reference to the region that had spearheaded the unification of Italy. Ukrainian activism in Galicia and the support it received from Vienna fueled Russian paranoia. At some point, the very existence of Ukrainian nationalism came to be perceived as an elaborate conspiracy by Austrian military intelligence. Whereas Austro-Hungarian authorities rightfully considered the Galician Russophiles an annoying but ultimately minor problem, for Saint Petersburg anything consciously Ukrainian was a mortal danger to the empire and the Russian nation. Thus, the conflict between Saint Petersburg and Vienna over Ukraine and Ukrainians was no less—and arguably even more—important than their struggle over the Balkans, which is typically seen as the key trigger for the outbreak of the Great War. The clash between the Russian and Austro-Hungarian empires over Galicia and the Ukrainian question more broadly was unavoidable.[9]

The outbreak of the Great War prompted a brief but powerful surge in patriotism across the Russian Empire and temporarily reconciled minority groups with the monarchy. Symon Petliura—editor of the Moscow-based journal *Ukrainian Life* who would later become the leader of the short-lived Ukrainian National Republic—wrote in the journal's proclamation that in war between Russia and Austria, Ukrainians had only one choice: Russia. This rapprochement did not last long, and soon the government was back to supporting and promoting exclusionary, xenophobic Black Hundreds' policies and publications and repressing the Ukrainian language and culture.[10]

The person leading Russia's war effort was the army's supreme commander, Grand Duke Nicholas (Nikolai Nikolaievich). At six feet six (nearly two meters), this grandson of Nicholas I was a towering figure who stood almost literally head and shoulders above his reigning nephew. A mediocre strategist, the grand duke was nonetheless an experienced soldier and a popular commander. His chief of staff was Nikolai Yanushkevich, a military bureaucrat who was previously the Russian army's chief of the General Staff but who had never led troops. Even by the standards of the time and their social class, the grand duke and Yanushkevich were extreme xenophobes. Both viewed the conflict as a holy war against external and internal enemies, which might partially explain the zeal—though not the actual purpose of—the Russian army's attacks against civilians.[11]

In addition to territorial expansion, for Russian elites the war against Austria-Hungary was an opportunity to finally unite all the ancient Rus' lands under their rule and remove what they perceived as the existential danger of Ukrainian nationalism. On August 5, Grand Duke Nicholas published an emotional address to the Ukrainians of Galicia. Referring to the Habsburgs' Ukrainian subjects as "Russian brothers who are being freed," Nicholas declared that "there is no force that can stop the Russian people in their outburst for unity. . . . You will find a place within the bosom of Mother Russia." The war, according to the grand duke, was the final stage in the long process of "gathering" the Russian lands that had started with Muscovite Prince Ivan Moneybags and would be completed by Nicholas II. A separate proclamation addressed the partitioned Poles, who in exchange for supporting Russia were promised postwar reunification and autonomy within the empire. General Alexei Brusilov, commander of the Russian Eighth Army, instructed his troops that Galicia is "a Russian land from time immemorial, populated . . . by Russian people." Nicholas II himself later stated that "there is no Galicia, rather [one] Great Russia to the Carpathian Mountains," and that annexing Galicia and Bukovyna would allow Russia to reach its "natural boundaries."[12]

Violence against civilians in Galicia and Bukovyna started almost immediately after the war broke out. The primary targets during the first days of the war were the Russophiles and anyone else suspected by Habsburg authorities of harboring pro-Russian sympathies. Such people were rounded up, imprisoned, and often shot or hanged by Austro-Hungarian troops. Rule of law and personal liberty ceased to exist, and practically any Ukrainian could find themselves accused of treason merely for using their language, which, like Russian, used a Cyrillic script. Estimates of the number of people executed by Austrian authorities during this brief initial period range widely, from 1,500 to almost 30,000. Up to 30,000 more were interned in the Thalerhof concentration camp in Graz in Austria. Yet as brutal and unjustified as it was, Austro-Hungarian violence paled in comparison to what the region would experience under Russian rule.[13]

When the Russian and Austro-Hungarian armies clashed in eastern Galicia, the two sides were roughly equal in strength. Habsburg forces enjoyed some initial success, but eventually poor strategic planning, tactical blunders, inept leadership, and inadequate logistics took their toll. The front soon collapsed, and Austro-Hungarian troops were in full retreat. In late August, the *Czernowitzer Allgemeine Zeitung*, a newspaper based in the Bukovynian regional capital of Chernivtsi, was still boasting of Habsburg troops achieving "victory after victory," but almost immediately after the article was published, Austrian authorities fled the city. With Chernivtsi undefended, on August 29 the first Russian soldier to reach it proceeded straight to a tavern and got drunk. More sober Russian units began occupying the town the following day, August 30. Lviv fell on September 3. Soon, all of eastern and large parts of western Galicia were in Russian hands. This disastrous campaign cost the Habsburg military close to four hundred thousand men killed, wounded, or taken prisoner.[14]

Austro-Hungarian citizens, originally unaware of Russia's plans to liberate them from the Habsburg yoke once and for all, quickly realized that the Russians had come to the region to stay. Julius Weber, editor of the *Czernowitzer Tagblatt*, recalled that during the surrender ceremony in Chernivtsi, the Russian commander, General Ariutinov, demanded that the Chernivtsi mayor speak Russian—a language the Austrian official did not know. When the mayor finished his part, Ariutinov shocked the crowd by declaring that Chernivtsi had now been fully incorporated into the Russian Empire.[15]

Russian authorities made no secret of the new ethnic and political hierarchy they planned to introduce. After securing control of the area, the military began releasing some Austrian prisoners of war (POWs) who hailed from the region; in particular, they selected Ukrainians—or, as official documents put it, "Russian Galicians"—who swore allegiance to the Russian emperor. By the spring of 1915, 4,290 Austrian POWs had been granted their freedom this way.[16]

Galicia and Bukovyna were on the front lines, and the Russian military enjoyed almost unlimited control over the region's affairs (as well as over originally Russian territory close to the front). Even if formal annexation was considered politically impossible during wartime, Russian authorities did their best to make the region a de facto part of the empire. This strategy violated international law and contradicted the obligations that the Russian Empire had accepted by signing the Hague Convention in 1899. The convention, which ironically owed its very existence to Russian diplomatic efforts, obligated occupying powers to protect civilian lives and property, maintain public order, and refrain from assigning collective responsibility and punishment for crimes. From the very beginning of their arrival in Galicia and Bukovyna, Russian authorities did exactly the opposite.[17]

Violence against civilians was the standard Russian way of doing things not only during wartime. Russian behavior in occupied Austro-Hungarian lands differed sharply from that in the occupied parts of German East Prussia. That region, neither a part of historical Rus' nor inhabited by Slavs, suffered some early marauding and violence at the hands of Russian troops, but there was no concentrated effort to annex the land, remake its ethnic composition, or change the identities of inhabitants. East Prussia experienced a mostly standard—if harsh and often violent—occupation; Galicia and Bukovyna did not.

Plunder was the trademark of Russian troops wherever they went. This was neither new nor unexpected; Russian forces had a penchant for wartime looting even when moving through their own territory. In Austria-Hungary, looting by Russian troops followed whenever they entered a town, no matter how destitute the locale. Sometimes plunder targeted more than just personal items, money, or valuables. In the University of Chernivtsi's Zoology Department, Russian troops destroyed the specimen collection by drinking the alcohol in which various reptiles and amphibians were preserved. The equipment of the chemistry lab was saved from destruction and transferred to Kyiv.[18]

Cossack units, brave but poorly disciplined, were the worst offenders, and eyewitnesses reported Cossacks riding through Galicia wearing women's clothes and furs. Jews were the chief victims, but Poles and Ukrainians were robbed as well. Resisting the often inebriated Russian soldiers was a futile and dangerous endeavor, and even at the Stavka officials openly spoke of civilians being murdered for trying to protect their property. Occasionally, if soldiers had already sobered up but not yet moved elsewhere, owners could convince them to return at least some of the loot, but such cases were rare.[19]

Purely criminal looting could be given a veneer of legality by rebranding it as requisition, but even here, xenophobia and disregard for the laws of war were the guiding principles. In theory, troops had to pay or at least leave receipts in case of requisitioning, but this rarely happened. An Austrian soldier who remained behind Russian lines was told by a

Russian noncommissioned officer that the troops had to pay Ukrainians and could, if they wished, pay the Poles, but they were instructed to simply take from the Jews outright.[20]

Looting went hand in hand with pogroms. Anti-Semitism was pervasive at all levels of the Russian military. Jews served in the Russian army but could not be commissioned as officers—not even if they converted to Christianity or had only one Jewish grandparent. Russian propaganda presented the war as a struggle not just against the Central Powers but also against the Jews, and the results of this framing were immediately apparent in Galicia. The first notable pogrom took place in Brody, a key trade and transportation hub just across the Austrian border. According to the Russian version of events, a local Jewish girl, possibly the daughter of a hotel owner, shot a Russian officer. In revenge, outraged Russian troops burned and destroyed the entire Jewish part of town. So massive was the carnage that it became a topic of conversation at the Stavka. When Grabar' suggested to his colleague, Prince Nikolai Obolensky, that the girl (who, we now know, might not have even existed) likely shot the Russian because he tried to rape her, the prince vehemently denied that a Russian officer could ever do such a thing.[21]

As Russian troops advanced deeper into Austrian territory, Jews, especially young women, developed a remarkably persistent habit of firing at soldiers who were already itching for violence, always from buildings that seemed to have valuables to plunder. The list of places where such a shooting was used to justify a pogrom grew so long that Russian officials simply stopped taking the story seriously. While excuses for pogroms were imaginary, the violence was very real. Jews "were killed, the women were raped in the streets, old women's breasts are slashed off and the people are left to die in the agony," described one Russian Jewish soldier. Eyewitness reports also suggest that sexual violence and rape, including gang rape, were especially common and particularly brutal during the pogroms. Fathers or husbands who tried to intervene were beaten; some were murdered. Religious Jews were publicly humiliated by Russian troops, their beards and side curls cut off.[22]

The most well-known, if not the bloodiest, pogrom of this wave of violence took place in Lviv on September 27, 1914. According to the official account, shots were fired at Russian troops from a house in a Jewish area and violence broke out. Between thirty-eight and forty-nine people, mostly but not only Jews, were murdered by Russian soldiers, and many more were wounded. Fearing such Russian violence, 250,000 to 300,000 people fled Galicia and Bukovyna, most often to Vienna, creating a refugee crisis in the Habsburg capital.[23]

With Galicia and Bukovyna under the Stavka's exclusive authority, the military ensured that as few outsiders as possible were allowed in, and almost no information about the pogroms and the looting made it out. Even the Russian government was largely in the dark about what was going on. Shloyme Rappoport, more widely known under his pen name S. An-sky, was one of the few Russians who saw the carnage firsthand. A proud Jew and Russian patriot, An-sky was a writer, ethnographer, and social worker with friends among the upper echelons of Russian liberal civil society. These friends secured him an assignment with a charitable organization giving aid to Russian soldiers. Visiting occupied Galicia in early 1915, An-sky kept a diary that paints a gruesome picture of Russian violence, mostly (though not only) against Jewish civilians.

> Rava-Ruska. Troops arrived there on [August] the 31st. For five days they wrecked the town, and also burned it. Sometimes the officers defended the residents but most pretended as if they didn't see. This was one scene: soldiers are tearing apart a trading stall. An officer passes by, flings himself at them: "What are you doing, so-and-so?" "Your Honor, it belongs to yids." "Ah, yids . . ." And he walks past.
>
> Mosti-Velki. Beating of Jews, the troops looted for five or six days, Ruthenians made off with the spoils.
>
> Niemirow. The whole shtetl was burned.
>
> Lubaczow. The center of the town is completely burned, not a single shop remains.

Cieszanow. Was turned into a hellhole.

[A Jew] showed me a . . . synagogue, a Hasidic one, which was securely boarded up after it was looted.

[Lawyer Boris] Ratner returned from Tuchow yesterday. He said the shtetl was completely burned and devastated.[24]

While looting and violence raged in Galicia, at the Stavka, Grabar' was taking part in lively debates about the future of "liberated" Austrian territories and their governance. On September 4, Grand Duke Nicholas ordered the creation of a special general governorship for Galicia, with the capital in Lviv. The governor-general was to be Lieutenant General Count Georgii Bobrinsky, who had little relevant experience besides sharing a last name with his cousin Vladimir Bobrinsky, Russia's most prominent supporter of the Austro-Hungarian Russophiles. The grand duke's chief of staff Yanushkevich also dispatched Nikolai Basily—deputy head of the Diplomatic Chancellery at the Stavka and a rising star at the Ministry of Foreign Affairs—to Galicia to survey the situation and to come up with suggestions for occupation policies in the region.[25]

While in Lviv, Basily realized that, all the Russian reunification propaganda aside, practical steps were needed for the occupation authorities to gain the loyalty of the Ukrainian population. Upon his return in mid-September 1914, Basily proposed a set of policies that boiled down to three things: Russifying the Ukrainians, neutralizing the Poles, and beating the Yids. Violence from below was to become a policy directed from above.

Ukrainians' support for Russia, Basily suggested, could be secured by confiscating the property of the Poles and the Jews and distributing it to Ukrainians, or using the proceeds of such property to provide social welfare to the Ukrainian population. When Basily presented this plan to the grand duke, the Russian commander was supportive but urged caution in dealing with the Poles. Dmitrii Chikhachev, a nationalist Duma member and a close associate of both Bobrinsky cousins, was assigned to Galicia as a civilian official and came up with a similar set of proposals. The Russian government was unwilling to antagonize the Poles too greatly, but Jews were fair game and could be abused in the service of turning Ukrainians into Russians. The Russian government's Ukrainian and Jewish "problems" thus became intertwined once again, now in occupied Galicia.[26]

Extreme anti-Semitism was not limited to the Russian military or card-carrying nationalists; the prejudice was widespread. At the Stavka, observed Grabar', only he and perhaps one other person ever used the word "Jews"; the rest referred to "kikes" exclusively. Over breakfast, refined diplomats and state officials, among the brightest in the Russian government, would discuss various ideas on how to deal with Galicia's Jewish population. According to one suggestion, Jews should be turned into serfs; another proposed expelling them to Austrian-controlled territory. These were the comparative moderates. The most radical voices advocated simply slaughtering all Jews because the war provided an opportunity to do so, whereas during peacetime the Duma might intervene. Like other members of the Russian elite, these people wanted to rule Galicia but were unwilling to accept the region for what it was: a complex and diverse place in which Ukrainians, Poles, and Jews lived side by side, not an imaginary land of nonexistent Austrian Russians. Tragically, these radicals also had the will and the means to use violence to try to transform the former into the latter.[27]

Galician Jewry was extremely poor, and the Yiddish pejorative term *Galizianer* came to mean abject poverty, uncouth manners, and religious fanaticism. But Galician Jewry also included a prosperous and well-educated middle class and, especially offensive for the Russian elite, owners of large agricultural estates. In Russia, Jews were banned from owning agricultural land, but in eastern Galicia at the beginning of the twentieth century some 18.5 percent of privately owned land belonged to Jews. This was a lot of land and property that could be distributed in exchange for local Ukrainians' support. Confiscating property of foreign citizens during wartime was legally problematic, but an unfazed Yanushkevich suggested simply granting Galician Jews compulsory Russian citizenship to circumvent this. Increasing the size of Russia's Jewish subjects by several hundred thousand might not have been the most intuitive policy for an anti-Semite like Yanushkevich, but buying the loyalty of Ukrainian peasants was even more crucial.[28]

After the initial wave of pogroms and plunder, Russian violence declined in intensity but, after the arrival in Lviv of the governor-general, also became more systematic. The focus of the repression also shifted. No longer a wave of uncoordinated attacks on hapless civilians, it became an organized effort to ethnically cleanse, and then Russify, the region's civic life, economy, and public administration. Galicia, in Governor Bobrinsky's words, was primordial Russian land and therefore had to be governed "according to Russian principles."

Russian principles meant dismissing all Jewish government and municipal employees and purging the courts, ostensibly to remove elements "potentially tendentious, harmful to the Russian population of Galicia." The Stavka also decided to install the lawyer Volodymyr Dudykevych, the leader of Galician Russophiles, at the helm of the region's judicial system. Dudykevych, who visited Grand Duke Nicholas in mid-September 1914, seemed to aim higher and sought to become the governor himself, but this position had to go to someone more Russian than him.[29]

Then the property confiscation began. Already during the early wave of pogroms Ukrainian and Polish peasants had helped themselves to plundered Jewish property, at times with the encouragement of Russian officers on the ground, but now this would become government policy. Initially, Russian authorities distributed among Ukrainian peasants the valuables and household possessions of Jews who had fled Galicia, but the much bigger prize was land. Bobrinsky started by confiscating the estates of Jewish landowners who escaped the region without leaving an estate manager in charge or appointing a legal caretaker, but the ultimate ambition was to confiscate and distribute everything. The governor-general was also very explicit about the perceived connection between Jewish land and Ukrainian loyalty. Newspaper editor Weber reported that, speaking to a large crowd of specially gathered Ukrainian peasants in Bukovyna, Bobrinsky assured them that "Austria is no more" and urged peasants to be "faithful sons of Russia and the Tsar." In exchange, when the war was over, they would receive the lands that belonged to the Jews and become, "with God's help and Tsar's assistance, wealthy people."[30]

Land transfer was just one part of the Russification policy. Another was eliminating any and all alternatives to Russian identity. One of the first things Russian authorities did after assuming control over Galicia and Bukovyna was to switch the region to Saint Petersburg's time zone and introduce the Julian calendar, which was used in the Russian Empire and differed from the Gregorian calendar of central Europe by thirteen days. This kind of policy was not unique—Austria-Hungary and Germany also practiced such measures in Russian and Serbian areas they occupied during the war—but it was an ominous signal of things to come.

After fixing the time and the date, Russian occupation authorities turned their attention to the alphabet and ordered all street signs switched from Latin script to Cyrillic. This was bound to create chaos because only Ukrainians used a Cyrillic alphabet, and even this was somewhat different from the Russian one. For those who spoke Polish, German, Romanian, or Yiddish, public spaces would now be impossible to navigate. Fearing the consequences of this measure, local leaders protested and tried to delay the change for as long as possible. There was simply no capacity to manufacture so many signs in Cyrillic letters so quickly, they argued. But the Russians remained unmoved. Having declared the region to be fundamentally Russian and a future part of the Romanov state, they simply could not go back on such a symbolic change.

In Lviv, Latin-script signs remained until the end of spring 1915, but eventually Cyrillic replaced them even there. Later, not just the signs but the street names themselves became a target. Names most closely associated with Austria-Hungary were replaced: in Chernivtsi, Austria Square was renamed Central Square; the square named after popular Habsburg monarch Franz Josef became the Emperor's Square. In burned-out towns, new street names appeared among the wreckage: Pushkin, Lermontov, Turgenev. "The irony of naming these horribly deformed streets after the luminaries of Russian culture had escaped the victors; they didn't realize how offensive it was to the memory of our great Russian authors," lamented An-sky. The occupation authorities also demanded locals adorn their houses with Russian flags and celebrate Russian holidays, such as the tsar's birthday. Wearing ribbons of blue and yellow, the colors of Ukrainian national movement, was forbidden.[31]

Russification meant not simply introducing Russian but also banning all things Ukrainian. While cleansing the judicial systems of Jewish judges and employees, the new masters of Galicia introduced Russian as the official working language of the courts, even though very few people within the system spoke it. The Ministry of Justice in Saint Petersburg went along with the purging of staff along ethnic lines but objected to the language switch because it was illegal under international law. They were ignored, and the measure went ahead anyway.[32]

Ukrainian media and publishing became another target of repression. In the Russian Empire, publications in Ukrainian were now allowed, but in the occupied Austrian lands Russian authorities closed all Ukrainian bookstores because the books they were selling were deemed "anti-Russian." The same fate befell Ukrainian-language newspapers, which were all shuttered. Even printing advertisements in Ukrainian was now forbidden. Antoni Siewinski, a Polish schoolteacher from Buchach, recorded in his diary that Russians "cannot stand the [Ukrainian] language, and I have seen Muscovites throwing books written in Ruthenian to the ground with great disgust." Repressions extended beyond papers and cultural institutions. Many Ukrainian journalists and artists were arrested, taken hostage to ensure the good behavior of the community, or exiled deep into Russia. Even writing letters and sending telegrams in Ukrainian was effectively forbidden, because the censors who perlustrated all mail were instructed to destroy any correspondence in that language. In short, in Galicia and Bukovyna the military authorities recreated the conditions that had existed in the Russian Empire after the Ems decree, even though Russia proper had already moved on from those measures. Governor Bobrinsky's office also began publishing a Russian-language and politically pro-Russian paper, but its circulation was limited, and the enterprise required substantial government subsidies to survive.[33]

Public education also became a target for repression. Initially, military authorities simply shut down all educational institutions in the occupied areas, from elementary schools to universities. By mid-September 1914 some were allowed to reopen, but only if they offered classes in Russian. Ukrainian was allowed in primary schools, but above that level all previously Ukrainian instruction had to switch to Russian. The problem was that there were almost no Russian-speaking teachers in the region, certainly not enough to support a functioning education system. To solve this, the authorities began dispatching educators and school officials from within the Russian Empire and organized crash courses in Russian for local teachers. The Petrograd (as Saint Petersburg was renamed at the war's outbreak) City Duma got involved and promised to fund Russian-language courses for teachers in the occupied zone as a patriotic gesture. The imperial government also planned to open nine thousand new Russian-language elementary schools in Galicia, fifty high schools, and twelve teachers' colleges within the next five years.[34]

The most heated battle in the campaign to Russify the region centered on religion. In Bukovyna most Ukrainians were Orthodox, but in Galicia the vast majority belonged to the Greek Catholic (also known as Uniate) Church. In the Russian Empire, the Uniates were persecuted and the government invested enormous effort into bringing Uniates into the fold of the Russian Orthodox Church. Many Russian officials recognized the importance of Greek Catholicism to Galician Ukrainians and urged caution in administration of religious issues. The more radical Russian nationalists, however, were convinced that making Orthodox Christians out of Uniates was essential to Russifying the region, and Yanushkevich argued that, to achieve this goal, "unofficial coercion" was well warranted. The hawks prevailed, and the task of turning Uniates into Orthodox was assigned to Archbishop Evlogii, a zealot with considerable experience fighting confessional conflicts in the empire's western borderlands. Evlogii was fully convinced that without religious conversion the unification of Galicia with Russia would never be stable.[35]

The Russians' religious adversary was the head of the Greek Catholic Church in Galicia, Metropolitan Andrey Sheptytsky. Born in 1865, Count Sheptytsky was a scion of a prominent Ruthenian family that had in the eighteenth century converted to Catholicism and assimilated into the Polish nobility. After a short stint as an officer in the Habsburg army, Sheptytsky abandoned secular life and returned to the religion and identity of his ancestors. By 1914, the metropolitan was not only a spiritual and moral but also a political leader of Galician Ukrainians. A staunch Austro-Hungarian patriot and the embodiment of the Ukrainian national movement in Galicia, Sheptytsky was despised by the Russian government even before the outbreak of war. Yanushkevich publicly promised to capture Sheptytsky "dead or alive." Shortly after occupying Galicia, Russian authorities arrested the metropolitan and deported him to Kyiv.

From the very beginning of the occupation, Galician Russophiles and Russian authorities tried to convert adherents of the Uniate faith by force. They shuttered churches, expelled Greek Catholic priests from parishes, and invited Orthodox clergy to take their places. According to Georgii Shavelskii, the Russian army's chief chaplain, a "huge percentage" of these imported Orthodox priests were zealous monks of the Pochaev Monastery, the religious center of Russian nationalism in Romanov Ukraine. Shavelskii described them as "half-literate, uncouth, boorish."[36]

When Archbishop Evlogii relocated to Lviv in November 1914, he fanned the flames of religious conflict by delivering on November 24 an Orthodox mass in the city's Greek Catholic cathedral and giving an inflammatory sermon in which he requested that Uniates embrace the "Russian spirit" of their ancestors and return to Orthodoxy. "Our common Mother—the great Orthodox Russia and our Holy Orthodox Russian Church—opens its arms to you," he preached.[37]

Reports about this campaign of conversion alarmed Grand Duke Nicholas, who, all his nationalist fervor notwithstanding, recognized that forced mass conversion might lead to a revolt and endanger the army's lines of communication and supply to the front. But not even the grand duke could stop Evlogii, whose efforts were supported by Tsar Nicholas

II himself. In February 1915, after receiving yet another complaint about Evlogii, the grand duke merely shrugged his shoulders and admitted that there was nothing he could do. In Galicia, the desire to Russify the region and eradicate the Ukrainian identity trumped even the war effort.[38]

The statutory conversion procedure was straightforward. If a village had people who wished it to switch to Orthodoxy, a vote would be held. If 75 percent of the village Uniates voted in favor of Orthodoxy, the parish would change churches. Things, however, did not go according to Evlogii's plans. He was impatient, radical, cantankerous, and constantly quarreled with Governor Bobrinsky and the army chaplain Shavelskii, wasting precious time and energy. More crucially, there was little real enthusiasm for Orthodoxy among the Uniates, who cared deeply for their church. Even the peas used in parish votes caused problems: Peasants voted for or against Orthodoxy by depositing peas in ballot boxes, a pea per person. But waiting in line to vote, bored peasants occasionally ate their peas, thus depriving Evlogii of the votes he needed for the final bean counting. Still, Evlogii and his allies were determined and continued dismissing and expelling Uniate clergy, even in places that voted against conversion to Orthodoxy.[39]

Such policies were bound to elicit resentment among the locals. An-sky recounts in his diary the story of a Ukrainian woman who sent her children into hiding for a long time for fear that they might be taken away and forcibly converted to Orthodoxy. No amount of potential material benefit from plunder could compensate the proudly Ukrainian communities of Galicia for having their language banned, their educational institutions shut down, their leaders arrested and exiled, and their religion attacked. By the end of 1914, despite all the pressure, just 0.85 percent of Uniates had converted to Orthodoxy. The chances of turning Galicia's Greek Catholic Ukrainians into Orthodox Russians en masse would always have been slim, even without the accompanying repression, but Russian heavy-handedness doomed the process from the very beginning.[40]

Amid property requisition and Russification policies that disrupted commerce, the region's economy nose-dived. During the Russian occupation, the number of pigs in eastern Galicia fell by over 70 percent, and almost half of all prewar horses and cattle disappeared. This predominantly agricultural area could no longer feed itself, and Russian authorities scrambled to organize soup kitchens and food distribution centers—by requisitioning any food that was still left in private hands—to prevent widespread starvation. In line with the plans discussed at the Stavka, Jews were excluded from using either welfare program. When local Jewish leaders in Chernivtsi complained to Russian governor Sergei Evreinov, he responded that Jews would continue to suffer until they had renounced their Austrian patriotism and become "good Russians" instead.[41]

The rhetoric of glorious unification also could not conceal the misery inflicted by Russian governance. For Russian officials in the metropole, even the most nationalistic ones, requests to dispatch a subordinate to help administer occupied territories presented opportunities to rid themselves of their most corrupt and least efficient staff. By early 1915, almost everyone in Galicia and Bukovyna, from peasants to generals, seemed to be complaining about the abysmal quality of Russian bureaucrats and police personnel. Even the loyal Russophiles lamented that Russian conduct was making things worse. This resentment went both ways, and at the Stavka some even began complaining that "Ruthenians" were in fact no better than the Jews.[42]

In May 1915, with tensions in Galicia and Bukovyna close to eruption, a German-Austrian attack (the Gorlice-Tarnów offensive) smashed through Russian lines and prompted what is now known as the Great Retreat. Russian occupation of the region ended as it started, with violence against civilians and widespread plunder. "Evacuation of Galicia due to the retreat of our valiant armies started in Drohobych [with] the destruction of oil production and removal [to Russia] of the more valuable machinery," noted the final report prepared by the Galician governor-general's staff. On June 9, Lviv was liberated, and by early July the occupation of Galicia and Bukovyna was mostly over, with only a tiny chunk of Habsburg territory still in Russian hands.[43]

Retreating Russian forces adopted a scorched-earth policy, pillaging and destroying as they pulled back. In 1915 the Russian authorities also became obsessed with the possibility of espionage and treason and were willing to take extreme measures to combat this perceived threat. In Galicia, Ukrainian activists, Jews, and to a lesser degree Poles were often accused of spying for the Austrians. Quite a few surely were, but by the time of the Great Retreat, Russian suspicions had turned into paranoia. Russian "spy mania" began in earnest in March 1915, when colonel of the gendarmes Sergei Miasoedov, a counterintelligence officer with the Russian Tenth Army in Warsaw, was arrested as a supposed German agent. According to the indictment, one of Miasoedov's key missions was inciting anti-Russian sentiments in Ukraine. The colonel was hastily tried and executed, though scholars now agree that he was innocent. The trial was the start of a mass hysteria, and Russian commanders and administrators began seeing treason everywhere. Along the entire front line, from the Baltic in the north to the Black Sea in the south, not just individuals but entire populations were labeled unreliable and dangerous. Already in January 1915, Yanushkevich had allowed military commanders to expel "all Jews and suspect individuals" from their zones of operation, and now every non-Russian was treated as Jewish or suspect or both. Mass deportations ensued, and official Russian documents ominously spoke of "cleansing" front-line areas.[44]

The exact number of people uprooted in this cleansing campaign remains unknown, and some were not expelled but willingly left with the retreating Russian troops. Yet the estimates are staggering: millions were on the move, most of them expellees. The deportations hit Galicia especially hard. At the beginning of the Central Powers' offensive, Eleventh Army commander General Dmitrii Shcherbachev argued that Russian authorities needed to concentrate all Galician Jews in one huge "reservation." Another proposal called for internment of all Jews in special camps. In the end it was practical, not moral or legal, arguments that thwarted these ideas. Unable to keep all Jews in one place under the army's watchful eye, Russian authorities opted for mass expulsion, which eventually came to target Jews and Ukrainians alike. By the end of 1915, more than four hundred thousand uprooted civilians, most of them from Galicia, passed through the Ukrainian region of Volhynia on their way into central and eastern Ukraine. In the process, tens of thousands died of hunger, disease, and exposure; thousands more were jailed, exiled deep into the Russian hinterland, or simply killed by Russian troops.[45]

In Volhynia, xenophobia and fear of espionage caused Russian authorities to expel tens of thousands of German farmers who had lived there for generations and were Russian subjects. Their seized farms were then given to Galician Russophiles and recent converts to Orthodoxy who had fled the region together with retreating Russian forces. Even attempts to help expellees became mired in nationalist disputes when a society set up to help Ukrainian refugees came under attack for emphasizing these refugees' non-Russianness. Russian nationalists had good reasons to worry about the refugees from Galicia: for many peasants in Ukraine, this was their first, eye-opening encounter with nationally conscious and politically active Ukrainians of their own social class.[46]

In the summer of 1916, the Russian army returned to Galicia. An offensive planned and led by General Brusilov began on June 4 and immediately broke through Austrian lines. On June 17, the Russian army reentered Chernivtsi and by the end of the month had reconquered most of Galicia. This time, Russian occupation authorities recognized their past mistakes and proceeded more cautiously. Repression and violence against civilians were more limited than in 1914–1915, and the occupation regime in general was more humane. But the end goal remained the same: in 1916 the Russian Empire was as determined to annex and integrate what it considered primordial Russian land as it had been two years prior. This time the occupation was short-lived, and in September Habsburg and German troops drove Brusilov's forces back.

Russian military authorities did their best to keep information about their occupation policies in Galicia and Bukovyna from getting out, but over time this became impossible. Visitors from the metropole such as S. An-sky shared what they saw, and while censors could prevent this information from being published, they were powerless to stop word of mouth. Nationalists predictably celebrated what they saw as the unification of Russian lands, but liberals were appalled. "A question might arise, why did the Russians take L'vov [Lviv] if instead of freedom they bring there oppression?" wondered the Kadet leader Pavel Milyukov in October 1914. A member of the party lamented that repressions against the Ukrainian language were spreading out from Galicia to the Russian Empire proper and claimed that the war—fought ostensibly for the liberation of oppressed nations—had become about the liberation of Ukrainians from their own culture. But even those Russian liberals who opposed the methods used by the Russian government in Galicia and Bukovyna accepted the annexation of these regions as a given. Some even saw it as a welcome opportunity to finally solve the problem of Ukrainian separatism or, less plausibly, to democratize the Romanov empire by demanding that all of Russia get the same political rights that Galicia had enjoyed in Austria-Hungary before the war. What the inhabitants of Galicia and Bukovyna themselves thought about their political future was seen as irrelevant.[47]

The Russian occupation of Galicia and Bukovyna, an attempt to destroy Habsburg Ukraine, failed. Russia had nothing to offer the region beyond violence and an unwavering belief in its own historical right to rule, a conviction that few locals shared. For Austro-Hungarian Ukrainians, unification with other Ukrainian lands was not an appealing enough proposition to accept giving up cultural rights, identity, and religion. Ukrainian identity was too established and too strong to surrender to Russification, especially within the brief period of the occupation. For local Poles and Jews, Russian rule meant nothing but repression, loss of rights, and inequality. These policies worked counter to Russian strategic aims, as they diverted resources and attention from the larger goal of winning the war, but in Galicia and Bukovyna identity trumped security. True, the Russian popular goal of beating the Yids was satisfied aplenty. The Jewish communities of Galicia and Bukovyna suffered enormously, but they did survive the ordeal of the Great War. The Russian Empire did not. Its collapse suddenly made Ukrainian statehood, unimaginable just four years prior, a reality.

CHAPTER 4

BLOOD AND CHAOS

O n May 25, 1926, a middle-aged, nondescript man was leaving Restaurant Chartier in Paris when a stranger approached him. "Mr. Petliura?" the stranger asked in Ukrainian, and then fired his pistol. The attacker did not escape. "I came to kill a killer," he declared. The murderer, Sholem Schwarzbard, was a Ukrainian Jew and an anarchist who had fought on the Bolshevik side during the wars that followed the collapse of the Russian Empire. Schwarzbard lost many relatives in the wave of pogroms that took place in Ukraine during the conflict and held Symon Petliura responsible for the violence. In November 1934, sixty-eight-year-old historian Mykhailo Hrushevsky was vacationing in the Soviet North Caucasus. After feeling ill, Hrushevsky, who by then was under constant surveillance from Soviet secret police, underwent a minor surgery but died several days later. The official cause of death was a blood infection, but some Ukrainians believe that Hrushevsky was murdered by the Soviet regime. On April 16, 1945, an Allied bombing raid on the Plattling rail station in Bavaria mortally wounded a seventy-one-year-old evacuee from Berlin named Pavlo Skoropadsky. He died on April 26, just days before the end of World War II in Europe. Petliura, Hrushevsky, and Skoropadsky had led Ukraine during its brief and chaotic independence following the collapse of the Russian Empire. None of the three were ready for this turn of events, and all failed to secure Ukraine's statehood.[1]

The question of Ukraine was central to the outbreak of World War I, but it was even more crucial to the fate of the Russian Revolution, the civil war that followed the empire's collapse, and the birth of the Soviet Union. Disagreements over the status of Ukraine seriously weakened the Provisional Government that replaced the Romanov dynasty. When the Bolsheviks overthrew the Provisional Government, the fate of Ukraine caused rifts between their opponents and thus helped the Communists to win the subsequent civil war. Ukraine was also at the center of the pivotal Polish-Soviet War (1919–1921). Amid all these events, Ukraine emerged as a sovereign, independent state. This period of statehood was brief and chaotic. Every major force vying for power in Russia saw preventing an independent Ukraine as a top priority, and the Ukrainians themselves were too weak and too divided internally to protect their newfound sovereignty; many in Ukraine were outright hostile to its independence.

These were years of confusion and blood. No region of the collapsing Russian Empire suffered as much as Ukraine in the period between the Russian Revolution in February 1917 and the emergence of the USSR in 1922. Different political and nation-building projects clashed. Armies—Reds, Whites, Greens, Ukrainians, Germans, French, Poles, revolutionaries, and marauders—came and went, alliances emerged and collapsed overnight, states were proclaimed and then evaporated. And, as always, it was the civilians who bore the brunt of the violence, warfare, and pogroms.

By early 1917, after two and a half years of total war, the Russian Empire was bruised and battered but still standing. The Great Retreat of 1915 reversed almost all the gains Russia's armies had achieved a year prior. Romanovs no longer controlled Galicia, Russia had been driven out of

Poland, and large swaths of the empire's northwest had been lost. The tsar had also dismissed Grand Duke Nicholas and decided to lead the war effort personally. The economy was struggling and, in Russia's urban centers, every tenth inhabitant was a refugee.[2]

The Russian Empire collapsed not because it was defeated on the battlefield but because of unrest at home. In this revolution, Ukraine played an important role. The main catalyst for the uprising was bread. Of the powers fighting in World War I, Russia was widely considered to be best shielded from the specter of food shortages. Ukraine, Europe's breadbasket, was expected to produce plenty to keep the Russian military and urban centers well supplied and protected from the shortages that plagued Germany and Austria-Hungary, which were being blockaded by the Entente powers.

Yet there were problems with food supply right from the beginning of the conflict. Some of these difficulties were inevitable consequences of war, because the government drafted large numbers of peasants and horses into the army. In Ukraine, almost three million men were mobilized; in some provinces, nearly 40 percent of peasant households were left without men. But no less consequential were the government's actions, which deliberately uprooted millions of noncombatants and turned Ukraine into a war zone, ravaged by plundering troops and traversed by masses of refugees searching for food and shelter. Even when food was produced, Russia's underdeveloped rail network struggled to manage its distribution to both the army and the home front. With military needs taking priority, in 1915 urban centers began experiencing acute shortages. Prices rose and food riots became more frequent and radical. Initially, protesters simply wanted food, but as time passed, they began demanding the removal of rulers who were proving unable to provide it.[3]

On March 8, 1917, an angry, mostly female crowd of Petrograd residents took to the streets protesting food shortages, long bread lines, and high prices. Slogans such as "Down with high prices!" quickly transformed into "Down with the tsar!" The next day, the city's workers went on strike. The soldiers of the Petrograd garrison refused to put down the rebellion by force and defected to the protesters' side. On March 15, Nicholas

II abdicated the throne, and just like that, the three-hundred-year-old Romanov monarchy was no more.

To avert anarchy, representatives of the Duma's various factions established the Provisional Government, in which the Kadets initially played the key role. Pavel Milyukov was appointed minister of foreign affairs and became the government's most prominent voice, not just on external relations but also on the all-important nationalities question. The Provisional Government saw its main goals as keeping Russia in the war and postponing all major decisions on the country's political structure and institutional design until a Constituent Assembly could be elected. Always committed to maintaining Russia's territorial integrity, Milyukov now went even further and publicly rebuffed growing calls for "peace without annexations," claiming that Galicia, which Russia no longer controlled, should become a Russian territory.[4]

This attitude was "the death knell of Russian liberalism." By insisting on continuing the war to sustain and enlarge the Russian Empire, the Provisional Government alienated millions of Russian soldiers who above all else wished to go home. The troops now wholeheartedly supported the idea of "peace without annexations and reparations." Ethnic minority soldiers were especially unenthusiastic about sacrificing their lives for the Russian state. In the months that followed the tsar's abdication, the rank and file of the military became not just pro-peace but also anti-imperialist. Slogans such as "For the self-determination of the peoples" became popular in the increasingly politicized army, and soldiers of one Ukrainian regiment on the Austrian front captured the overall mood when they refused to hold the line because they "did not need hilltop 1064." And while the Provisional Government kept supporting the war, Vladimir Lenin and his Bolshevik party opposed it and thus rapidly grew in popularity.[5]

Another key priority for the Provisional Government was to prevent the establishment of self-governance in Ukraine. Unfortunately for those in Petrograd who desperately wished to avoid making tough decisions until the war was over, the collapse of the tsarist regime triggered a wave of political mobilization across the empire. In Ukraine, emotions ran especially high.

When the news of the tsar's abdication reached Kyiv, the city was deeply divided on how to proceed. The Russian nationalist newspaper *Kievlianin* lamented the "massive explosion" in the empire's affairs and warned about the dangers of public disturbances and unrestrained political activism, lest they undermine the war effort. But what Russian nationalists saw as a great danger was to Ukrainian activists a rare opportunity.[6]

At the beginning of World War I, the Ukrainian national movement in the Russian Empire had declared full support for the war effort, but this rapprochement with the central government did not last long. In addition to harming Ukraine's economy, unleashing a refugee crisis, and trying to eradicate the Ukrainian identity in Galicia, Petrograd had returned to its pattern of repression against all things Ukrainian within the empire. Cultural associations and political organizations were banned, and Hrushevsky, who had returned home from Lviv when the war broke out, was exiled to Moscow. In 1917, with the oppressive tsarist government gone, the Ukrainian political movement could be revived.

Ukrainian activists had few preexisting organizational structures, no clear leadership, and little funding. They had neither a name nor an agreed-upon overarching program for their movement. Some—a small minority—wanted Ukraine to become independent, but most envisioned Ukraine remaining within a democratic, post-tsarist Russia. The main disagreement was whether Ukraine should receive autonomy and self-governance rights or whether the Russian state should be transformed completely and become a federation. Eventually, by March 16, a small group of Ukrainian activists in Kyiv converged on a name, the Central Rada (council), and chose Hrushevsky (still in exile in Moscow) to lead their new organization. The name was more aspirational than a reflection of reality: there was nothing for the Rada to centralize and no other groups with which to create a council. Yet the idea of securing political and cultural rights for Ukraine was very popular, especially among peasants and soldiers. Hrushevsky accepted the position offered to him and arrived in Kyiv on March 26, after surviving a fire in his train compartment en route.

Hrushevsky's views on the political status of Ukraine fluctuated throughout his career, but by 1917 he had come to support Ukraine's autonomy within a transformed Russian state. Yet the Ukrainian leader also believed that the time had come to demand more than just cultural and linguistic rights for Ukraine. The Provisional Government disagreed and sought to postpone any decisions on political rights for minorities until the Constituent Assembly had been convened. In part, this was because the Provisional Government did not feel it had the legal and political legitimacy to make such monumental decisions on the future of the state. Some politicians also recognized that the topic was so fraught that it could easily bring the government down if they engaged with it. But the key factor was that the Kadets, who dominated the Provisional Government, simply objected to granting political rights to national minorities, especially to the Ukrainians. "Russian liberalism ends where the Ukrainian question begins," lamented Ukrainian writer and politician Volodymyr Vynnychenko, who served as Hrushevsky's deputy. Lenin, on the other hand, supported national minorities' right to self-determination, though he viewed it simply as a step toward eventual Communist revolution. Still, the Bolsheviks' support for national rights was a powerful weapon, which they skillfully deployed to undermine the Provisional Government.[7]

On the question of Ukraine, the Provisional Government moved carefully and very slowly. The new regime abolished all restrictions on individual and cultural rights, appointed many officials recommended by the Central Rada, and allowed Ukrainian language instruction in elementary schools, but was reluctant to go any further. When Ukrainian activists sought the appointment of a special commissar for Ukrainian affairs, this request lingered in the government's Judicial Commission and eventually died there, because the commission was chaired by a Kadet who opposed national autonomy.[8]

For Hrushevsky and the Central Rada, these measures were not nearly enough, and they threatened to convene a separate Constituent Assembly for Ukraine. The mood in Kyiv became steadily more militant, and increasing numbers of people came to support not just autonomy but complete separation from Russia. In April, a congress of Ukrainian soldiers demanded the creation of a Ukrainian army formation: the Bohdan Khmelnytsky regiment. A monument to Petr Stolypin, Russia's influential prime minister who was assassinated in Kyiv in 1911, was removed from its pedestal in front of the City Duma.

To prevent a complete break from the Provisional Government, a Rada delegation led by Vynnychenko was dispatched to Petrograd in mid-May, but their proposals were flatly rejected and the negotiations were called off. Vasily Shul'gin, the well-connected editor of *Kievlianin* and a vocal opponent of the Central Rada, wrote that the then head of the Provisional Government Prince Georgii L'vov told him that Petrograd "under no circumstances would agree to Ukrainian demands prior to the Constituent Assembly. Autonomy for Ukraine is the business of the entire Russian people. . . . The government is not even confident that the group of people that call themselves Ukrainians . . . in fact represent the desires of the population of South Russia."[9]

By early June, the Rada had given up on reaching a negotiated settlement with Petrograd. On June 23, it unilaterally published a declaration of Ukrainian autonomy, which became known as the First Universal.* This document affirmed Ukraine as a part of the Russian state but also outlined a framework for future relations between the central government and Ukraine. Russian politicians were apoplectic, and a newspaper affiliated with the Kadets called the statement "a link in the German plan to dismember Russia." Yet no matter how furious the Provisional Government was, the publication of the First Universal forced it back to the negotiating table. On July 16, the Second Universal announced a new compromise reached by the Rada and the Provisional Government. According to this agreement, Petrograd recognized Ukraine's right to autonomy, but the formal decision on Ukraine's status was left to the Constituent Assembly.[10]

---

* "Universal" was the term for an especially important proclamation by Polish kings. Cossack leaders later also adopted the tradition of calling a key proclamation a "universal."

Yet despite the agreement, relations between Petrograd and Kyiv remained acrimonious. A clash between the new Khmelnitsky Regiment and a Russian cavalry unit that was determined "to show Ukrainians their autonomy and . . . introduce the old military order" left sixteen Ukrainian soldiers dead. In September, Kyiv hosted a congress of Russia's ethnic minorities, all of whom were dissatisfied with the Provisional Government and committed to transforming the state into a federation. Speaking at the event, Symon Petliura, the Rada's military commissar, accused the Provisional Government of sidelining non-Russians in state affairs and insisted that Ukraine needed its own, separate army. Preparations to hold a Ukrainian Constituent Assembly also began.[11]

When the Provisional Government chose to keep Russia in the war, it alienated the soldiers who wanted to go back home. The policy was unpopular, but it could be justified by referencing the commitment made to Russia's allies and the need to abide by the country's treaties. The Provisional Government's policies toward Ukraine were driven by imperialistic nationalism, not constitutional constraints or the need for wartime allied solidarity. This intransigence made minorities more likely to support the Bolsheviks and alienated and radicalized the Ukrainian national movement. If in March 1917 almost all Ukrainian activists merely wanted autonomy within Russia, by late fall independence had become a popular idea.

When on November 7 the Provisional Government was deposed in a Bolshevik coup d'état, the Rada initially hedged its bets. Even though Lenin supported the right to self-determination, the Rada was no friend to the Communists. But Kyiv also saw little reason to support the Provisional Government, which Ukrainian leaders now perceived as simply a vehicle for Russian chauvinism. Eventually, Ukrainian authorities came out against the Bolshevik coup. In Ukraine, three armed factions—Ukrainian units, the Bolsheviks, and troops still loyal to the Provisional Government—now faced each other. The civil war in Ukraine had begun.

After a brief but vicious bout of fighting between the Bolsheviks and Provisional Government troops, the Central Rada assumed control in Kyiv. It then published the Third Universal, which proclaimed the establishment of the Ukrainian People's Republic (Ukrains'ka Narodna Respublika, UNR), though it still envisioned Ukraine as part of a future, non-Communist, federal Russian state. The UNR was meant to be a liberal, progressive entity with a mandatory eight-hour workday, no death penalty, an independent judiciary, and autonomy for national minorities. To underscore the multiethnic composition of Ukraine, the Third Universal was issued in four languages: Ukrainian, Russian, Polish, and Yiddish.

Russian nationalists were predictably furious, and an editorial in *Kievlianin* even spoke of a foreign "Ukrainian occupation" of the land. But for many in Ukraine, even those lukewarm to the idea of Ukrainian statehood, the UNR was the least of the available evils, and they grudgingly reconciled themselves to this new reality. "The dominance of Hrushevsky and Vynnychenko was revolting but more tolerable than that of the Bolsheviks," recalled the future prominent Soviet writer Mikhail Kol'tsov. Ukrainian leaders took their promises seriously. They set up courts, established ministries, and legislated. The National Autonomy Law, adopted in January 1918, fulfilled the Third Universal's promise to make Ukraine tolerant and inclusive. This was "one of the best moments of mutual existence for the various nationalities in Ukraine," recalled Vynnychenko, a period of hope and optimism: sincere, contagious, but unfounded. The Central Rada's days were numbered.[12]

Unfortunately for Ukrainian activists, state building required governance, and few in the Ukrainian camp had the necessary experience. Decades of Russification and repression meant that the existing state apparatus in Ukraine was not only Russian speaking but also ideologically tied to the imperial Russian state, Russian identity, and, often, Russian chauvinism. The Rada leaders were scholars, journalists, writers, and activists; the Ukrainian national movement was blessed with an abundance of intellectuals but lacked capable administrators and technical experts. It could issue universals but not implement them. "When a great edifice has been torn apart, it cannot be restored by spreading over it a new roof; the foundations must be rebuilt," observed Arnold Margolin, a former member of

Menachem Mendel Beilis's defense team who now served as a judge on Ukraine's Supreme Court. Rebuilding the state required not only time and effort but also commitment, which was in short supply. A native Russian speaker, Margolin learned Ukrainian with a private tutor. In the absence of alternatives, many Russian bureaucrats in Ukraine might have followed Margolin's example, learning the Ukrainian language and adapting, exactly as the Rada leaders hoped. But alternatives did exist, and instead of helping build the UNR, the Russian-speaking middle class awaited the arrival of a Russian anti-Bolshevik army that had recently formed just across the Ukrainian border.[13]

Southern Russia, especially the Don Cossack Host, quickly emerged as a locus of anti-Communist opposition. On November 20, 1917, shortly after the Bolsheviks came to power in Petrograd, the Don Cossacks—fierce, proud, unruly, and very conservative—declared their independence from newly formed Soviet Russia. Former tsarist generals and officials also began making their way south from Petrograd and Moscow. There, under the leadership of generals Mikhail Alekseev, Lavr Kornilov, and Anton Denikin, they began organizing troops to fight against the "Red" Bolsheviks. Soon, the region became a kind of mecca for those determined to fight against or just trying to escape Soviet rule. The Volunteer Army, the main anti-Bolshevik "White" force in southern Russia and Ukraine, was organized in December 1917 under the command of Kornilov and, after his death in battle in April 1918, Denikin.[14]

Despite the still popular misperception to the contrary, the main goal of the White movement that fought against Lenin's Bolshevik government was not the restoration of the monarchy. Many Whites were undoubtedly deeply committed monarchists who sought the return of the Romanov dynasty, but others supported—or at the very least were willing to accept—other forms of government. The one goal that bound the Whites together and undergirded their policies was a commitment to the territorial preservation of the Russian state: "Russia, one and indivisible" was their rallying cry. This aim inevitably pitted the Whites against minorities' national movements across the former empire, just as it had for the

Provisional Government. Unsurprisingly, many Kadets became devoted supporters of Denikin when the civil war began.[15]

From late 1917 to early 1918, the Soviet government saw the Whites as a more pressing concern than Ukraine, but the clashes between the Bolsheviks and their opponents were destined to involve Ukraine because of Ukraine's proximity to south Russia and because of the Donbas's industrial capacity, which all sides desperately needed. Neither Russian faction had any intention of tolerating the emergence of a genuinely independent Ukrainian state from the empire's collapse. The Whites, at least, were honest about their goals.

The Bolsheviks supported national self-determination, but only if they were to rule the new entities that would emerge. According to Lenin, "We will tell Ukrainians: as Ukrainians, you can organize your life as you wish. But we will extend a hand to Ukrainian workers and tell them: together with you, we will fight against your and our bourgeoisie." The Central Rada, the Communists maintained, was bourgeois and therefore an enemy. On December 16, 1917, Lenin and Leon Trotsky, the Bolshevik commissar of foreign affairs, penned an address to Ukrainian people. In this document, the Soviet government acknowledged Ukraine's right to self-identification up to and including secession, but at the same time it refused to recognize the Central Rada because of its bourgeois composition and policies hostile to Bolshevik aims. Ukrainian authorities were given forty-eight hours to change their behavior or risk war. The Rada rejected Lenin's ultimatum out of hand.[16]

The Communists were unpopular in most of Ukraine, but in the Russian-speaking, industrial Donbas they had a foothold. On December 24–25 in Kharkiv, representatives of the Kyiv Bolsheviks and Donbas workers declared the creation of a Soviet Ukrainian government and announced their goal of the "complete unification of Ukrainian and Great Russian democracies." This was a genuinely local initiative that took Lenin by surprise, but he also could not refuse to support a Soviet Ukraine. This made war between the Rada and the Soviet governments, both Russian and Kharkiv-based, inevitable.

When Bolshevik troops marched on Kyiv, both they and the city's defenders were poorly armed and looked more like militias than true armies. The Bolsheviks, however, were bolder and better organized. While the Rada deliberated, Bolsheviks in Petrograd and Kharkiv seized the initiative and acted. The Rada's political moderation and caution also cost it many initial supporters, who increasingly switched allegiance to the Soviets because they promised radical reforms and sweeping redistribution of land.

On January 22, the Fourth Universal declared Ukraine's full independence, but it made little difference on the ground. Kyiv became the site of pitched street battles between local pro-Soviet rebels and UNR forces, which also included units organized from Ukrainian-Austrian former POWs. The Communist revolt in Kyiv was suppressed, but this did not stop the Soviet advance. Russian patriots in Kyiv, many of them with military experience, hated the Bolsheviks but despised Ukrainian statehood even more and thus remained neutral. By early February 1918, the Soviets had prevailed. The Rada fled to Zhytomyr in central Ukraine and Soviet troops entered Kyiv, where they promptly unleashed a reign of terror against religious leaders, priests, capitalists, former tsarist officers, Rada supporters, and all other enemies of Soviet Russia—real or imagined. At least five thousand people were executed by the Reds. Among them were officials involved in the Beilis trial and Vera Cheberyak, the most likely murderer of Beilis's alleged victim. With UNR troops defeated, Kyiv in Communist hands, and the Whites wishing to revive the old regime, only a foreign power could save independent Ukraine. That power was Germany.[17]

Lenin was committed to extracting Russia from the Great War, and his government initiated an armistice with the Central Powers, followed by peace negotiations that were scheduled to open on December 22, 1917. Held in Brest-Litovsk, the headquarters of the German Eastern Front, the talks brought together a remarkably colorful mix of aristocratic generals and refined diplomats on one side and full-time revolutionaries, many of them recently imprisoned, on the other. As Soviet delegates preached revolution and broke all rules of diplomatic protocol, the Germans and Austro-Hungarians grew tired of their antics and started to doubt the utility of the whole enterprise. But then, on January 1, 1918, a Ukrainian delegation arrived to negotiate a separate peace between the Central Powers and the UNR.

Trotsky stalled and hoped that the revolution he believed was imminent in Berlin and Vienna would force his opponents to offer better peace terms. He was also aware of the situation in Ukraine and expected the Bolshevik capture of Kyiv to neutralize the danger of a separate peace between the Central Powers and the UNR. To add to the confusion, a Soviet Ukrainian delegation also made it to Brest but quickly became an appendage of the Soviet Russian one. Trotsky's intransigence backfired and created an opening for the Rada. Germany and its allies knew that the UNR was on its last legs, but Ukraine had what Germany and Austria-Hungary, plagued by severe food shortages at home, needed the most: grain. On the night of February 9, 1918, the UNR and Central Powers signed a peace treaty.[18]

The Rada received international recognition of Ukrainian statehood and the military support it needed to survive, while in a secret addendum to the treaty Ukraine committed to delivering a million tons of grain to the Central Powers. Trotsky vocally protested that the Rada, defeated on the battlefield, could not represent Ukraine, but he was ignored. There were also desperate attempts to keep at least some Bolshevik foothold in Ukraine in the form of the hastily proclaimed and short-lived Odesa (January 31) and Donetsk-Kryvyi Rih (February 12) Soviet republics, but Bolshevik forces were no match for the German divisions that entered Ukraine on February 18. Kharkiv, the capital of Soviet Ukraine, fell to the German advance on April 7. The UNR, now a German client state, was still standing, albeit barely and not for long.[19]

German de facto rule was unpopular in Ukraine, especially in the countryside, which had already been devastated by years of war and refugee crises. Ukrainian peasants had hoped that the fall of the monarchy would lead to land redistribution, and the Bolsheviks enthusiastically promised them as much. Now, instead of receiving land, they had to work to feed foreign rulers in Berlin and Vienna, and few peasants liked this arrangement. Peasant resistance to the new system meant the UNR's government needed to assume control over the countryside to levy taxes and, if necessary, expropriate grain, because exports to the Germans simply had to be maintained. In other words, the Rada had to govern, but this was precisely what it was incapable of. German representatives grew increasingly irritated with the Rada's inability to control the situation, and—after several members of the UNR government hatched a remarkably harebrained plot to kidnap a banker with whom the Germans worked closely—they decided enough was enough. On April 28, 1918, German military authorities shut down the Central Rada. The next day Ukraine had a new ruler, Pavlo Skoropadsky, who assumed the position of hetman. A new state, the conservative and dictatorial Hetmanate, replaced the UNR.[20]

Pavlo Skoropadsky was the scion of a prominent aristocratic family from eastern Ukraine that had produced an eighteenth-century Cossack hetman. A product of the empire's most prestigious educational and military institutions, Skoropadsky was a lieutenant general in the Russian army and even served as Nicholas II's aide-de-camp. The new hetman was politically and economically conservative and represented the interests of major landowners in Ukraine. The new government reversed many of the Rada's social reforms. The eight-hour workday was abolished and striking banned. Also gone was the National Autonomy Law, the symbol of independent Ukraine's ethnic tolerance and inclusion. The hetman was also much more comfortable with use of the Russian language than with Ukrainian.

Skoropadsky's brief rule was even less popular than that of the Rada and completely dependent on the backing of the German military. Peasants ambushed and killed German troops sent out into the countryside to confiscate grain, and the German top officer in Ukraine, Field Marshal Hermann von Eichhorn, was assassinated. But compared to Russia, where the civil war raged unconstrained, Ukraine was an island of peace and stability during this period. Under Skoropadsky, Ukraine also became a place of refuge for Russian politicians escaping Bolshevik repression, and the hetman's cabinet included prominent Kadets. Milyukov himself moved to Kyiv, but even after having lived there the Kadet leader remained convinced that Ukraine was just "a fiction concocted by a bunch of intellectuals; the Ukrainian national movement does not exist" and that there was no Ukrainian language, only jargon. Russia, he and other White leaders maintained, would reemerge as a unitary state. Suggestions of federative arrangement or self-governance for Ukraine were ridiculous, indeed offensive.[21]

When in November 1918 Germany lost the Great War, Trotsky immediately ordered the Red Army to march into Ukraine. Deprived of German protection, Skoropadsky suddenly became a supporter of reunification with Russia. On November 14, three days after Germany's surrender, the hetman published a manifesto that envisioned Ukraine joining a future non-Communist Russian Federation. The aim was to woo new allies: namely the White movement and its supporters, France and the United Kingdom. Yet the White leader Denikin was unwilling to accept anything less than a unitary Russian state and rebuffed Skoropadsky's overtures. At the same time, for pro-independence forces, the manifesto was an offer by Ukraine's leader to sell out his country. Led by Vynnychenko and Petliura, Ukrainians rebelled. On December 14, as the last German units prepared to leave Kyiv, the hetman abdicated and fled, disguised as a wounded German officer. The UNR, now led by a Directory with Petliura at the helm, was back, and for many in Ukraine this was a tragedy.

Mikhail Bulgakov, a titan of Russian and Soviet literature, was born in Kyiv in 1891. Bulgakov was a typical member of the city's Russian intelligentsia; his father was a history professor, his mother a high school teacher. *The White Guard*, a mostly autobiographical novel Bulgakov published in 1925, tells the story of the Turbins, a proudly Russian family in Kyiv living through the transition from the Hetmanate to Directory rule. The Turbins, the embodiment of Russian Kyiv, are proud, caring, and devoted. They do their best to navigate the horrors of revolutions and war with dignity and honor. The Turbins are also unabashedly monarchist, nostalgic about the old regime, anti-Communist, and xenophobic. For the Turbins and their class, Kyiv is a Russian city, while Ukrainian is a "vile language that does not exist," and it being an official language "terrorizes" the Russian speakers.

The Turbins despise the UNR but also hate Skoropadsky, for they believe that if he had organized the Russian army in Ukraine—instead of engaging in an "abominable comedy with the Ukrainians"—this army would by December 1918 have taken Moscow, crushed Trotsky like a fly, and, even more crucially, made sure that not even a hint of Petliura remained in Little Russia. People of Bulgakov's and the Turbins' social class hoped for the victory of the White movement in the civil war, but above all they wanted the Ukrainians to lose. In 1982, Soviet authorities put a commemorative Russian-language plaque on Bulgakov's home in Kyiv, which celebrated the "famous Russian Soviet writer." Only in May 2023, after public pressure and calls to close the museum, was the plaque changed, and the new Ukrainian-language inscription describes Bulgakov as a "notable Kyiv resident, physician and writer."[22]

The year 1919 was one of breathtaking chaos, constant volatility, and exceptionally brutal violence for Ukraine and its people. At least nine different armies fought in Ukraine, and, in some areas, governments came and went on an almost weekly basis. Kostiantynivka in the Donbas changed hands twenty-seven times between February and May 1919 alone. Even in the 1980s, people in Ukraine were still telling stories and naughty jokes about those who opened their front doors not knowing which army—Red, White, Yellow-Blue, or Green—was now ruling the town. Each change of regime invariably brought reprisals against the supporters of the previous one, forced requisition, plunder, sexual violence, and murder.[23]

Lacking the support of the Russian-speaking urban working and middle classes and plagued by the same organizational and logistical woes that bedeviled the Rada, the Directory government could not hold Kyiv for long. In February 1919, it lost the city to the Bolsheviks, who throughout 1918 had held on to power in Russia and were now a formidable military force—in large part thanks to the efforts of former tsarist officials and generals such as Brusilov, who were willing to serve any Russian government regardless of ideology. Bulgakov's Turbins despised the Bolsheviks, a government full of "kikes and commissars," but between a Russian

Communist government they oppose and a Ukrainian one they abhor, they prefer the Soviets.

The return of Soviet power to Ukraine inevitably meant the return of the Red Terror too, on a much grander scale than in 1918. This time, Ukrainian activists, rather than White supporters or the Russian bourgeoisie, were the prime target. Soviet secret police (CheKa) files show that the vast majority (in some places up to 90 percent) of those executed were connected to the UNR. Veterans of the Ukrainian army were shot on the spot, and the Ukrainian language itself was considered "counterrevolutionary." Mistrustful of the locals, the Soviet government dispatched overwhelmingly Russian Red Army units and brought in officials and clerks from Russia to govern Ukraine.[24]

As Ukrainian, White, and Red troops tussled over the cities of central and eastern Ukraine, large swaths of the countryside were controlled by well-armed and well-organized anarchists, local militias, or no one in particular. The Directory, after losing Kyiv, relocated to the city of Kamianets-Podilskyi, 350 kilometers (217 miles) to the southwest. There, attacked by both the Reds and the Whites, the UNR had just one more chance to revive its fight for independence—by joining forces with the remnants of a Ukrainian state that had briefly emerged in Galicia.

The Habsburg empire did not survive its defeat in World War I and splintered into multiple pieces, some absorbed by members of the victorious Entente, others striving to achieve an independent statehood of their own. Eastern Galicia was claimed by Ukrainians and Poles, and both groups sought recognition from the collapsing government in Vienna, the British, and the French. On October 18, 1918, a group of Ukrainian leaders declared the establishment of a "Ukrainian territory" that would unite all the Habsburgs' Ukrainian lands into one entity, affiliated with the then-still-extant Austro-Hungarian Empire. The Sich Riflemen, a Ukrainian military unit created by the Austrians in 1914, became the core of a new national army. Originally the riflemen were a small infantry outfit with limited training and questionable combat effectiveness, but after incorporating Ukrainian soldiers and officers from other Austrian army units, they became a formidable force.[25]

Declarations alone could not bring a state into being; actions were needed. In a surprise move, on the night of October 31, 1918, a group of about 1,500 Ukrainian fighters seized power in Lviv and announced the creation of a new state, the West Ukrainian People's Republic (Zakhidnoukrains'ka Narodna Respublika, ZUNR). The city's Polish population immediately rebelled against the new government. Fearful of increasingly anti-Semitic Polish nationalism but also skeptical of the Ukrainians' chances of success, the city's large Jewish community adopted a position of armed neutrality. In practice, this clearly benefited the Ukrainian side. The Jewish community's refusal to declare against the ZUNR conferred legitimacy on the new regime and deprived the Poles, initially the weaker party, of the substantial resources and manpower the Jewish community possessed. The ZUNR thus welcomed the Jews' neutral stance, while the Polish leadership complained that the two once-subordinate communities had formed a de facto alliance against the traditionally dominant Poles.

The Polish refusal to accept Ukrainian control of Lviv was predictable, yet the Ukrainian side inexplicably failed to prepare for the coming showdown. Polish volunteer militias—a motley yet highly motivated crew of patriotic students, demobilized soldiers, professionals, and even quite a few underworld figures—successfully challenged the new Ukrainian authorities. Urban warfare in Lviv became increasingly vicious, but neither side was powerful enough to gain control over the entire city. The tide turned in the Poles' favor when Polish units from western Galicia secured control over the crucial rail hub of Przemyśl and then rushed to Lviv. On November 22, Ukrainian troops withdrew from the city, and the ZUNR government moved to Stanyslaviv (now Ivano-Frankivsk) 115 kilometers (71 miles) to the southeast.

After securing Lviv, Polish troops unleashed an anti-Jewish pogrom, which, depending on the source, claimed between 73 and 150 lives. Widely reported in international media, this violence complicated Poland's bid to secure international recognition of its statehood, and Polish authorities thus did their best to deflect the blame onto criminal hoodlums, untrained volunteer fighters, and even the treacherous behavior of the

Jews themselves. The most immediate outcome of Polish anti-Semitic violence was to convince Galician Jews to embrace the ZUNR.

Ukrainian-Jewish cooperation in Galicia was a marriage of convenience. The Ukrainian national movement in the Habsburg empire had not been free from xenophobia, but the ZUNR leadership, in the Habsburg tradition of tolerance, took ethnic diversity and the Jews' legal equality for granted. Anti-Semitic violence did happen under their rule but was condemned and prosecuted by the authorities. Beyond individual equality, the ZUNR also recognized Jews as a minority group entitled to collective rights.

To a large degree, ZUNR benevolence toward Galician Jews stemmed from a recognition that Ukrainians needed the Jews on their side for both symbolic and practical reasons. Jewish support increased the ZUNR's legitimacy and, being primarily a peasant community, Ukrainians simply did not have enough urban blue- and white-collar workers to sustain a modern state on their own, especially while fighting the Poles, who traditionally dominated the region's economy and bureaucracy. The Jewish community reciprocated; Jews served in the ZUNR army and played an important role in its public administration, financial sector, judicial system, and law enforcement, though not as actively as Ukrainian authorities wanted them to.

In many respects, the West Ukrainian state was, during its existence, more successful than the UNR. There was no general anarchy in Galicia, and the ZUNR organized a functioning (if sometimes corrupt) bureaucracy, established public order, provided education and public services, and opened diplomatic missions abroad. Led by Yevhen Petrushevych, a political moderate, the ZUNR sought to establish a political system that ensured the representation of all its main ethnic groups. Had it survived, the ZUNR might have built an ethnically tolerant and inclusive polity, a rarity in interwar Eastern Europe and a productive new model for Ukrainian-Jewish relations.[26]

Unfortunately for the Ukrainians, the ZUNR was simply too small to sustain a long war against the much larger Poland, which was also heavily supported and armed by France. The ZUNR joining forces with the Directory could help both Ukrainian republics, and on January 22, 1919, the

UNR and ZUNR signed a unification treaty. It was, however, a mostly symbolic move, and both governments continued to operate independently.

Throughout the first half of 1919, the Polish army inflicted numerous painful defeats on the Ukrainians and forced the Petrushevych government into exile. In July 1919, the ZUNR finally collapsed and the remnants of the Sich Riflemen—almost fifty thousand well-disciplined and motivated troops—crossed the Zbruch River that separated West Ukraine from the UNR to keep fighting for what remained of Ukraine's statehood. The strength of the Ukrainian armies thus increased to about one hundred thousand, a considerable force indeed.[27]

The arrival of the Galicians gave the Ukrainian forces the strength to march once again on Kyiv. The White Volunteer Army also advanced on the city. On August 30, the Soviets abandoned Kyiv, and the Ukrainians even held a victory parade, but fighting soon broke out between the Whites and the UNR. The Volunteer Army would not compromise on its ideal of one, indivisible Russia, even if this meant fighting both the Ukrainians and the Bolsheviks simultaneously. For the Whites, Petliura was no less of an enemy than Lenin. Ukrainian independence was "a tempest in a teapot," and even Bolshevik gains were presented as evidence of the region's Russian nature. Outgunned, Ukrainian forces withdrew from Kyiv.

Under Denikin's rule, White terror replaced the Red. Members of the Ukrainian intelligentsia were arrested, tortured, and killed; statues of Ukrainian cultural figures desecrated; libraries and reading rooms destroyed; Ukrainian schools and newspapers shut down; and the sale of Ukrainian-language books—even those allowed under the tsar—banned. White authorities also ordered shopkeepers to remove all signs in Ukrainian and replace them with Russian; those who failed to do so faced heavy fines. This unwillingness to accept even a modicum of Ukrainian self-rule eventually doomed the Volunteer Army. As Denikin focused on his confrontation with the UNR, the Bolsheviks were able to regroup, exploit the divisions among their opponents, and retake the lost territory. By December 16, 1919, Kyiv was once again in Soviet hands.[28]

The White movement's commitment to preventing Ukrainian statehood at all costs also had an international impact. The UNR was bedeviled by a lack of foreign support, both political and material. Western powers were determined to counter the threat of Communist revolution at home and stop Bolshevik Russia from fomenting disorder abroad, but none looked to Ukraine to serve this goal. Instead, they supported Denikin. The Whites, in the meantime, actively lobbied their supporters in London, Paris, and Washington against establishing closer relations with the Ukrainians. For most Western diplomats and military strategists, the Ukrainian state was at best a curiosity and at worst a problem.

Arnold Margolin, by this time the UNR deputy minister of foreign affairs and part of the Ukrainian delegation to the Paris Peace Conference, identified two prevailing Western attitudes toward Ukraine: ignorance, and the adoption of a Russo-centric perspective. According to Margolin, British and American diplomats—including supposed regional experts—told him they knew little about Ukraine, their knowledge shaped mostly by interactions with Russian scholars and aristocrats from Petrograd and Moscow. "On the other hand, linguists and urbane and polished gentlemen were considerably less numerous among the non-privileged, non-Russian nationalities of Russia," lamented Margolin. His interlocutors, including US secretary of state Robert Lansing, insisted on Ukrainian federation with Russia as the best—and, for them, easiest—solution. "Russia was our ally," Lansing stated, and demanded that Ukraine submit to the authority of the Whites. Attempts to explain why Ukrainians desired recognition and support as an independent country were rebuffed. As a result, Western military, political, and humanitarian support went to the Whites, and this policy cost the UNR dearly.[29]

The Ukrainian state was nowhere near strong enough to fight the Poles, the Soviets, and the Whites simultaneously, and the UNR and ZUNR could not even agree on who their worst enemy was. For the Galicians, it was the Poles. For Petliura and the Directory, the key threat emanated from Russia, whether it was the Bolshevik government or the Whites. This internal disagreement could not be reconciled, and soon it caused rifts among Ukrainian forces and doomed their campaign. Ukrainian unification turned out to be a mirage, and it ended in bitter acrimony between Petliura, Petrushevych, and their respective followers. Some even feared that open fighting might erupt between the two camps. If all this was not enough, a typhus outbreak decimated Ukrainian units just as they were turning on each other.[30]

In a desperate move, Galician troops first recognized Denikin as their supreme commander before switching to the Bolshevik side. On February 10, 1920, Galician soldiers elected their own soviets, started addressing officers as "comrades," and declared themselves the "Red Western Ukrainian Army."[31]

For Petliura, on the other hand, Poland held the only hope for the UNR's resurrection. By 1920, Polish and Soviet troops had already engaged each other in Belorussia and Lithuania, but the German presence prevented this conflict from spreading south into Ukraine. Throughout 1919, Poland was preoccupied with consolidating its borders and fighting other neighbors, but by early 1920, it was ready for a major war with Russia. Józef Piłsudski, the Polish leader, wanted this war to secure the country's eastern borders and ultimately sought to create a federation of Eastern European states that would ally with Warsaw and serve as a buffer between Warsaw and Moscow. Unfortunately for Piłsudski, the only ally he could actually find was the UNR, which by now governed just a small strip of territory in central Ukraine and was desperate for external support.[32]

The Polish offensive began on April 25, 1920. The Red Army was unprepared for the attack, and by May 7, Polish troops and their UNR allies were already in Kyiv. The fall of Kyiv to the Poles and Ukrainians was a shock that reconciled many Russians who were previously hostile to the Bolsheviks with Soviet regime. By fighting Poland and defending Kyiv, the Soviets became, in the minds of these nationalists, the guardians of Russian land. Thousands, including many former tsarist officers, volunteered to serve in the Red Army, and there was a popular sense of "national unity" in the face of external danger.[33]

In mid-May, the Red Army regrouped and counterattacked. Polish units, overstretched and exhausted, were pushed into retreat. As Soviet troops advanced westward, Lenin's appetites grew. The destruction of Poland would open for the Red Army a direct route to Berlin and Paris. But to get to Warsaw and go on to ignite a worldwide Communist revo lution, the Soviet government first had to control Ukraine. Ukraine thus became paramount not only for the Soviet state's defense but also to fulfill the Communists' ideological destiny. By August, the Red Army had advanced almost to Warsaw and came close to capturing it, but a decisive Polish counterattack, the "miracle on the Vistula," drove them back.

The war produced some unexpected encounters. The Poles had the support of Western advisors and volunteers. A young French major named Charles de Gaulle was there, and a squadron of American volunteers flew in combat for Poland. One of the American pilots was Merian C. Cooper, the future creator of *King Kong*. In July 1920, Cooper was shot down and captured. While Cooper was in a Soviet POW camp, a writer came to interview him.

The writer, Isaac Babel, was a native of Odesa and spent the war as a journalist with the Soviets' illustrious First Cavalry Army. *Red Cavalry*, a collection of short stories Babel wrote about the war, catapulted him to global fame. The Ukraine that Babel saw and described was a ravaged place where civilians and soldiers were trying to survive amid chaos, petty squabbles, painful death, looting, rape, senseless violence, and war crimes. On all sides, ideological commitments were weak, discipline nonexistent, and pogroms erupted as the armies advanced and retreated.

During the civil war, more than a thousand anti-Jewish pogroms took place in Ukraine. Exact numbers are unavailable, but according to most estimates, at least one hundred thousand Ukrainian Jews died due to this violence. Many more were wounded or became refugees, and two-thirds of Jewish houses in the country were looted or destroyed. Every army fighting in Ukraine engaged in anti-Semitic violence, but the scale of destruction inflicted and the motivation for it differed. The Volunteer Army was the most committed and used violence against civilians—including mass rape—as a weapon of war. For the White forces, anti-Semitism was a policy, not a problem. Nonetheless, a great number—about 40 percent—of pogroms took place in UNR-controlled territory or were carried out by Directory troops.[34]

The Directory was not an anti-Jewish government and Petliura was not an anti-Semite. Indeed, both the Central Rada and the Directory adopted policies to accommodate Ukraine's Jewish community. Though Jews were overrepresented in the Communist Party, as a whole they were originally mostly supportive of Ukrainian statehood, or at the very least viewed it as less threatening than the prospect of Soviet or White rule. But many Ukrainian soldiers and officers harbored anti-Jewish attitudes. A toxic mix of prejudice, fear of treason, poor discipline, insufficient oversight, brutalization after years of war, and frustration because of mounting losses eventually exploded in a wave of anti-Jewish violence in 1919–1920. Pogroms were not an official policy for the UNR, but their impact was disastrous nonetheless.[35]

In Ukraine, no government or army was fully immune to anti-Semitic violence in its ranks. The crucial test was what they did after it happened. The ZUNR not only condemned but also punished perpetrators. Petliura eventually condemned the pogroms, but his government did little to stop the violence even when it grew to become a major problem. The largest UNR-perpetrated pogrom took place in Proskuriv on February 15, 1919; there had been an attempted Bolshevik uprising, which the city civilian authorities had no trouble putting down. The regional UNR military commander, Ivan Semosenko, blamed the entire Jewish community for the Communist uprising and ordered a massacre. At least 1,500 Jews were killed, but the Directory did little to prevent the slaughter or punish the perpetrators. Eventually Semosenko was arrested and executed by the UNR, but for a different offense.[36]

Petliura's later justification for this inaction was that the Directory was powerless and had little control over its own army. Furthermore, Petliura presumably could not punish his troops for committing pogroms because the UNR's very survival depended on the soldiers' support. Most likely,

Petliura indeed could not prevent the outbreak of pogroms, but he also did little to stop them, and the consequences of this inaction were disastrous for both the Jews and the Ukrainian state. The Directory troops' violence against Jews killed the UNR's own citizens, destroyed communities, took precious time and resources away from fighting the Soviets and Denikin, and corroded what little discipline and morale remained in the army. The pogroms left an immense moral stain on the reputation and heritage of the Ukrainian national movement and complicated its efforts to gain foreign support. Violence also turned a large and important community within Ukraine into sworn enemies of the UNR.[37]

The Bolsheviks also had their share of anti-Semites, and xenophobia was common among the Communist rank and file. Yet Soviet leadership, committed as it was to the idea of internationalism, tried to combat anti-Semitism and did a better job of controlling and disciplining its troops than the UNR. This made the Soviet camp more attractive to Ukraine's Jews, even though most of them were ideologically hostile to Communism. Devastated by pogroms, driven by revenge, and seeking security, many Jews volunteered for the Red Army in Ukraine. There were so many signing up that the Red Army established a dedicated Yiddish-language Jewish War Section. As support for the UNR shrank, that for the Soviets expanded. Later, many of these Jewish volunteers, highly committed and typically better educated than Ukrainian peasants, would join the Soviet secret police and public administration and become key drivers of Soviet policies and repression.[38]

In March 1921, the Polish and Soviet governments signed a peace treaty in Riga, the capital of now independent Latvia. The treaty ended the war and divided Ukraine among the victors. The brief period of Ukrainian statehood was over. Its leaders and soldiers either went back home or fled in exile to Paris, Berlin, Vienna, or Prague. Poland kept Galicia and Volhynia; the rest of Ukraine became Soviet.

For Lenin and the Bolsheviks, who after years of brutal violence had replaced the Romanovs as Russia's overlords, control over Ukraine was crucial for both ideological and security-related reasons. Lenin needed

Ukraine's territory to protect the nascent Communist revolution from foreign invasion from the West and as a springboard to export the revolution to Warsaw, Berlin, and Paris. For the White movement that opposed the Bolsheviks, identity was paramount in their desire to control Ukraine. They simply could not fathom a Russian state without it. For many Whites, Russian control over Kyiv was more important than which ideology ruled Russia. Neither camp was willing to tolerate an independent Ukraine; it had to be eliminated or subjugated.

In the 1920s and 1930s, a younger generation of Ukrainian nationalist activists would decide it was the moderation of the UNR's and ZUNR's leaders and their internal divisions, lack of willpower, and avoidance of radical measures that had doomed Ukrainian statehood. In fact, the key internal challenges for independent Ukraine in the civil war period were weak state capacity, failure of governance, and insufficient public support for independence. Some of these problems were an inevitable product of Russian imperial rule, others a result of the UNR's own missteps and divisive policies. Yet even if independent Ukraine had been more popular, more capacious, and better governed, there was still no guarantee it could have prevailed against so many powerful foes.

The years of sovereign statehood—chaotic and bloody though they were—transformed Ukrainian society and made Russification from above, as the Romanovs had practiced, no longer viable. These changes were especially pronounced in the countryside, where peasants now perceived their Ukrainian identity not just in linguistic or cultural terms but also in political ones. Ukrainian identity and the Ukrainian countryside posed a challenge for the Soviet state, and Moscow would need a new approach. It came first as accommodation, then as starvation.

CHAPTER 5

MAKING A MODEL REPUBLIC

In 1930, sixteen-year-old Victoria Kalynovych was exiled from her home village in central Ukraine to Tomsk in Siberia. Her only transgression was being born to a wealthy peasant family. Kalynovych's parents had lost most of their land in the early 1920s, and by 1930 her father was long dead, but the other family members were still considered class enemies of the Soviet government, which was busy forcing peasants into collective farms. Kalynovych and her mother soon escaped Siberia and returned to Ukraine but found only famine and devastation. In one of the most fertile regions of the world, Kalynovych saw people with bellies swollen from hunger. She witnessed young children "dried up," how a hungry person "walks, all bloated, hungry, walks, walks, falls and dies." She saw villages emptied and roads covered with weeds from lack of use and feared falling prey to cannibals. But in the district town, Kalynovych also found stores laden with food that peasants were not allowed to buy and witnessed Communist Party representatives, many of them villagers like her, take grain from starving farmers. Kalynovych survived, but her mother died in what Ukrainians came to call the Holodomor (death by hunger).

This massive famine, lasting from 1932 to 1933, killed somewhere between 3.5 and 5 million people in Ukraine, almost all of them in the countryside. Later, another member of Kalynovych's family was arrested by the Soviet secret police and taken to Vinnytsia, the regional capital, "and from Vinnytsia no one returned."[1]

Victoria Kalynovych's story encapsulates the experience of millions of Ukrainians during the 1920s and 1930s. Alongside the creation of the USSR came a blossoming of Ukrainian language and culture, followed by a violent crackdown that lasted for almost a decade. For Joseph Stalin, the Soviet leader during most of the interwar period, peasants were class enemies, Ukraine a constant security concern, and Ukrainian language and culture conduits for dangerous nationalism. In the 1930s, these fears led Stalin to initiate a massive campaign of violence that Victoria Kalynovych became caught up in. The Kremlin's goal was to subdue, control, and exploit Ukraine by killing many but sparing and co-opting others, continuing Russia's time-tested strategy of dividing and repressing Ukrainians.

Stalin's paranoias, security fears, and determination to fully subordinate Ukraine to Moscow and deny it a distinct identity were in line with the goals of the Romanov emperors. The methods he chose to achieve these aims, however, represented a drastic break from past repressions. Tsarist officials banned books, prevented publications, instigated pogroms, targeted the Ukrainian language, and imprisoned and exiled activists, but they would have shuddered at the idea of executing hundreds of thousands, starving millions, and eliminating entire social groups. Stalin had no such qualms.

The post–civil war Soviet Union was an extremely violent state, and many groups and regions, not just Ukraine, suffered tragedies in which millions perished. Indeed, for decades scholars argued whether the Holodomor and repressions were just part of the broader pattern of Stalinist violence or whether Ukraine was deliberately singled out for especially murderous treatment. Now there is little doubt: even in the overall violent USSR, Stalin was especially determined to destroy Ukraine as an identity project and a political idea, and this intent to destroy escalated into the murder of millions of Ukraine's residents of different backgrounds. This was a genocide that not only killed people but remade Ukrainian society, and made it compliant, Russified, and secure for Moscow for more than half a century.

———

The end of the Polish-Soviet War in March 1921 forced Lenin to shelve his dreams of using Ukraine as a springboard from which to launch world-wide Communist revolution, but it also allowed the Kremlin to shift to eradicating the few remaining internal threats to Soviet rule. That same month, the Red Army completed its conquest of Georgia, a former territory of the Russian Empire that had declared independence in 1918. Neighboring Armenia and Azerbaijan had been subjugated even earlier, in 1920. The Kremlin gave up on bringing the Baltic states and Finland back into the fold, for now anyway, while the war in Central Asia continued. By 1922, however, the violence that followed the Russian Empire's collapse was mostly over, and the Bolsheviks emerged as the undisputed victors. Despite all their talk of internationalism and nations' right to self-determination, Lenin and his party were committed to salvaging as much former Russian imperial territory as possible. Some White Russians even believed that the Soviet state was like a radish: a thin red veneer covering a large, solid-white core.

With the war won, the key question was how to organize the new state. On this, Lenin had a fundamental disagreement with his commissar for nationalities, Joseph Stalin. Born in Georgia in 1878, Joseph Dzhugashvili had been a seminary student and trained to be ordained as an Orthodox priest until he discovered Marxism and instead became a revolutionary. In 1912, Dzhugashvili took the name Stalin. Stalin was not charismatic, but he was smart, ruthless, and a good coalition builder. During the civil war, he served as the Kremlin's representative in the Volga region and then in the Polish-Soviet War, an experience that attuned the future dictator to the strategic importance of Ukraine.

Stalin sought to create a unitary state that would put the "genie of national states unleashed by the Great War . . . back in the bottle." His plan was to have the Russian Soviet Federative Socialist Republic (RSFSR) absorb Ukraine, Belorussia, Georgia, Armenia, and Azerbaijan, which were at the time formally independent but ruled by Communists. This new, enlarged state would formally be a federation, in which the central government oversaw the economy, security, and foreign relations. Unfortunately for Stalin, only the Communist leaders of Armenia and Azerbaijan went along with this plan, while the central committee of Ukraine's Communist Party refused to even consider it. Ukraine's leaders would rather be their own bosses than Stalin's subordinates.[2]

Instead of Stalin's plan, Lenin proposed a union, which the RSFSR would join alongside the other Communist-ruled republics, and in which every unit would have equal status, the formal right to secede, and control over its own affairs. Unlike Stalin, Lenin recognized that nationalist sentiments ran high in the former Russian Empire, first and foremost in Ukraine. The Ukrainian peasantry, the backbone of the UNR, was unlikely to submit to a new Russian state without a major struggle, and in 1922 Lenin could not afford an all-out war against rural Ukraine. The champion of the working class needed the country's farmers and the food they grew.

Food shortages had sparked the 1917 revolution that destroyed the Russian Empire, and the Kremlin knew that to survive the Communist regime had to feed the cities and the army. Lenin's Communist utopia had little to offer the socially and economically conservative peasantry, and the Bolsheviks had low support in the countryside. Amid the civil war, economic crisis, and political instability, peasants also had little incentive to sell grain to a government that paid in currency that by tomorrow might be replaced by that of a different regime. But the state needed grain, and to procure it Soviet authorities resorted to their tool of choice: violence.

In early 1918, the Kremlin declared a "food supply dictatorship," which, simply put, meant forced expropriation. Peasants with surplus grain who did not hand it over to the state were declared by Lenin "enemies of the people" and treated accordingly. Bolshevik authorities established ruthless, armed Food Detachments and subsequently the Food Supply Army (*Prodarmiia*), tasked with requisitioning grain and other produce. At its peak, the Food Supply Army had 77,000 men under arms, and more than 150,000 people served in its ranks throughout the war. Lenin went so far as to suggest renaming the War Commissariat the War and Food Supply Commissariat. Trotsky expressed a similar sentiment when he stated in April 1918 that "civil war is the struggle for bread."[3]

Control over Ukraine, its soil, and its produce was therefore essential for the Kremlin. For Lenin, the connection between Ukrainian grain and Soviet survival was direct and explicit. "For God's Sake! Use all energy and all revolutionary measures to send grain, grain, and more grain!! Otherwise, Petrograd might starve to death. Use special trains and special detachments. Collect and store. Escort the trains. Inform us every day. For God's sake!" Lenin implored the Communist authorities in Ukraine in early 1918. According to another source, "At every mention of Ukraine, Lenin asked how many [kilos of grain] were there, how many could be taken from there, or how many had already been taken."[4]

The impact of War Communism, as Soviet food policies came to be known, was immediate: peasants stopped sowing. In Ukraine, Soviet requisition also had a national dimension: the armed detachments who took the peasants' grain not only belonged to a different class but also came from far away and spoke a different language. The conflict over grain increased nationalist sentiments. War Communism devastated the countryside and sparked peasant revolts throughout Soviet-controlled territory. Lenin realized that the government had gone too far, endangering the regime. In 1921, he introduced the New Economic Policy (NEP), replacing War Communism. A tax in kind replaced food requisition, while the government relinquished its grain monopoly and legalized the trade of food. But it was too late to avert disaster. Lack of incentives to farm, the general devastation and chaos of war, and a severe drought in 1921 combined to produce a famine. The Volga region, southern Russia, and Ukraine were hit especially hard. Witnesses and survivors recalled horrific scenes of mass starvation, and multiple instances of cannibalism were recorded across famine-stricken areas. As the tragedy unfolded amid civil war and state collapse, the death toll remains unknown, but estimates range from 1.5 to 5 million.[5]

The Communist regime survived, barely, saved by the Americans. The American Relief Administration (ARA), a humanitarian organization established by future US president Herbert Hoover, undertook a massive relief effort. Soviet authorities allowed the ARA to operate in the Volga region, but Moscow and Kharkiv (Soviet Ukraine's capital) initially tried to conceal that there was a famine in Ukraine and to prevent the ARA from expanding operations there. The official justification was that Ukraine was de jure a separate country, but this excuse fooled no one. Lenin even tried to take food out of Ukraine to ease the famine in Central Russia. "Workers and peasants of the Volga region ... expect help from the Ukrainian farmers," he implored. Ukraine's strategic location, the Soviet obsession with secrecy, and, quite likely, a cynical willingness to weaponize starvation to subdue Ukrainian resistance to the still nascent Communist government were the actual reasons for trying not to let the ARA in. In 1922, the food situation improved, but the Kremlin knew that another major famine might destroy their regime. For now, the desires and identity of Ukrainian farmers had to be accommodated.[6]

To ensure Ukrainians enjoyed some token self-rule and were not wholesale swallowed by Russia, the RSFSR, Ukraine, Belorussia, and the Transcaucasian Socialist Federative Soviet Republic (which included Armenia, Azerbaijan, and Georgia) in December 1922 proclaimed the Union of Soviet Socialist Republics. The arrangement, however, came with a catch: while USSR members retained the formal trappings of self-rule, real political power remained in the hands of the Communist Party, which was fully, centrally controlled by the Kremlin. The new state would be "federal in form, centralized in content."[7]

Having created Communist Ukraine, the authorities set out to create Communist Ukrainians. In 1923, the Soviet Union introduced the *korenizatsiia* (indigenization) program, aimed at defanging the still potent nationalist sentiments. It involved promoting local languages in education, government, and culture at the expense of imperial Russian. An auxiliary goal was to educate the rural population, who largely did not speak Russian, increasing their loyalty to the regime and easing the peasants' transformation into urban proletariat. In Ukraine, the policy was known as Ukrainization, though non-Russian minorities within the republic also received their national districts, newspapers, cultural institutions, and schools. By 1926, ethnic minorities in Ukraine, predominantly Poles, had eleven officially recognized minority regions and almost three hundred autonomous villages. In the city of Dnipropetrovsk, the thirty-six ethnically Hungarian residents had their own government-funded newspaper. As historian Terry Martin aptly put it, the USSR became an "Affirmative Action Empire."[8]

In July 1923, the Ukrainian government issued a decree that mandated gradually switching all government business at the republican level into Ukrainian. Officials were required to learn Ukrainian and pass a language test; those who failed faced punishment, up to dismissal. Street signs and notices in public spaces were changed into Ukrainian. By 1927, 80 percent of primary education in the republic was in Ukrainian. This trend also went hand in hand with a rapid expansion of literacy.[9]

The investment in the Ukrainian language sparked a cultural explosion, and a new cohort of writers and artists completely transformed Ukrainian literature and poetry. Most were deeply committed Communists, but even though they believed in Lenin's ideals, they worshipped neither Russia nor Russian. Instead, they perceived Russian culture as colonial and overbearing, and their views were occasionally tinged with borderline racist condescension for Russia's "Asiatic" character. The most prominent member of this cohort, the brilliant modernist writer and poet Mykola Khvylovy, urged Ukrainians to turn away from Moscow and embrace Western Europe culturally and psychologically. Another prominent artist, Mykhailo Boichuk, echoed the sentiment, advocating for erecting a Chinese-style "great wall" separating Ukrainian culture from Russia.[10]

Science and research could now be conducted in Ukrainian, and in 1924 Mykhailo Hrushevsky, the most prominent Ukrainian historian and former head of the Central Rada, made his peace with Soviet Ukraine and returned to Kyiv from self-imposed foreign exile. Ukrainization also turned the tables in Galicia's relationship with the rest of Ukraine. If previously Galicia had been the center of Ukrainian culture that inspired Ukrainians across the border in the Russian Empire, now the goal was to make Soviet Ukraine the center of attraction for Galicians, whose culture was under attack by the Polish government. At a time when the Kremlin viewed Poland as a major security threat, such diaspora outreach had strategic implications and benefits.[11]

A major goal of Ukrainization was to secure the support of the Ukrainian-speaking peasantry for the regime. In 1922, there were about 55,000 members of the Ukrainian Communist Party, but by 1933 membership skyrocketed to more than 550,000. More crucially still, the percentage of ethnic Ukrainians in the party ranks almost tripled, from 23 percent to 60 percent. The policy also transformed Ukraine's cities. The share of Ukrainians in government posts expanded, and there emerged substantial Ukrainian-speaking middle and working classes. Yet ethnic Ukrainians, who were 80 percent of the republic's population according to the 1926 census, were still underrepresented in the party, government, and security services. Russians remained the most powerful group, and Jews were heavily overrepresented. But Ukrainians were catching up, and several of the so-called national Communists became prominent in the republic's leadership.[12]

Not everyone was happy with these larger and more assertive Ukrainian-speaking middle and working classes. Ukrainization challenged Russians' cultural and political superiority in the republic. Ethnically Russian or Russian-speaking professionals and bureaucrats had little interest in speaking Ukrainian, and now they found themselves at a disadvantage and faced competition from Ukrainian upstarts. Many parents resented their children being educated in Ukrainian, because they still perceived Russian-language education as a gateway to more and better job opportunities.

Ukraine's republican leadership supported Ukrainization in public but was lukewarm about its implementation; it was never a major priority for the government. Some prominent Communists looked down on the Ukrainian language and saw the republic as a battlefield between the urban—and therefore progressive and superior—Russian culture and the rural, socially backward, and inferior Ukrainian one. Compliance with the new rules was superficial. Bureaucrats dragged their feet, passively resisted, complained, and grumbled. The greatest resistance came from within the Communist Party itself. According to one evaluation of government employees, 44 percent of those who were not party members knew Ukrainian well, whereas among card-carrying Communists in government service, the share was a mere 18 percent.[13]

Even more crucially, by the end of the 1920s, Soviet leadership decided that the push to promote local languages and cultures had gone too far, creating centrifugal forces, fueling the danger of nationalism, and reducing the Soviet Union's cohesion and governability. Ukraine was firmly under the Communist thumb, but specifically *Russian* control over it was in danger. Lenin, who backed indigenization, died in 1924; after several years of collective rule and power struggles, Stalin emerged as the country's new leader.[14]

A consummate bureaucrat, Stalin had not forgotten his 1922 plan to create a unitary state, and his suspicion of Ukraine had not abated either. If anything, it had only increased during the years of Ukrainization. Already in 1926 Stalin began attacking the extent of Ukrainization, which, he warned, had veered into a fight "against Russians in general, against Russian culture and its highest achievement, Leninism." Stalin was especially infuriated by Khvylovy's calls for rejecting Moscow in favor of Europe and complained bitterly about the backing the poet received from Ukraine's leaders.[15]

The Russian public also shared (or was taught to accept) some of Stalin's anti-Ukrainian prejudices. In 1926, author Mikhail Bulgakov adapted his vehemently anti-Ukrainian novel *The White Guard* into a stage play, titled *Dni Turbinykh* (*The Days of the Turbins*). Bulgakov's prejudices were so blatant that the prominent German intellectual Walter Benjamin, who saw the play during a visit to Moscow, described it as "an absolutely revolting provocation." But Russians loved it. The play became a hit and was performed almost a thousand times in Moscow alone. When the authorities tried to ban the production for its glorification of the Whites, Stalin intervened personally to save it. A fan, he watched the play more than twenty times between 1926 and 1941.[16]

Stalin was, meanwhile, also concerned about the Soviet Union's geopolitical situation. He was certain that the capitalist West had not given up on its goal of destroying the USSR, and therefore worried that the country was under constant threat. A 1926–1927 war scare made many in the Kremlin fear imminent invasion. After the crisis—which was mostly a product of the leadership's own imagination and internal struggles—was over, Stalin came to believe that the USSR was not ready for a confrontation with the West. To protect Communism, Stalin concluded, the union had to be recentralized, modernized, industrialized, and guarded from enemies, both foreign and domestic. The post–civil war, market-oriented NEP was to be replaced with an ambitious "revolution from above."

Industrialization required both working hands and money. The growing urban proletariat needed food, and foreign technology had to be paid for. Peasants were supposed to fulfill both needs by feeding the cities and providing the government with grain for export. Stalin explicitly spoke of peasants paying tribute and perceived the countryside as a hostile territory to be conquered. To squeeze more from the farmers, in 1927–1928 the government reduced the price paid for procured grain while leaving the prices of industrial goods, which peasants needed, intact. But instead of selling for less, farmers began hoarding grain, which also made sense if war was, as the Kremlin warned, on the horizon. A procurement crisis ensued, and food supplies to the cities were threatened. Importing grain was not feasible, as the Kremlin had little hard currency to spare and was determined to spend what it had on technology, not food. Instead, Stalin decided to subject the countryside to central planning, the cornerstone of the Communist economic system. Now the state would decide what, how, and in what quantities the peasants would produce for the government. The means to achieve this control over grain production was the collectivization of agriculture.[17]

In 1929, collectivization—a "campaign of domination and destruction, which aimed at nothing less than the internal colonization of the peasantry"—hit the countryside. The government sent party activists and officials—mostly urbanites with little respect for the peasantry—to convince or cajole farmers into joining collective farms (*kolkhoz* in Russian, *kolhosp* in Ukrainian) where land, livestock, tools, and labor would belong to the collective, and what to grow and how would be determined by the state.[18]

Poorer peasants, who had little to lose, typically joined up gladly, but among the wealthier or more individualistically minded of them, few were excited about the new arrangement, in which everything would belong to everyone, and therefore to no one. When promises and arguments failed to convince farmers, the collectivizers switched to threats, destruction of churches, and open violence, but the majority of peasants still resisted. Collectivization was perceived as a new form of serfdom and provoked bitter resentment. Many peasants preferred slaughtering their livestock to giving it to the state.

In Ukraine, achieving collectivization was especially challenging for the authorities. Russian peasants had long traditions of communal farming, whereas Ukrainian farmers were known for individualism and fierce attachment to their property. By October 1929, despite all the government's efforts, only 16 percent of Ukraine's peasantry had been collectivized. In the western parts of the republic, thousands of farmers fled to Poland by crossing the porous border that divided Ukrainians and separated Communism from capitalism.[19]

The Kremlin's response was, as ever, more repression. The border with Poland was sealed. A chance victim of this change was Hanna Pinchefsky, a resident of Tel Aviv, who in summer 1929 had returned to her native Khmilnyk, just forty kilometers (twenty-five miles) from the Polish border, to attend her grandson's wedding. Hanna crossed the border illegally, without obtaining a Soviet entry visa, and by the time she wanted to return to Palestine, it had become impossible. Hanna Pinchefsky got stuck in the USSR and later died in the Holocaust. But the money Hanna received from abroad saved her great-grandson, my maternal grandfather, who purchased a fake identity card and survived the Holocaust posing as an ethnic Ukrainian.

The chief target of Soviet collectivization violence was the wealthy peasant: *kulak* (literally "fist") in Russian and *kurkul'* in Ukrainian. In Communist thinking, wealthy farmers were the most reactionary segment of the peasantry and implacable foes of Soviet rule. The kurkul', in Soviet propaganda, oppressed the village poor (the Communists' natural allies), corrupted "middle peasants," and sabotaged collectivization. There was no standard definition of a kurkul'. The government had once used economic criteria, but increasingly all those who opposed, or were suspected of opposing, collectivization could be branded as kurkul' and targeted. In December 1929, Stalin vowed to "eliminate kulaks as a class," and eliminate them he did. From January to April 1930, more than 110,000 peasants, among them Victoria Kalynovych, were deported from Ukraine for the crime of being wealthy farmers and hindering collectivization by their actions or very existence.[20]

Unsatisfied with the pace of "collectivization from below," in January 1930 Stalin ordered that all main agricultural regions be collectivized by the fall, then shortened the timeline to the beginning of the spring sowing season. Local cadres enthusiastically pledged to meet this highly ambitious goal. The only way to do so on schedule was via massive, brutal coercion of peasants. Thanks to this pressure and violence, the pace of collectivization increased, but so did the peasants' opposition. Soon, large parts of the Soviet countryside were in open revolt.[21]

Ukraine was the epicenter of rural violence, and about a half of all Soviet anti-government peasant disturbances took place in the republic. In March 1930, just in the small district of Tulchyn in central Ukraine, 153 villages experienced unrest, and local Soviet authorities were completely expelled from fifty communities. Some villages armed themselves, dug defensive trenches, sang Ukraine's national anthem, and, according to government reports, shouted slogans like "Down with Soviet power, long live independent Ukraine." The unrest became so intense and widespread that the Kremlin worried Poland might seize the opportunity and invade. Regime stability, national security, and Stalin's increasingly Russian nationalist worldview all came under threat in Ukraine. The dictator backed off and the collectivization drive halted, though this was only a tactical temporary retreat.[22]

The Ukrainian nationalist sentiments that accompanied peasant resistance unnerved the Kremlin. Soviet leaders had long believed that "every Ukrainian is potentially a nationalist," and Stalin himself was convinced that the national and peasant questions were one and the same. The events in Ukraine in 1929–1930 reinforced this perception and made Stalin even more determined to reimpose Moscow's dominance, not just politically but also socially and culturally.[23]

The assault on the peasantry went in hand in hand with the rollback of Ukrainization; securing Ukraine meant asserting better control not just over peasants' economic behavior but also over Ukrainians' identity. The person in charge of securing Ukraine for the Kremlin was Vsevolod Balitsky, Ukraine's head of the GPU (State Political Directorate), as the Soviet security service was now named. Balitsky, "Ukraine's guillotine," was born to a middle-class family in 1892 in eastern Ukraine and grew up in Luhansk. He studied law in Moscow but never graduated and served as a warrant officer in the tsarist army during World War I. Politically active since 1913, Balitsky joined the Soviet security service in late 1918 and spent most of his career in Ukraine. Sometimes he listed his ethnicity as Ukrainian, sometimes as Russian, a matter of political expediency but also a testament to the fluid identities of the Donbas Russian-Ukrainian border area. Since the early days of his career, Balitsky had been especially concerned about Ukrainian nationalism and relished the chance to crush this enemy once and for all.[24]

Unfortunately for Balitsky, there was very little actual underground nationalist activity in Ukraine at that time. Most Ukrainian intellectuals, even those who had participated in the short-lived independence experiment ten years prior, were frightened enough to stay out of politics or, like Hrushevsky, had made peace with Soviet rule thanks to Ukrainization. No matter: if a conspiracy did not exist, it would be concocted. The first Ukrainian nationalist organization invented by Balitsky's GPU was the Union for the Liberation of Ukraine (*Spilka Vyzvolennia Ukrainy*, SVU). The SVU, like many other conspiracies invented by Soviet intelligence, was not entirely fictional. An organization with that name had existed in Austria-Hungary during World War I. Most of its members were Ukrainian activists from Romanov-controlled Ukraine, and their activities mostly consisted of publishing anti-Russian propaganda. But this real SVU folded in 1918 and was never active in Soviet Ukraine.

The SVU that Balitsky invented and then diligently exposed was a massive, well-hidden nationalist conspiracy to infiltrate Soviet Ukraine's cultural and educational institutions and poison the minds of the next generation. Indeed, the SVU purportedly even had a youth branch, the Association of Ukrainian Youth. Since the GPU itself invented the plot, the ideology Balitsky assigned to the conspiracy is a good indicator of how Soviet leadership perceived Ukrainian nationalism in the late 1920s and early 1930s, and what the Kremlin and its agents feared the most.

The SVU, Balitsky informed his superiors, rejected the Soviet system and believed that Communist rule would lead Ukraine into social and cultural decline and turn it into a Russian colony. The organization sought to topple the Soviet government in Kharkiv and reestablish an independent Ukrainian People's Republic. From the perspective of Communists like Balitsky, this Ukrainian state would be a hellish place indeed: democratic and respectful of private property, with equality before the law, freedom of religion, and no class-based privileges. Nationalized enterprises would be returned to their owners, and the lands of collective farms to individual peasants.[25]

The trial of the SVU opened on March 9, 1930, in Kharkiv. It was a public spectacle, literally "theater in the theater," for it was held at the city's opera house. Hearings were conducted on the main stage in the morning, with ballet and opera in the evening. *Pravda*, the All-Union Communist

Party's mouthpiece, ran over thirty articles on the trial. On the docket were forty-five carefully chosen defendants, all accused of counterrevolutionary activities, ranging from the distribution of flyers commemorating Petliura's murder by a Jewish Ukrainian assassin to planning the murder of Ukrainian and Soviet leadership (including Stalin) and preparing a mass uprising. Most defendants were intellectuals or people with advanced education: professors, researchers, teachers, writers, priests, lawyers, and students. Some had been prominent in pre-Soviet Ukrainian politics; the SVU included a former prime minister of the UNR, its minister of foreign affairs, and several members of the Central Rada. None of the defendants were members of the Communist Party. Three of the alleged Ukrainian nationalist conspirators were women and two were Jews. Serhii Yefremov, a prominent scholar and one of the leaders of the UNR, was assigned the role of SVU leader. Yefremov had it the worst, not just because of the danger of punishment but also because GPU interrogators demanded he provide extensive information on a conspiracy he knew nothing about. Eventually, he simply told the GPU everything they wanted to hear.

On April 19, 1930, all the defendants were convicted but received relatively lenient sentences. At this stage, Stalin's goal was to put the Ukrainian national movement itself on trial, rather than physically eliminate dissenters. The Kharkiv trial was just the beginning, though; eventually, up to thirty thousand people would be arrested for belonging to the SVU. The SVU affair did not mark the end of Ukrainization, but it did signal that the Ukrainian intelligentsia was about to be brought back under the state's full control.[26]

Meanwhile, the GPU got busy inventing and then uncovering other subversive groups. Between 1931 and 1934, Soviet authorities prosecuted suspected nationalists for belonging to the Ukrainian National Center (UNT, 1931–1932), Ukrainian Military Organization (UVO, 1933), and Organization of Ukrainian Nationalists (OUN, 1934). Like the Union for the Liberation of Ukraine, the UVO and OUN were real organizations active in Poland and in the diaspora, but the conspirators arrested by the GPU had nothing to do with these groups. Instead, those targeted by the

Soviet government were community leaders, intellectuals, former activists of Ukrainian socialist parties, and members of the Communist Party of Western Ukraine who had moved to the USSR. Hrushevsky also found himself in the GPU's crosshairs. He was arrested and viciously attacked for his nationalist views but escaped prosecution. Instead, in 1931 the government simply sent Hrushevsky into unofficial exile in the RSFSR, where he died in 1934. His historical writings were banned, and most of his colleagues and students were persecuted.[27]

As well as targeting imaginary Ukrainian subversives, the GPU moved against the Poles. Polish educational institutions and administrative units were gradually dismantled and, alongside the UVO investigation, Soviet security services uncovered the Polish Military Organization, which was actively plotting against Soviet authorities in Ukraine. The Polish Military Organization was real and played a prominent role in creating the Polish state, but it had ceased to exist more than a decade before being "uncovered." In Poland, Ukrainian nationalists (first the UVO and then the OUN) fought the Polish government, but in the USSR the two bitter enemies apparently cooperated harmoniously against Communist rule. The improbability of this supposed alliance, one of many that the GPU and its successors would concoct over the years, did not bother the Soviet government in the slightest.

Culture and education, especially primary and secondary education, were the cornerstones of Ukrainization and therefore key targets for Stalin's Kremlin. Soviet officials viewed education as "the third front," after the military and economic domains, and believed that children should be taught to be "fighters for communism or not to be schooled at all." Now Communism and Ukrainization were viewed as incompatible, and in 1933, 10 percent of all Ukrainian schoolteachers were arrested for political offenses. In the higher echelons of public education, the purges were much more extensive. All the regional heads of the Ministry of Public Education were purged during 1933. At the district level, the share was 90 percent. Mykola Skrypnyk, Ukraine's minister of public education until February 1933, was the target of an unrelenting campaign accusing him of bourgeois nationalism and other transgressions. Skrypnyk was the personification of Ukraine's internal divisions and contradictions. One of Ukraine's most prominent national Communists, he was heavily involved in repressions as a former prosecutor general. For instance, in 1932, Skrypnyk advocated for the death sentence for sixteen district-level officials charged with not fulfilling unrealistic grain procurement quotas. A disciplined Bolshevik, Skrypnyk acknowledged his transgressions when accused, but nothing helped; the campaign against him continued, and on July 7, 1933, Skrypnyk committed suicide.[28]

Skrypnyk was not alone. On May 13, 1933, Khvylovy, the writer who had urged Ukrainians to turn away from Moscow and infuriated Stalin, unable to bear the ever increasing purges, took his own life. Khvylovy remained a devoted Communist until the very end, but for Stalin, Communist rule and a Ukrainian-language culture that was not fully subservient to the Kremlin could not coexist. Dozens of writers and poets, a cohort that would later be named the "executed Renaissance," would perish simply because they wrote in Ukrainian. From 1933, Ukrainization was wound down by the government in Ukraine and ceased altogether among the large Ukrainian minority in the RSFSR.[29]

The fallout of the central government's attack on culture and education was felt immediately. In the Donbas, almost the entire school system switched to using Russian, and technical schools went as far as treating Ukrainian not as a second language but as a foreign one. In Luhansk, renamed Voroshilovhrad, the Institute of Public Education responsible for training teachers, though named after Taras Shevchenko, taught classes only in Russian and did not have even a single book of Shevchenko's Ukrainian-language poetry in its library. The situation in the rest of Ukraine also slid toward total Russification. In 1936, a German diplomat in Kyiv tried to send a telegram in Ukrainian but was told by a post office employee that "one speaks Russian in the Soviet Union." The same diplomat reported he could not find a Russian-Ukrainian dictionary anywhere because they were simply no longer available. In some areas of central Ukraine, even Ukrainian language study groups were branded as "nationalist." Switching to using Russian and abandoning any trappings of Ukrainian culture was the safest choice.[30]

This shift aligned well with a broader change occurring in Soviet ideology, as well as with Stalin's own emergence as a Russian nationalist—though the dictator was ethnically Georgian. Throughout the 1930s, the Soviet Union moved away from its original Leninist internationalism and adopted a more Russo-centric populist and nationalist view that, among other things, elevated military heroes of the imperial past. Russians were presented as the core and most important group in the state, first among equals and elder brothers to all other Soviet ethnicities, including Ukrainians. The *Short Course of the History of the USSR*, adopted as the main Soviet history textbook around this time, was mostly a standard old Russian narrative that traced Russians' origins through Kyiv and then Muscovy, the Russian Empire, and the USSR. Under such conditions, expressing Ukrainian culture, let alone advocating distance from Moscow, became unthinkable, even deadly.[31]

In March 1934, the Kremlin also decided to move the capital of Ukraine from Kharkiv to Kyiv. From a purely strategic, national security perspective, this was a strange move, given that the Kremlin was obsessively worried about an attack from the West and subversive Ukrainian nationalism. Kharkiv was an industrial city, full of loyal, Russian-speaking proletariat, and far from the border. Kyiv was neither. It was only about 250 kilometers (155 miles) from Poland, had limited industry, and was home to a diverse population of uncertain loyalties. It was also a potent symbol of Ukrainian nationalism, and some of its landmarks made the Communist authorities squirm. The statue of Khmelnytsky, for instance, was boarded up during public celebrations of Soviet holidays, and there were discussions about removing it permanently.

The decision, however, made perfect sense if one considers the Kremlin's political and ideological concerns, rather than just national security. Moving the massive, thoroughly loyal, and increasingly Russified workforce of the government to Kyiv would Russify the city, change its ideological makeup, and dilute its nationalist past. Eventually even Khmelnytsky was rehabilitated in the government's eyes, when the focus shifted from his submission to monarchic rule to his unification of Ukraine with the Russian elder brother, a narrative that only reinforced the dominant Russo-centric ideology.[32]

Repression of Ukrainian identity and leadership in the cities unfolded in parallel with a renewed assault on the countryside. The 1930 decision to halt collectivization, presumably because it had gone so well that officials became, in Stalin's words, "dizzy with success," was merely a tactical pause. The Kremlin regrouped and struck again, this time more slowly but also more systematically and ruthlessly. Pressure to join collective farms grew again, this time not through open violence by outsiders but via heavy taxation and unrelenting pressure on those who clung to independent farming.[33]

As levels of collectivization grew, the food situation worsened. The 1931 harvest was a failure, and not just in Ukraine. In some regions of Russia, bad weather was indeed a contributing factor, but collectivization was the main culprit. Collective ownership reduced peasants' incentives to work, farm managers were often incompetent, the tractors and modern technology promised by the government never arrived, and the kulaks, who had typically been well-off for a reason, were gone. Yet ambitious state procurement quotas still had to be filled; Stalin was determined to continue exporting grain even if peasants starved. Expropriation became easier when production was centralized, supervised by the government, and overseen by loyal officials.

While Ukraine's situation was not unique, it was worse off than other regions—deliberately so. There was a clear anti-Ukrainian bias in procurement targets. Regions with the same production levels had to deliver more grain to the state if they had a higher share of ethnic Ukrainians, which meant that Ukrainians were left with less to eat compared to other Soviet farmers. Already in spring 1932, secret police reports began mentioning famine in some parts of Ukraine. The leadership in Kyiv realized the extent of the danger and asked the Kremlin for reprieve. Stalin refused and, in July, dispatched his most obedient lieutenants—Lazar Kaganovich, a Ukrainian Jew and a former party boss of Ukraine, and Vyacheslav Molotov—to bring the republic to heel. For Moscow, there would be neither concessions to nor compromises with Ukraine's unreliable and opportunistic leaders who could not get their act together. Molotov and Kaganovich did as instructed, browbeating the Ukrainian leaders and accusing them of being "capitulators." Procurement quotas remained unchanged, and Ukrainian party officials readily complied. Even the Kremlin's enforcers were surprised at how weak the Ukrainian leaders' resistance was.[34]

But for Ukrainian peasants, the capitulation of the republican leadership meant hunger. Starving people tried to get calories wherever they could, including from collective farm fields and granaries. To the Kremlin, these desperate, small-scale survival tactics were theft of public property, which was more valuable than human life. A law adopted in August 1932 became known as the "five ears of grain law," because it punished taking even tiny amounts of state property, including grain that peasants themselves grew and the state had appropriated, with ten years' imprisonment or death. The Kremlin was deadly serious; by the end of the year, 4,500 people had been executed and over 100,000 sent to labor camps.[35]

As the food situation in Ukraine deteriorated and local-level officials started to voice their concerns about procurement plans being both inhumane and unrealistic, Stalin exploded. He knew the situation was catastrophic, but he blamed the Ukrainians themselves. His fear of Western invasion, determination to extract as much as possible from the peasants to support industrialization, deeply ingrained hostility toward Ukraine, and belief that peasants were hoarding food combined to produce a response that doomed the Ukrainian countryside. "Ukraine now is the most important thing," Stalin wrote Kaganovich on August 11, 1932.

> Things in Ukraine are terrible. . . . About 50 [party] district committees spoke up <u>against</u> the grain procurement plan, called it <u>unrealistic</u>. . . . What is this? It is not a Party but a parliament, a caricature of a parliament. . . .
>
> If we don't start improving the situation now, we might lose Ukraine. . . . Also keep in mind that in Ukraine's

Communist Party (500,000 members, ha-ha) there are not a few (yes, not a few!) rotten elements, conscious and unconscious Petliurites.

Ukraine, Stalin concluded, "ought to be turned into a true fortress of the USSR, into a truly model republic." Simply put, unreliable and noncompliant Ukraine had to be subdued, punished, disciplined, and secured for the Kremlin, no matter the cost.[36]

Turning Ukraine into a Soviet fortress meant delivering as much grain as Moscow demanded, regardless of the consequences. Everything—seed grain for the next harvest, grain reserves, livestock, all other food—had to be collected and delivered. Kaganovich came to Ukraine himself to ensure compliance. Taking seed grain meant sabotaging the next harvest and ensuring future starvation, but Kaganovich would not budge. Underperforming communities were blacklisted, which meant public shaming, losing access to crucial manufactured and industrial goods (even matches and salt), bans on migration and trade, denial of loans, and other sanctions. Blacklisting was used not just in Ukraine, but in heavily Ukrainian regions of the North Caucasus, the practice was especially widespread, much more so than in ethnically Russian areas.[37]

But no amount of repression could deliver grain that simply did not exist, and to fulfill procurement quotas in the winter of 1932–1933, the government resorted to even more drastic measures. Search brigades made up of officials, party cadres dispatched from the cities, local Communists, members of the party's youth branch, and collective farmers of both sexes began combing through houses and farmsteads. They broke walls, destroyed stoves, made holes in roofs, and could take any food or livestock they found, even if this left victims with nothing at all. When a search brigade came to the house of Anastasiia Lysyvets', they took all the remaining flour, "everything. . . . Not even a handful [was left]. Father was trembling and mother was crying and asking" how she would feed her children the next day. Soon, both Anastasiia's parents and two of her three siblings died.[38]

Many thousands of similar tragedies were unfolding throughout Ukraine. It was then that the famine became the Holodomor, peaking in the spring of 1933, when close to thirty thousand people died every day. Demographers estimate that most of the famine deaths in Ukraine happened in 1933, the outcome of a campaign of searches that took the last remaining food. Entire villages began to die, and cannibalism—unknown since the famine of the early 1920s—returned. It became so ubiquitous that the authorities felt compelled to prepare and distribute a special poster that proclaimed, "EATING CHILDREN IS BARBARISM."[39]

Search brigades—whom peasants often referred to as "the Red broom," for they swept away everything—could keep part of what they found and therefore had very strong incentives to confiscate food. Most rank-and-file perpetrators were members of the same communities as the victims; while some starved, others protected themselves by condemning neighbors to death. But some perpetrators came from the outside. Lev Kopelev, a young Communist from Kharkiv and a future dissident, was sent to the countryside in December 1932. He participated in searches, took away food, witnessed violence, and saw helpless peasants intimidated, but he believed in Communism fanatically and questioned neither the policy nor his own behavior. Kopelev could silence his reason and conscience but not his stomach. The countryside *was* starving, but unlike the peasants whose homes he searched, Kopelev could get food in the city. After completing his mission, the first thing he did was go to a party district committee cafeteria in the nearest town and get a real lunch: soup with meat and an entire loaf of rye bread. There was also a piece of lard, sugar, canned fish, and beer. Peasants starved so that Communists and urbanites could eat. Living in the city meant food coupons, and food coupons meant life. In a time-tested fashion, the government repressed some in Ukraine but spared and even elevated others, thus ensuring internal division and compliance to Moscow's rule.[40]

Peasants were left with nothing and did not have coupons, but they still went to the cities—if not to buy then to beg. But outside the party elites, urbanites, though not starving, also suffered from food shortages, and the number of beggars was simply overwhelming. In cities across Ukraine, the bodies of dead peasants who had tried and failed to find food became so ubiquitous that people simply stopped noticing. Hundreds of thousands of peasants tried to flee Ukraine altogether, but in late January the government closed the republic's borders with the rest of the USSR, thus preventing starving people from leaving to parts of the Soviet Union that had food. By the end of March, about two hundred thousand Ukrainian peasants would be stopped at the republic's border and sent back home to starve. The writer Vasily Grossman recalled an encounter with a famished peasant near the Russia-Ukraine border: "Swarthy from hunger and illness, she walked toward the express train, looked up at me with her wonderful eyes, and said with her lips, without any voice, 'Bread.'"[41]

By 1933 the Kremlin could no longer deny the occurrence of massive famine, but instead of fighting the tragedy, it fought the truth about it. When trains passed through afflicted areas, passengers were ordered to lower the blinds and stay away from windows. Those who did look, like British writer Grant Carveth Wells, saw "small children with stomachs enormously distended" eating grass. The word "famine" itself was banned, and Western journalists in the USSR were carefully monitored and prohibited from traveling to Ukraine. Some, like the *New York Times* Moscow correspondent Walter Duranty, who believed that one cannot "make an omelet without breaking eggs," willingly aided the misinformation campaign. "Russians hungry but not starving," Duranty wrote. "There is no actual starvation or deaths from starvation but there is widespread mortality from diseases due to malnutrition," he continued. Duranty's sophistry and denials won him a Pulitzer Prize in 1932. Eventually the West learned the truth about the famine, in large part thanks to the Welsh journalist Gareth Jones, who broke official rules and walked through eastern Ukraine on foot to witness the carnage. But within the Soviet Union the Holodomor remained a taboo, and its very existence was denied until 1987. In the rare cases when the tragedy was mentioned, the authorities spoke euphemistically about "difficulties in the countryside."[42]

Unfortunately, we still know much more about the course and mechanics of the famine than about Stalin's motivation and decision-making. Stalin clearly cared deeply about securing control over Ukraine, and he prioritized industrialization and workers' pantries over peasants' lives. But was the Holodomor Stalin's goal?[43]

Since the 1990s, several researchers have blamed bad weather and pests for the poor harvests that caused the famine, but recent statistical analyses using better data and more advanced methods have demonstrated that temperature and climatic conditions in Ukraine predicted a harvest in 1932–1933 largely in line with the 1924–1929 average. It was government policy, not climate, that caused the catastrophe. The famine was man-made, the result of Stalin's policies, phobias, and actions carried all the way down to local officials and party activists in Ukrainian villages.[44]

Yet there is little reason to believe that the Holodomor, which did result from Stalin's actions, was deliberately, intentionally preplanned. The Kremlin wanted Ukrainian peasants to be compliant, productive, reliable, and well monitored. Ukraine had to be made secure, loyal, weak, and compliant but not starving, unable to work, and begging for help. The dictator, however, was shrewd, opportunistic, and brutal enough to spot an opportunity to break the Ukrainian peasantry once and for all by exploiting and exacerbating the famine when it began to unfold through policies such as blacklisting and the closure of borders. The toll was terrible, but Stalin succeeded. Soviet Ukraine would indeed become a model republic: industrialized, productive, compliant, and Russified.

Still, did Ukrainian peasants, the vast majority of the victims, die because they were Ukrainians engaged in agriculture, or because they were peasants who happened to be Ukrainians? Until recently, attempts to solve this question involved trying to decipher Stalin's mind and intentions, and answers inevitably differed. But recent comprehensive statistical analysis has uncovered a substantial anti-Ukrainian bias in government policies during the Holodomor. This bias explains roughly 92 percent of famine deaths in Ukraine and caused mortality rates that were four to six times higher than those in Russia. Moreover, even the low harvests of the famine years were sufficient to feed all of Ukraine's population, and had the food grown in Ukraine during the famine been kept in the republic, it would not have triggered starvation elsewhere in the USSR. Rather, the Kremlin's policy of deliberate *overextraction* from Ukraine caused the famine. We might now have the answer: Ukrainian peasants, not just the kurkul' class enemies but also poor and middling peasants, died because they were Ukrainians, not because they farmed. This was a radical break from previous Russian repressions. In the past, the intent to destroy Ukraine centered on targeting culture, institutions, and activists. Ordinary Ukrainians were either to be transformed into Russians or silenced, not exiled, imprisoned, or starved to death because of their identity. Under Stalin, the desire to destroy Ukraine as an identity and an idea escalated into the physical destructions of Ukrainians.[45]

After the Holodomor and repression of suspected Ukrainian nationalists came Stalin's Great Terror, which reached its peak in 1937–1938. In the RSFSR, both the famine and earlier campaigns of repression were shorter, more limited in scope, and more geographically concentrated. In contrast, Soviet Ukraine—all of it—simply could not catch a break. Even though the pool of potential anti-Soviet conspirators had already been greatly reduced by the famine and previous repression, Ukraine was one of the deadliest areas during the Great Terror. At least 267,579 people were arrested in the republic in 1937–1938 alone, and more than 122,000 were executed. Once again, formerly wealthy peasants and suspected nationalists were the main targets, though this time almost anything smacking of traditional Ukrainian culture could get one in serious trouble. Playing the bandura, a traditional Ukrainian string instrument, became potentially deadly, for banduras, as one Kyiv-based Red Army commander explained, "have a Petliurist soul." Writing poetry about or even merely mentioning the famine was considered a counterrevolutionary, nationalist crime.[46]

Ukraine's national minorities were hit especially hard by the Great Terror. According to the head of the Ukrainian NKVD (successor to the GPU), all Germans and Poles in the republic were "spies and saboteurs." Poles, a mere 1.5 percent of Ukraine's population, accounted for almost

20 percent of those arrested in 1937. Germans, similar in number to the Poles, represented another 10 percent. This ethnically motivated repression would be the first major step toward homogenizing Ukraine and presaged the ethnic cleansings and genocide that Ukraine would experience in the 1940s.[47]

Finally, the Communist Party, the government, and especially the security services were extensively purged of old cadres, many of whom had been active perpetrators of collectivization violence, the Holodomor, and various anti-Ukrainization campaigns. Ukrainian GPU chief Balitsky was arrested in July 1937 and executed four months later, accused of participation in a fascist conspiracy and plotting an armed uprising. His replacement as the head of Ukraine's NKVD, Israel Leplevskii, was arrested seven months after taking the job, supposedly for belonging to a conspiracy group within the NKVD itself. Aleksandr Uspenskii, the next in line, faked his own suicide and went into hiding after nine months at the helm because he, too, was about to be arrested. The specific charges often made no sense—a Jewish NKVD operative who survived several civil war–era pogroms (likely perpetrated by UNR troops) was accused of being a Ukrainian nationalist—but they were not intended to. The more ridiculous the charge, the more complete and humiliating was the submission of the society that accepted it. Nikita Khrushchev, who became the party boss of Ukraine in 1938, survived by zealously carrying out any and all of Stalin's policies, including aggressive Russification.[48]

The purges of the party, bureaucracy, and security services changed their ethnic makeup and outlook. The impact on the NKVD was especially pronounced. Jews, who were heavily overrepresented in the Soviet security apparatus prior to the Great Terror, were purged and their numbers plummeted. The proportion of Ukrainian operatives, in the meantime, increased from 5 percent in 1934 to almost 20 percent in 1939, but ethnic Russians remained by far the largest and most dominant group, even though they were a minority of Ukraine's population. The purging of old cadres also meant that, for the new generation of Soviet secret policemen in Ukraine, the formative experience was not fighting the Whites but collectivizing the Ukrainian peasantry, confiscating food during the Holodomor, and undoing Ukrainization. They would continue worrying about and repressing nationalist enemies for the rest of their careers.[49]

The Holodomor and accompanying rounds of repression changed Ukraine forever. Twenty years after its attempt at independence, Ukraine was subdued and fully back under Russian control. Stalin's violence made the republic smaller, poorer, and deeply traumatized. Peasantry, the backbone of Ukrainian identity and anti-Communist sentiment, was collectivized and starved into submission. New populations from Russia and Belorussia were brought in to replace the dead. Repressive policies originated in the Kremlin, but implementation was local, and even those who disagreed learned to obey.

Famine stunted development, hamstrung economic activity, and diminished social cohesion for decades; some legacies of the Holodomor can be felt even now. It also ensured the republic's compliance, and, from the Kremlin's perspective, this trumped everything else. The end of Ukrainization and the purging of intellectuals shattered Ukrainian-speaking culture, while the Great Terror purged any remaining national Communists and sympathetic local-level officials. The outcome was total Russian dominance and growing Russification of government and society.[50]

Despite Stalin's fears, he did not lose Ukraine. But by the end of the 1930s, the Ukrainian nation was still divided between the USSR and its western neighbors, especially Poland, and substantial Ukrainian nationalist sentiment persisted in Galicia. World War II and the Soviet invasion of Poland and annexation of Galicia, Volhynia, and, later, Bukovyna and Transcarpathia—which had previously belonged to Romania and Czechoslovakia—would create the borders of contemporary Ukraine (except for Crimea). But the incorporation of these territories and their Ukrainian-speaking communities into Soviet Ukraine would also introduce an important counterbalance to Russification. Eventually, the existence of such western Ukrainian enclaves would fuel the push for independence and help to destroy the model republic that Stalin killed so many people to build.

CHAPTER 6

UNITE AND RULE

In November 1940, twenty-two-year-old Yisrael-Leib, a Jew from Galicia, was drafted into the Red Army. The soldier's first concern was learning Russian, the army's language. By then, the USSR had ruled western Ukraine for more than a year, but Yisrael-Leib was too busy making ends meet to take advantage of the educational and social opportunities the Soviets offered. Russian was his fourth language, after Yiddish, Polish, and Ukrainian. His second concern was his name. Yisrael-Leib was not a good one for a soldier, let alone an officer, of the increasingly Russo-centric and chauvinist Soviet state. So, first Yisrael-Leib became Leib, then Leonid, and eventually Lev. He fought in the Arctic and served in the Soviet far east. When Junior Lieutenant Lev Finkel, my grandfather, finally left the service in 1946 and returned to Lviv, he discovered that his entire family—parents, four sisters, brothers-in-law, nieces, and nephews—had been killed in the Holocaust. The MGB, the Ministry of State Security and predecessor of the KGB, offered him a job. They needed people like my grandfather—local, presumably loyal, with combat experience and little to lose—to fight the Ukrainian nationalist guerrillas still active in western Ukraine. He refused the offer, married, settled down. Like his name, his entire identity gradually Sovietized, and Russian became his primary language. Of the very few Galician Jews who survived World War II, almost all left the Soviet Union in the 1940s and 1950s; our family was among the last remnants of this once large, poor, proud, and vibrant community. Now it is no more.

Also almost entirely gone from western Ukraine are the Poles, Czechs, and Germans who lived in the region for centuries. In Crimea, the Tatar community is now a faint, threatened shadow of its former self. All these tragedies are the outcomes of World War II and the immediate postwar violence against civilians committed by the Nazi and Soviet states, their collaborators, the Ukrainian Insurgent Army (UPA), and other, smaller forces. Ukraine was ground zero of World War II violence against civilians, and every community and settlement suffered, albeit unevenly. The same person could be both a victim and a perpetrator, and the lines separating freedom fighters from collaborators with foreign occupiers, and heroes from villains, blurred before collapsing entirely.

But after the war and the postwar violence, Ukraine entered a period in which Moscow's control and the stability of the Soviet system were taken for granted. Ukraine ceased to be a major security or identity concern for the Kremlin, and it stagnated with the rest of the USSR—though aggressive overreaction to any hints of Ukrainian nationalism still characterized Soviet policy. Ukraine's residents became Soviet and Russified, preoccupied with economic concerns, and, except for a small circle of dissidents, uninterested in politics, identity, or language issues. Ukraine itself turned into a piece of the larger, Russian-dominated Soviet whole.

Things changed abruptly in the late 1980s. Perestroika and the deep crisis of the Soviet system began to make Ukrainian independence a real possibility. In response, identity-driven obsession with Ukraine returned to Russia. Now, however, it combined the shared origin story of the Kyivan Rus' with an equally potent myth centered on World War II and the postwar Soviet struggle against the UPA.

On August 23, 1939, Stalin drank to Hitler's health. The occasion was the signing of a nonaggression treaty between the USSR and Nazi Germany, the Molotov-Ribbentrop Pact. War was brewing in Europe and the dictators came together to carve up the continent. The secret protocol of the agreement partitioned Poland between the two states and consigned the Soviet Union's neighbors to the rule of Moscow. In a matter of months, the USSR would expand to swallow up western Ukraine and Belorussia, occupy the Baltic states, grab Bukovyna and Moldova from Romania, and invade Finland.[1]

In this massive expansion, western Ukraine was part of the broader effort to move Soviet borders westward and, in so doing, enhance the Communist regime's security. The identity-based motivation behind the Kremlin's policies, though less important than security concerns, was also hard to miss. On September 1, 1939, Nazi Germany invaded Poland and started World War II. The Polish army fought bravely but was no match for the German Wehrmacht.

On September 17, the USSR invaded Poland from the east. The Kremlin's justification was that the Polish state had ceased to exist, and Moscow therefore had a duty to intervene to protect Russia's "brothers of the same blood, Ukrainians and Belorussians." Some propagandists went even further, describing western Ukraine and Belorussia as "primordial Russian lands." In reality, on September 17 the Polish state was still very much in existence, and it was the Soviet invasion that doomed Poland's resistance against Hitler. The justification for the Soviet attack also invoked the same themes and symbols as Russian imperial rhetoric preceding the invasion of Galicia in 1914. Stalin, increasingly a Russian nationalist, was poised to achieve what no Romanov emperor ever could: uniting all Kyivan Rus' lands under Russian rule.[2]

The Soviet invasion force of half a million troops easily conquered western Ukraine. Soviet troops emptied the stores, paying with unfamiliar rubles or, occasionally, not paying at all. "The Russians liberated us, they liberated us from butter, from sugar, from milk, from meat," a former resident of eastern Poland recalled sarcastically. The wives of Soviet officers, who wore unfamiliar, newly purchased nightgowns as if they were evening dresses, became the butt of local jokes.[3]

Yet the attitudes of the Ukrainians, Poles, and Jews in the region were not universally hostile. Most locals, regardless of identity, simply wanted to get by and avoid trouble. Poorer members of the three major communities hoped to benefit from the new regime, and many did. Jews had additional reason to welcome the Soviets because the Red Army offered protection from the Nazis. The attitude of the Poles, who almost overnight lost both their state and their prominence in the local social hierarchy, was the most negative.

Ukrainians, the region's largest community, were divided. Many welcomed the unification of all Ukrainian lands, even if it was under Communist rule. The region's new rulers also embarked on a policy of Ukrainization, mirroring that of Soviet Ukraine in the 1920s. Lviv University was renamed after Ivan Franko, a Habsburg-era Ukrainian writer and politician, and multiple other cultural and educational institutions switched from using Polish to Ukrainian, creating employment and career opportunities for the Ukrainian middle class. Indeed, there was no shortage of Ukrainians willing to cooperate with Soviet authorities, hoping they would continue to prioritize Ukrainians and the Ukrainian language.[4]

But other parts of the Ukrainian community viewed the onset of Soviet rule as a colonial occupation. The main proponent of this view was the Organization of Ukrainian Nationalists. The OUN had emerged out of two existential crises. The first was the failure to secure durable Ukrainian statehood in the aftermath of World War I, most importantly the demise of the ZUNR. Many Ukrainian activists, especially younger ones, believed that the ZUNR had failed not because it was too small, inexperienced, and fighting the much larger and better-equipped Polish army, but because it was too democratic, too moderate, too tolerant, and too restrained in its use of violence. They vowed to never repeat these mistakes and embraced action-oriented, violent radicalism as the answer to Ukraine's problems.

The second crisis was the Second Polish Republic's repression of Ukrainians, particularly their political and social life, in Galicia and Volhynia. Minorities constituted about 30 percent of interwar Poland, with Ukrainians, Germans, Belorussians, and Jews being the largest groups. Minorities faced discrimination, and the end goal for the Polish government was to assimilate everyone besides the Jews, by force if necessary. In Galicia and Volhynia, this policy meant repression, heavy censorship, police surveillance of Ukrainian activists, and efforts to limit Ukrainian-language education. Thus, from 1919 to 1923, the number of Ukrainian-language schools fell from 1,050 to 433, and most of those that remained were later forced to become bilingual, Polish-Ukrainian institutions. The government restricted the admission of Ukrainian students to Lviv University and abolished its Ukrainian chairs. It also started importing Polish colonists (predominantly army veterans) into the region that was already experiencing a land shortage, thus heightening tensions further.[5]

Ukrainians initially responded with boycotts and protests, but in the late 1920s the standoff exploded into violence, which was brutally put down by the Polish government in a campaign of "pacification." There were voices on both sides calling for compromise, but these had only limited appeal. In 1929, various Ukrainian nationalist organizations, most of them based outside Poland, joined forces to establish the OUN. The OUN's first leader was Yevhen Konovalets, a native of Galicia and an Austro-Hungarian army officer during World War I. Konovalets played a key role in organizing Ukrainian military forces amid the disintegration of the Russian and Habsburg empires, and after the UNR collapsed, went into exile in Western Europe.

The ideology of the OUN was heavily influenced by Dmytro Dontsov, a publicist and political thinker born in 1883 to a mixed Russian Ukrainian family in Melitopol in southern Ukraine. Dontsov began his career as a Marxist but soon moved over to the extreme, racist, and authoritarian right. Dontsov and the OUN believed that because Ukraine had historically been colonized by external powers, only uncompromising, violent total struggle against these colonizers and their collaborators would secure an independent Ukraine. For the OUN, the chief enemies were the Poles and the Russians; Jews were a secondary but still dangerous adversary, because the OUN viewed them as tools of the colonial powers on the ground. The independent Ukraine the OUN sought to create was to be an ethnically homogeneous, single-party dictatorship where all political life, institutions, and decision-making would be subordinated to the will of a supreme leader. OUN members were radical, uncompromising, and famous for their total devotion to the cause of establishing an OUN-governed Ukrainian state.

Historians still argue about whether the OUN was ideologically fascist. Yet even those who promote different terms to describe its worldview—such as "integral nationalism" or "Ustashism," after the Croatian Ustaše regime that collaborated with Hitler—agree that the OUN came extremely close to, and in some ways was even more radical than, fascism. Many OUN leaders publicly expressed their admiration for Benito Mussolini and were especially fond of Hitler's hostility toward Poland and determination to dismantle the interwar international order created at Versailles. The organization was also in close contact with several European intelligence services, most notably those of Lithuania and Germany, which, like the OUN, saw Poland as an enemy.[6]

Violence was the OUN's tool of choice for gaining fame, attracting supporters, and eliminating opposition. Among its most prominent victims were Polish minister of interior Bronisław Pieracki and the Polish parliamentarian Tadeusz Hołówko, who promoted Polish-Ukrainian rapprochement. Yet during the 1930s, most victims of OUN violence were neither Poles nor Russians but fellow Ukrainians who opposed the OUN's radicalism.[7]

The OUN was also divided internally between the older, diaspora-based activists like Konovalets and the younger, more radical members in Galicia led by Stepan Bandera and Roman Shukhevych. In 1938, Soviet intelligence—worried about the OUN's potential ability to mobilize Soviet

Ukrainians against Moscow in a future European war—assassinated Konovalets with a bomb concealed in a chocolate candy box. The killer was Pavel Sudoplatov, an NKVD officer who, like Dontsov, hailed from a mixed Russian Ukrainian family from Melitopol. After this assignment, Sudoplatov would play key roles in other Soviet assassinations, most notably that of Leon Trotsky.

In 1940, the OUN split into two separate factions: OUN-M, led by Konovalets's close associate and brother-in-law Andriy Melnyk, and the larger OUN-B, led by Bandera. Historian Timothy Snyder has described OUN-B as a "nationalist terrorist organization, led by immature and angry men." These OUN-B men (and women) were indeed young, violent, and angry, but their experience operating underground in Poland allowed the OUN to survive after western Ukraine came under Soviet rule and the authorities tried to eradicate the organization.[8]

The era of relative Soviet tolerance and genuine Ukrainization in western Ukraine was short-lived. After securing control of the region, Soviet authorities continued promoting Ukrainians to high-level positions, but these were no longer locals but Ukrainians brought from the east. Many Russians also arrived to staff Soviet government institutions, especially the security services and law enforcement. The new authorities nationalized businesses, expropriated houses, closed religious institutions, cracked down on expressions of nationalism, and disbanded civic groups. Only Soviet organizations and ideas were allowed to proliferate. In one remarkable episode in Drohobych, near Lviv, the NKVD arrested the famed local Jewish artist and writer Bruno Schulz for using suspiciously large amounts of blue and yellow (the colors of the Ukrainian flag) in a mural devoted to "the liberation of Western Ukraine." Most banned organizations trying to continue working illegally were inexperienced, made rookie mistakes, and were quickly discovered and destroyed. The OUN, which was well acquainted with clandestine operations, had a clear advantage.[9]

The government also started deporting people en masse from western Ukraine to the Soviet hinterland, mostly Siberia and Central Asia. The first wave of deportations targeted prewar elites, political activists, state officials, and local leaders. Most of the victims were ethnic Poles. Later, the focus switched to refugees, predominantly Jews, who were arriving in western Ukraine from Nazi-occupied Poland and refused to accept Soviet citizenship because they hoped to return home after the war. Those Jews who remained in western Ukraine joked that Soviet liberation commuted a death sentence under the Nazis to life imprisonment. On June 22, 1941, Germany invaded the USSR, and this dark joke became prophetic.

The Nazi invasion of the USSR and the staggering violence that followed completely reshaped the demography of Ukraine. Of those Jews who did not escape alongside the retreating Red Army, almost all perished in the Holocaust, killed by the Germans, by their Hungarian and Romanian allies, by their local collaborators, and in various pogroms that broke out in western Ukraine after the Soviet retreat. After all other Ukrainian groups had been destroyed by the Soviets, the OUN quickly emerged as the leading political force among western Ukrainians. Scholars still argue about the full extent of local and OUN participation in the pogroms and the Holocaust, though few deny the very fact of the group's involvement. The most detailed recent study by Canadian Ukrainian historian John-Paul Himka shows that the Ukrainian and OUN contribution to the Holocaust took different forms. OUN-led militias actively partook in, and in some places led, anti-Jewish pogroms during the summer of 1941. Many Ukrainian nationalists also joined Nazi-organized police units. Their motivations for signing up ranged from securing better food rations to gaining military training and weapons, which would be needed to fight for independent Ukraine, but serving in the police also meant guarding ghettos and participating in mass shootings and deportations of Jews to the death camps. Later, guerrilla Ukrainian-nationalist UPA units also murdered Jews on their own, without any German supervision.[10]

It is also undeniable that, prior to and during the early stages of the German invasion, the OUN collaborated with the Nazi government in the hope that this collaboration would be rewarded with the creation of a Nazi-allied Ukrainian state. Indeed, the OUN even proclaimed such a state on June 30, 1941, after German troops occupied Lviv. Hitler, however, had other plans for Ukraine; the OUN "government" was quickly disbanded and arrested. Bandera himself was detained on July 5 and spent most of the war in Sachsenhausen concentration camp.

The arrest of Bandera did not automatically transform the OUN-B into anti-Nazis. Throughout most of the German occupation, Nazi authorities and the OUN-B coexisted, alternating between cautious cooperation and open confrontation. The OUN-M was openly pro-German, but it was also smaller and less influential. In August 1943, after the Soviet victories at Stalingrad and Kursk, German defeat and the return of Soviet rule seemed inevitable, and so the OUN-B changed tack. Hoping to attract American and British support in the anticipated fight against the USSR, the OUN-B moderated its rhetoric and abruptly changed its official vision for Ukraine's future from an ethno-nationalist dictatorship to a democracy with full minority rights. On the ground, however, the UPA—which was not identical to but closely overlapped with the OUN-B in its leadership and membership—used the quickly closing window of opportunity to start an ethnic cleansing campaign against the Poles, predominantly in Volhynia. UPA attacks often led to Polish retaliation that also targeted civilians, but the death toll from UPA violence was substantially higher, about fifty thousand to sixty thousand dead in Volhynia, and between seventy thousand and one hundred thousand in all of western Ukraine. Proclaiming commitment to minority rights was easier when the largest minority groups, the Poles and the Jews, were destroyed. Stalin completed the ethnic cleansing; after the war, Poles from western Ukraine were expelled to Poland.[11]

In 1944, the Red Army returned to western Ukraine. The Soviet Union had changed during the war years. It was now a fully Russo-centric polity in which Russians were elevated above everyone else. But Soviet propaganda also invoked non-Russian heroes and mythologies, including Ukrainian ones. However, in the Ukrainian case, the symbols, images, and heroes used for propaganda purposes were explicitly chosen with the goal of strengthening the perception of a shared origin and special bond between Russians and Ukrainians.[12]

The UPA's guerrilla war against the Soviets is the most well-known of its kind, but it was not unique; similar insurgencies were waged in the Baltics. Yet the UPA—led by Roman Shukhevych, who had earlier served in military and police units organized by and subordinate to Nazi Germany—was by far the largest and most violent group. At its peak, the UPA had up to forty thousand fighters and as many as four hundred thousand people involved in total. The struggle was bloody, vicious, and, most crucially, flew in the face of the official narrative of Soviet liberation and the brotherhood of Russians and Ukrainians. "Bandera" and "Banderites" quickly entered the Soviet and later Russian lexicon as shorthand for perfidious treachery, fanatical nationalism, and violence. Not many Russians have ever heard of the Baltic "forest brothers," but almost everyone knows—and most Russians passionately hate—"the Banderites," despite knowing very little about the UPA's actual history. "Banderite" also became a general pejorative term for western Ukrainians and, more generally, supporters of Ukraine's independence, including those who were democrats and rejected the OUN's radical ideology.[13]

Soviet authorities had great difficulty suppressing the UPA, and the insurgency continued into the 1950s. The insurgents adopted small-unit stealth tactics and enjoyed the support of many locals. Soviet repression was ruthless, and heavy punishments were meted out to captured UPA fighters. The families of real and suspected nationalist guerrillas were deported to the Soviet hinterland. Shukhevych died during the insurgency, most likely committing suicide to avoid capture. According to Soviet records, the campaign against the UPA killed more than one hundred thousand people. In the late 1940s and early 1950s, between a third and half of inmates in special Gulag camps for political prisoners were Ukrainian nationalists.[14]

But rank-and-file UPA fighters who surrendered often received amnesty and had their families released. Slowly, the tide shifted in favor of the Soviet counterinsurgency. What ultimately doomed the UPA was the combination of Soviet repression and the insurgents' own violence against Ukrainians suspected of collaboration with the Soviet authorities. The UPA's definition of collaboration was expansive and included not just state officials but also the families of soldiers drafted into the Red Army, peasants forced into collective farms, and everyone who worked for the Soviet state in any form, down to janitors and doormen. Out of more than thirty thousand people killed by the UPA between 1944 and 1956, the majority were not Soviet troops but Ukrainian civilians. This violence led many Ukrainians to begin supporting the Soviet government, and soon the number of those the UPA viewed as collaborators far exceeded that of the nationalists and their supporters. The Soviet counterinsurgency also used so-called destruction battalions, made up of local Ukrainians, including pardoned UPA fighters, who sought to protect themselves and their families from nationalist violence or to avenge killed relatives. Without this local—even if reluctant and forced—support for Soviet rule, the insurgency might have continued even longer.[15]

At the end of their violent struggle, the OUN and UPA had achieved little. The Ukrainian state of which they dreamed was as distant a prospect as ever. They entered the history books as symbols of uncompromising struggle for Ukrainian statehood, but the human and moral cost of the violence they unleashed was enormous. The OUN, and especially the UPA, killed tens of thousands of civilians. Soviet, and later Russian, propaganda skillfully linked all supporters of independent Ukraine to genocidal violence and collaboration with the Nazis.

The OUN remained active in the diaspora but splintered still further into several bickering factions. By the end of the 1950s, Bandera (whom the German government had released in 1944) was as committed, authoritarian, and radical as ever, but his standing and support among Ukrainian nationalists were much diminished. In 1959, he was assassinated by the KGB in Munich. Ironically, it was the assassination that turned Bandera from a failed rebel and minor politician into a martyr and icon of Ukraine's anti-Soviet struggle. In death, Bandera became a much larger threat to the Kremlin and its control over Ukraine than he ever was in life.[16]

Soviet repression went beyond just fighting the UPA: It eradicated Ukrainian national symbols and historical narratives, such as the memory of the ZUNR. It also crushed the Greek Catholic Church, the cornerstone of Galician Ukrainian identity. But Communist rule did more than repress; it was also flexible and pragmatic enough to accommodate some local demands in order to buy public support for the regime. Deeply ingrained popular commitment to Ukrainian culture in Galicia forced the authorities to make Ukrainian the dominant language of public life, education, and culture in the region at a time when the rest of Ukraine was Russified. Lviv and western Ukraine would remain an island of Ukrainian language and a distinct (if repressed and Sovietized) identity in a large, Russian-speaking ocean. The existence of this rebellious, Ukrainian-speaking enclave challenged the dominant Soviet, Russian-speaking narrative that denied any politically meaningful distinctions between Russians and Ukrainians and would play a major role in Ukraine's future development.[17]

Stalin's death in 1953 was celebrated in the Ukrainian diaspora—a photo of a diner in Washington offering free borscht, Ukraine's traditional beet soup, to mark the occasion became iconic—and, more quietly, among many in western Ukraine. But in the rest of Ukraine, the dictator's death prompted confusion and genuine grief, even among those who would later become prominent dissidents. After a short period of collective rule by Stalin's lieutenants, Nikita Khrushchev, the former party boss of Ukraine who grew up in the Donbas, became the new Soviet leader. Khrushchev eased restrictions on Ukrainian language and culture, ended large-scale repression, and gradually released most political prisoners. The eleven years of his rule are often referred to as "the thaw."[18]

Nineteen fifty-four, the year after Khrushchev came to power, was the three-hundredth anniversary of the Pereiaslav treaty, when Bohdan Khmelnytsky and the Cossacks pledged allegiance to the tsar. With Ukraine's former boss now in the Kremlin, and the UPA guerrillas finally subdued, the anniversary was an important opportunity to promote and fully cement in the public imagination the idea of unity between Ukrainians and Russians, and Russia's role as the dominant but caring "elder brother."

Proskuriv, a regional capital in central Ukraine and site of the most famous civil war pogrom, was renamed Khmelnytsky, and a deluge of celebratory publications, films, and proclamations were disseminated in Ukrainian and central Soviet media, praising the unification and its legacy. But the most important and lasting consequence of the anniversary was the transfer of Crimea, then part of the RSFSR, to Ukraine.

During World War II, Crimea saw heavy fighting. The German army captured Sevastopol after a bloody eight-month siege, and the Red Army did not return to the peninsula until May 1944. After the Red Army liberated Crimea, security services began hunting down Nazi supporters. In Simferopol, the peninsula's main city, "trees lining the streets were used as gallows, so great was the number of executions." Soviet authorities immediately accused the Crimean Tatar community of wholesale collaboration with Germany. Some Tatars did indeed collaborate with the Germans, but so did members of every community besides the Jews, who were almost all exterminated (though there were collaborators even among the Karaites, a small Jewish community whom the Nazis considered racially Turkic). Tens of thousands of Crimean Tatars were at the time fighting in the Red Army.

The charges against the Tatars were driven more by long-standing prejudices connected to their Muslim faith and the government's desire to remove the Tatars from the strategically important "Soviet paradise" of the peninsula. Stalin was also contemplating an invasion of Turkey, and having a Turkic-speaking, Muslim community in Crimea was therefore seen as a security risk. On May 10, 1944, Lavrentii Beria—the powerful chief of the NKVD—suggested that Stalin deport the entire community. No Tatars, even those fully loyal to Soviet rule, were to remain in Crimea.[19]

On May 18, 1944, Captain Amet-khan Sultan was home on leave, visiting his parents in the just liberated Crimea. He was a Crimean Tatar, a model Soviet citizen, and a fighter ace who had received the Hero of the Soviet Union award, the country's highest decoration. In the middle of the night, Sultan heard a commotion, went outside, and saw armed soldiers holding his mother. After noticing the pilot's rank and medals, the soldiers paused and took Sultan to the NKVD officer in charge, who explained that

145

all Crimean Tatars were being expelled from the peninsula. Not even the parents of a Hero of the Soviet Union would be exempt.[20]

The majority of Crimean Tatars, about 150,000 in all, were deported to Uzbekistan. They were transported in box and cattle cars, with barely any food or water and without medical care. Thousands died on the journey and many more in the first years after arrival, because Tatars had no immunity to local diseases, little land to farm, no experience of local conditions, and were met with hostility by neighbors and local authorities. About a third of the Crimean Tatar nation perished during and in the years immediately following the deportation.[21]

Amet-khan Sultan continued serving the Soviet Union but stopped being a Crimean Tatar; military documents began listing his ethnicity as simply "Tatar," a related but different group. Just as the pilot was no longer Crimean, Crimea ceased being Tatar. Soviet authorities embarked on an extensive campaign to erase all signs of Tatar presence. Almost all mosques were demolished or turned into movie theaters, clubs, or warehouses, and Crimean Tatar–language textbooks were destroyed. Place names, including those that predated the Tatar presence in Crimea, were changed. The government also permanently altered the demographic makeup of the peninsula by bringing in ethnic Russians and Ukrainians. Unlike other nations deported from their homelands by Stalin, Crimean Tatars were not allowed to return after Stalin's death and had to wait until 1989.[22]

The mass deportation devastated Crimea's economy. The new Slavic arrivals were unfamiliar with local conditions and farming systems, and Russia's republican authorities did not care about the distant province. As the peninsula fell into dilapidation, Khrushchev's solution was to combine the Pereiaslav treaty anniversary with cold economic logic and transfer Crimea to Ukraine. Crimea, the thinking went, was closer to Ukraine than to Russia both economically and geographically, and Kyiv was therefore better positioned to develop the peninsula. Besides, within the now highly centralized Soviet state, such a change of internal borders meant little in practice. The transfer of Crimea to Ukraine was of so little consequence that the government likely did not even follow existing Soviet legislation. Crimea became nominally Ukrainian, and besides the small group of Russian nationalists who quietly grumbled, nobody cared.[23]

Khrushchev was energetic but erratic, and most of his reforms and pet projects failed. In 1964, senior Communist Party officials banded together to oust Khrushchev in a bloodless coup d'état. His replacement was Leonid Brezhnev. While Khrushchev had grown up and spent much of his career in Ukraine, he was a Russian native. Brezhnev was born in eastern Ukraine proper, and his and Khrushchev's rise to power were clear signs of the region's significance to the Soviet state and the important role Ukraine's Communists played in leading the Soviet Union. Eventually, most reforms initiated by Khrushchev were rolled back, and Brezhnev's era of "stagnation" replaced Khrushchev's "thaw."

Yet the Brezhnevian emphasis on stability was not enough to ensure the allegiance of the Soviet population, and the regime needed new political myths and symbols. World War II quickly emerged as one such myth. Under Stalin, Soviet victory over Germany had quickly lost political prominence. Indeed, after 1948, Victory Day, celebrated on May 9, was a regular working day, not a national holiday. This changed after Brezhnev took power. Beginning in 1965, a massive, pompous military parade in Moscow's Red Square became an annual tradition, May 9 was enshrined as one of the main annual holidays, and the defeat of Germany came to surpass even the Bolshevik Revolution as the most important event in the Soviet historical narrative.[24]

Used extensively to inspire patriotism and loyalty to the Communist Party, the war became, and remains, more than a crucial myth; it turned into an obsession. This obsession elevated Sevastopol's status to that of a sacred place and entrenched a conviction in the inherent, timeless righteousness of the Russian cause and the undefeatable might of the Russian army and nation. When the victory over Nazism came to overshadow everything else, Russia's enemies, regardless of ideology or geography, became seen as akin to—and, eventually, literally—Nazis, in the public imagination and ultimately in official rhetoric.

The increasing prominence of the commemoration of the war in the late 1960s coincided with the formative teenage years of Vladimir Putin, twelve years old when military parades returned to Red Square. According to Putin, a film about a heroic Soviet spy in Berlin during the war, one of many such post-1965 productions, steered him toward a career in the KGB.

The growth of the war myth also cemented the leading status of the Russian nation within the USSR because, the argument went, Russians had played the main role in the Soviet war effort. Ukrainians came second in the ethnic hierarchy, but Banderites now deserved even greater scorn. The war myth and the Russo-centric orientation of the Soviet state also made the Kremlin increasingly sympathetic toward Russian nationalists who viewed the entire USSR as a Russian nation-state, vehemently rejected Western liberalism, and were especially interested in rehabilitating Russia's imperial past and the Orthodox Church.[25]

Brezhnev's rule also almost completed the Russification of Ukraine. Outside of western Ukraine, it became almost impossible to hear Ukrainian spoken on city streets, and even in the countryside, it gradually gave way to Russian. By the end of the 1970s, over half of schoolchildren in Ukraine attended Russian-language schools, up from 30 percent in 1958. In eastern Ukraine, many towns no longer had even a single Ukrainian-language school. Those who protested this growing Russification were immediately labeled nationalists and faced punishment. *Internationalism or Russification?*, a 1965 pamphlet authored by writer Ivan Dziuba, eloquently expressed the frustration and fears of Ukrainian speakers as their language and culture became marginalized and gradually vanished.[26]

Many prominent Ukrainian-language artists of Khrushchev's "thaw" era evolved from supporters of the system to dissidents. The price of this activism was high. Security concerns connected to Ukraine's strategic location mixed with the long-standing fear of Ukrainian "bourgeois nationalism" to produce especially heavy—by the standards of the day—punishments. No other dissidents in the USSR, with possible exceptions of Zionists and Crimean Tatars, were repressed as heavily as Ukrainian activists. By the early 1980s, Ukrainians represented the largest group of political prisoners in Soviet prisons; some dissidents, such as the poet Vasyl Stus, died in prison and became martyrs for Ukrainian opposition to Soviet rule. But outside the small circles of dissidents, most peo ple in Ukraine were either genuinely loyal Soviet citizens or simply could not imagine any alternative to the existing system. The Soviet Union and Soviet Ukraine seemed stable and permanent. One history of the period described the stagnant Soviet reality as "everything was forever, until it was no more."[27]

The USSR collapsed like the man going bankrupt in Ernest Hemingway's famous story: first slowly, then suddenly. In the five short years of Mikhail Gorbachev's reforms between the Chernobyl nuclear disaster in April 1986 and the Communist hard-liners' failed coup attempt in August 1991, the recently unimaginable—the breakup of the Soviet state and Ukraine achieving independence—became conceivable and then inevitable. By the end of 1991, the mighty USSR had ceased to exist. Ukraine did not kill the Soviet Union, but it played a crucial role in burying it. And as the USSR was in its death throes, Russians' sense of ownership over Ukraine, their desire to control it, and their territorial claims on Crimea and eastern Ukraine—which had lain dormant during Soviet times—returned with gusto among Communists, nationalists, and even supporters of democracy.

By 1985, the Communist system was in deep trouble. The Cold War against the United States had escalated and demanded massive investment in military and industrial capabilities, even though the Kremlin had little money to spare. The Soviet economy was plagued by inefficiencies, shortages, and reams of red tape, and it was skewed toward military production. According to a popular joke, no matter what Soviet plants tried to manufacture, the end product was invariably a tank. Agriculture was in even worse shape than industry, and the government had to spend gargantuan amounts of foreign currency on food imports to feed the growing urban population. Despite encompassing Ukraine, which had been

Europe's breadbasket less than a century prior, the USSR was at this stage the world's largest grain importer. But even that was not enough, and the country was plagued by constant food shortages. Soviet citizens no longer spoke of buying food; they used the term "to obtain," because it required so much more than just showing up at the store and paying.

Even more damning for the regime, very few people still believed in Communist ideals, and even fewer were willing to make sacrifices for them. Yet despite all those problems, radical change still seemed impossible. The Soviet Union limped along but did not tumble. Those who pushed for change from below were labeled "bourgeois nationalists." In Ukraine, the definition of "bourgeois nationalism" was especially expansive and encompassed much more than political activism. Petro Veksliarov, the iconic and beloved Grandpa Panas of Ukrainian TV's *Good Night, Kids!* program, came under suspicion because he wore a *vyshyvanka*, a traditional Ukrainian embroidered shirt. Ironically, the actor himself, who became an unofficial mascot for Ukrainian folk traditions, was Jewish; he had changed his name from Pinkhas Veksler to protect himself when taken as a POW by the Germans during World War II. The Holocaust and ethnic cleansings of the 1940s notwithstanding, Soviet Ukraine remained a diverse place, though not nearly as much as before.

Real change would have to come from above. Yurii Andropov, the dour KGB chief who became Soviet leader after Brezhnev's death in November 1982, sought to introduce economic reforms, coupled with a campaign of repression aimed at improving workplace discipline. He might have succeeded had he lived longer, but Andropov died in February 1984. His successor, Konstantin Chernenko, had an even shorter term, dying in March 1985. As a child, I remember using toy soldiers to reenact elaborate state funerals, though I often mixed up the names of the beloved leaders I was burying. As I later discovered, many adults were just as confused by this quick succession of dying statesmen.

Chernenko's replacement was the much younger Mikhail Gorbachev. A native of the Stavropol region in southern Russia, Gorbachev was born to a poor peasant family of mixed Russian Ukrainian heritage.

After studying law in Moscow, he returned to Stavropol to embark on a party career and quickly rose through the Soviet bureaucracy. He became a protégé of Andropov, who in 1978 brought Gorbachev to the center of Soviet power in Moscow. Like his mentor, Gorbachev recognized the urgent need for reform but, like everyone else, could not grasp how hard it would be to reinvigorate the system without destroying it. Gorbachev never wanted to dismantle Communism, let alone cause the disintegration of the USSR. His goal was to return the system to its original Leninist ideals and dreams.[28]

Gorbachev's efforts, which came to be collectively known as perestroika (restructuring), included glasnost (increased openness and public discussion of existing problems and shortcomings). This was originally meant to occur within strictly defined limits, neither threatening the regime nor demanding political freedoms. Gorbachev started promoting glasnost as the key component of his reform package at the Twenty-Seventh Communist Party Congress in February–March 1986. Less than two months after the congress, events in Ukraine tested the limits of glasnost and found them to be extremely narrow indeed.

At 1:24 a.m. on April 26, 1986, a mismanaged safety test triggered a massive explosion in Reactor 4 of the Chernobyl Nuclear Plant, north of Kyiv. In retrospect, it was a disaster waiting to happen. To meet deadlines imposed by Moscow, the plant was built in violation of multiple safety standards and without conducting all necessary tests. The reactor model used at Chernobyl was capricious and unstable, and there had been previous incidents that were swept under the rug. These structural problems were exacerbated by the tight schedule of the test, the hubris of the engineer in charge, and the inexperience of key members of the test team. Beyond the immediate damage caused by the explosion, the disaster released a huge amount of radioactive particles into the atmosphere, which began drifting toward Kyiv, Belorussia, Poland, Western Europe, and Scandinavia.[29]

The Soviet government's response to the disaster was scandalous. Initially, plant management and local leadership tried to minimize the damage and pretend that things were under control, even when they manifestly were not. It took some time for the authorities in Kyiv and Moscow to comprehend the scale of the danger posed to millions of Soviet citizens. Even when they did, the Soviet reflexes of secrecy, denial, and disregard for human life immediately kicked in. The government prevaricated about the need to quickly evacuate the highly exposed town of Pripyat, where the nuclear plant's workers lived, and concealed information from the public. When routine radiation tests conducted in Scandinavia and Western Europe all pointed to a nuclear disaster in the USSR, Gorbachev, rather than admitting what happened, accused the West of spreading disinformation.

Kyiv presented a special problem for the government. On May 1, massive celebrations, rallies, and parades were traditionally held across the Soviet Union, and 1986 was no exception. Local health authorities argued that the parade in Kyiv would expose tens of thousands of people to high levels of radiation. But the May Day procession was an important symbol of state power, and canceling it would be an admission of the gravity of the situation. According to one popular version of events, Volodymyr Shcherbytsky—Ukraine's conservative Communist boss and a close Brezhnev ally who had led the republic since 1972—tried to convince Gorbachev to call off the procession. Gorbachev refused and threatened to fire Shcherbytsky and expel him from the party. Shcherbytsky obeyed, and the parade was held as planned. For Communist mandarins, human lives were always subordinate to the regime's goals.[30]

The disaster, its mishandling by the government, the blatant lies despite the promises of openness, and the disregard for Kyivites' health for the sake of a parade bred deep resentment among Ukrainians. For the few dissidents who were not currently in jail, ecological concerns provided an opening for criticism of the system without being accused of nationalism, and even many previously loyal citizens and intellectuals were genuinely outraged.

Already by June 1986, the KGB was reporting on the "ethnonational interpretation of the disaster." That Chernobyl was managed directly from Moscow, bypassing Ukraine's republic-level government, only strengthened the perception of Soviet internal colonialism in Ukraine and amplified desires for increased local autonomy. The ecological campaign was led by Ukrainian writers and intellectuals, including many previously loyal to the system; for some, it would be a stepping stone to more explicitly political activism. Initially, the authorities tried to suppress the movement, but as Gorbachev's reforms in Moscow expanded beyond the economy to encompass political and social issues, Ukraine's nuclear trauma and the mobilization it triggered eventually solidified into anti-regime opposition.[31]

The *Rukh* (movement), which became the main pro-democracy faction in Ukraine, was explicitly a product of the Chernobyl disaster, and its first and foremost goal was the closure of the plant and achieving a nuclear-free Ukraine. Later, the opposition's focus came to include a broader set of political and social reforms: first, support for perestroika, and then, in 1990, Ukraine's independence. Many of the Rukh leaders were former dissidents, and it became the principal grouping of Ukrainian "national democrats" who sought to create a democratic, independent state. The opposition also sought to resist Moscow's domination of Ukraine and its history and culture, for instance by protesting the Russo-centric 1989 commemoration of the 1709 Battle of Poltava, in which the Russian army had defeated the Swedes and their Cossack ally Hetman Mazepa. The conservative Shcherbytsky, who despised perestroika and had little patience for the Rukh, originally tried to suppress the movement—Yurii Shcherbak, one of its leaders, was smeared as simultaneously a Ukrainian nationalist and a Zionist—but was in September 1989 himself removed from power.[32]

Perestroika exposed and exacerbated the structural failures it was meant to overcome, and by 1990, the various economic problems had combined into one deep crisis. Food shortages grew worse, and when glasnost allowed people to express themselves freely, the extent of popular discontent could no longer be hidden. Nationalism, previously suppressed by the KGB, reared its head. Lithuania, Latvia, and Estonia were demanding independence, which they had lost because of the Molotov-Ribbentrop Pact. Armenians and Azeris clashed over Nagorno-Karabakh, and

Crimean Tatars finally began returning to the peninsula. But the most important nationalist mobilization was unfolding in Russia itself.

Conflict between Gorbachev and Boris Yeltsin, former party boss of Sverdlovsk in the Urals and later Moscow city, led Yeltsin to embrace the Russian cause within the union. Russian nationalists had long believed that the Russian Federation subsidized the rest of the USSR and complained that, unlike the other republics, Russia did not have formal symbols of identity such as a flag or republican Academy of Sciences. Now, in his bid for power, Yeltsin wanted Russia to have what Ukraine and Belorussia had. Yeltsin's efforts undermined Gorbachev's campaign of reforms, weakening the Kremlin and scaring other republics. The other members of the USSR now had to contend with Moscow not just as the seat of the already overbearing central government but also as the capital of the union's largest, strongest, and increasingly assertive republic. Yet the struggle between Gorbachev and Yeltsin also presented an opportunity for other republican elites as the Kremlin's authority weakened. Gorbachev's efforts to preserve the union were not yet doomed but were facing very serious headwinds.[33]

In March 1990, Ukrainians went to the polls to elect a new republican parliament, the Supreme Soviet, which in 1991 would be renamed the *Verkhovna* (supreme) Rada. Opposition candidates could compete for the first time, but the elections remained neither fully free nor fair, for the Communist Party still controlled the mass media and government and used this control to gain an advantage at the polls. Communists won a majority of the seats, while the Democratic Bloc—encompassing the Rukh and several smaller groups—came second. Volodymyr Ivashko, who had replaced Shcherbytsky, was duly elected as the chamber's Speaker, but he soon moved to Moscow to become Gorbachev's party deputy and, in July, Leonid Kravchuk became the Speaker and Ukraine's leader. Kravchuk was born in 1934 in a village in Volhynia, then still part of Poland. As a child, he had witnessed both the Holocaust and Polish-Ukrainian violence during World War II. After graduating from university, he embarked on a successful career in the Communist Party. His beat was ideology, but

Kravchuk was no ossified doctrinaire and successfully reinvented himself as a national Communist when times changed.

In summer 1990, both the Russian and Ukrainian parliaments adopted declarations of sovereignty that proclaimed de facto independence from the Soviet central government. The Ukrainian declaration was the product of an alliance between the Rukh and the national Communists in the parliament. It specifically addressed the legacy of Chernobyl and declared Ukraine's commitment to becoming a nonnuclear state. The Russian one was driven by Yeltsin's ambitions and the wide support he enjoyed from the population and the republic's pro-democracy movement.[34]

Ukraine's push for sovereignty was more symbolic than practical, but it went hand in hand with public discussions that strengthened the perception of Ukraine's distinctness from Russia and understanding of its mistreatment by the government in Moscow. Many Ukrainians learned, for the first time, about the Holodomor; even those who had known about the famine from hushed family histories finally discovered its true extent. Stalinist repression, the persecution of Ukrainian dissidents, Petliura, and the UNR, OUN, and UPA also became topics of public (if initially very confused) discussion. On January 22, 1990, a human chain of almost half a million people was formed from Lviv to Kyiv to commemorate the official unification of the UNR and ZUNR in 1919. In November 1990, in a move that underscored Gorbachev's growing irrelevance, Russia and Ukraine signed an agreement recognizing the border between the two sovereign polities.

Gorbachev was apoplectic at these developments but still believed in his ability to bring about a reformed USSR. He had reason to be optimistic. In March 1991, Gorbachev organized a referendum on the preservation of the USSR, as a prelude to the Union Treaty he planned to negotiate. Several republics boycotted the vote altogether. In Ukraine, the question on the preservation of the USSR was accompanied by a vote on making Ukraine's Declaration of Sovereignty the basis for the country's participation: 70.5 percent voted yes on Gorbachev's question, but 80.2 percent also agreed that the Declaration of Sovereignty was a necessary condition. Both

Gorbachev and Kyiv viewed the results as a victory, but it was less clear how Gorbachev's vision of a new union could be squared with the de facto independence that the Declaration of Sovereignty outlined. Kravchuk dragged his feet and was reluctant to sign on to a new state that, he feared, would offer Ukraine less than the 1922 treaty that created the USSR.[35]

The Kremlin also had the United States on its side. Despite the popular myth that the United States conspired to destroy the USSR, Washington in fact did all it could to preserve its former adversary. President George H. W. Bush enjoyed close personal relations with Gorbachev and, more crucially, worried about the consequences of the USSR disintegrating into multiple nuclear-armed, potentially warring units. Diplomats at the newly opened US consulate in Kyiv were instructed to "gently encourage democracy and market reforms, but to do nothing that would be seen as encouraging Ukrainian independence." In August 1991, in what became known as the Chicken Kiev speech, Bush himself warned the Ukrainian parliament that "Americans will not support those who seek independence in order to replace a far-off tyranny with local despotism. They will not aid those who promote a suicidal nationalism based upon ethnic hatred." Most pivotally, on the question of Ukraine, Gorbachev and Yeltsin agreed. Yeltsin told Bush that Ukraine "must not leave the Soviet Union," because if it did, the USSR "would be dominated by non-Slavic republics." As the prospect of Ukraine going its own way became increasingly realistic, identity-based concerns became more prominent in Russian thinking, and the determination to prevent such a scenario intensified.[36]

Even at this stage, all was not yet lost for the USSR. The economy was in free fall, politicians were bickering, and ethnic violence was spiraling out of control in the Caucasus, but Ukrainians and Russians mostly still supported the idea of a reformed union. In the end, neither the democratic opposition nor the United States triggered the downfall of the USSR; the Communists themselves did. On August 19, 1991, as Gorbachev vacationed in Crimea, conservative hard-liners in the Kremlin launched a coup in an attempt to prevent the Soviet Union from disintegrating. The plotters, who formed the State Committee for the State of

Emergency (GKChP) were more adept at creating acronyms than seizing power. They failed to effectively use TV and radio stations (which they controlled), could not suppress dissent, did not arrest Yeltsin or other opposition leaders, and were averse to using force until it was far too late. Yeltsin quickly emerged as the leader of the anti-coup opposition, and after three days, the plot collapsed. Kravchuk, meanwhile, sat on the fence until the very last moment.

After the coup, Gorbachev returned to the Kremlin, but he was now a much diminished figure, while Yeltsin rose meteorically. The Communist Party was collapsing in Russia, and it was fully banned in November 1991. Kravchuk found himself in hot water, attacked by the democratic opposition for not fighting the coup, alarmed by Yeltsin's ascendance, and worried about the Communist Party's fate—and his own—in any future union. Full independence, not just sovereignty, offered a solution. The bid for independence reconciled the erstwhile party apparatchiks with the nationalist opposition, protected Kravchuk from events in Moscow, and offered more power than playing second fiddle in the potential Yeltsin-dominated union. On August 24, the Ukrainian parliament voted for independence. There were just two dissenting votes. Even the Communists supported independence, primarily to distance themselves from the GKChP coup. The move was to be confirmed in a national referendum, scheduled for December 1 in conjunction with presidential elections.[37]

Moscow was furious. Yeltsin issued a statement declaring that if any republic left the union, Russia reserved the right to raise the question of borders, even though Ukraine and Russia had just signed an agreement recognizing their shared border. Vladimir Lukin, a key member of Yeltsin's team, demanded Russia use economic pressure to force Ukraine to return Crimea, which had an ethnic Russian majority (conveniently overlooking the fact that this majority was a product of ethnic cleansing and the decades-long refusal to allow the survivors of it to return home). Yeltsin's vice president, Aleksander Rutskoi, a former air force general, was even more blunt, using the derogatory term *khokhly* to refer to Ukrainian leaders.[38]

These statements sparked a scandal. Kravchuk phoned Yeltsin to complain, and Western ambassadors became increasingly worried that Russia might take an imperialist turn. Liberal media compared the rhetoric to Hitler's claims on the Sudetenland. Kazakhstan feared that Russia would claim its northern regions, where many ethnic Russians lived. Yeltsin backed down.[39]

The Russian president stopped making claims on Crimea and eastern Ukraine, but others did not. Georgy Shakhnazarov, Gorbachev's advisor, suggested that his boss should mobilize Russians and Russian speakers in Ukraine against "Galician nationalism." He believed that Moscow should declare that Crimea, the Donbas, and southern Ukraine were "historical parts of Russia, and Russia does not intend to give them up, in case Ukraine leaves the Union." Gorbachev himself remained fixated on ethnic Russians in Ukraine and their fate if the country broke away.[40]

The most prominent voice among Russian nationalists was Aleksandr Solzhenitsyn. The writer—a Nobel laureate and a former Gulag prisoner—had complex relations with Ukraine. His mother was an ethnic Ukrainian from southern Russia, and Solzhenitsyn genuinely respected the Ukrainian nationalists he had met in the Gulag. Solzhenitsyn also recognized the unjustness of the tsarist repression of Ukrainian language and culture, but nonetheless he fully accepted the idea of Russians, Ukrainians, and Belorussians being a single people. Solzhenitsyn viewed Ukraine's borders as artificial and even seriously considered the possibility of war between Russia and Ukraine. The solution, he believed, was a new state that comprised the three East Slavic peoples, potentially with Kazakhstan too. If Ukraine really wanted independence, Solzhenitsyn argued, then it should be considered region by region, as he was certain that eastern and southern Ukraine and Crimea would want to join Russia.

The refusal to accept Ukrainian independence extended well beyond politicians and nationalist intellectuals. Rodric Braithwaite, the British ambassador in Moscow, observed that "perfectly sensible Russians froth at the mouth if it is suggested that the Ukraine (from which they all trace their history) might go off on its own." Statements that denied Ukraine's right to independence or challenged its borders focused on topics like language, ethnicity, and history rather than on Russia's defense. In 1991, Russians' desire to control Ukraine was wholly about identity, not security.[41]

The aggressive posturing in Moscow strengthened Ukrainian nationalists' case about Russian imperialism and the dangers of Kremlin rule. To fully drive the point home, Ukrainian TV broadcast a film about the Holodomor shortly before the December 1 independence referendum. The referendum delivered a resounding mandate vote for statehood. The turnout was 84 percent, and over 90 percent voted yes. Predictably, support was the highest and almost unanimous in Galicia, but even in the Donbas almost 84 percent approved. In Crimea, the numbers were more modest but still a clear majority. In the coup's aftermath, most Ukrainians simply gave up on any notion of reforming the union and just wanted away from the dysfunction and economic collapse.

As it had in 1917, chaos in the empire's capital drove Ukrainians away from the Russian-dominated state and forced them to adopt increasingly radical political positions that eventually led to independence. They also shared a widespread (if mistaken) belief that Ukraine was subsidizing the rest of the USSR and that the country's rich soil and industrial capacity would quickly bring prosperity. Politicians—even those who knew better—did not discourage such thinking, but regardless, the pressure to escape the collapsing Soviet empire was simply too great. Meanwhile, Kravchuk easily won the presidential election. His main rival—the former dissident and political prisoner Viacheslav Chornovil, a Rukh member and now the head of the Lviv regional council—failed to win any region outside of Galicia.

The results of the referendum were so decisive that they marked the end of any hopes of saving the USSR. Yeltsin refused to participate in a new union without Ukraine, and there certainly would be no union without Moscow and Kyiv. On December 7, 1991, the leaders of Russia, Ukraine, and Belorussia met at a hunting lodge in Belovezha in Belorussia. The Russians proposed various ideas for reorganizing the Soviet space in light of Ukrainian independence. They explored options for future relations ranging from a loose federation to a confederation à la Switzerland, but Kravchuk was determined that Ukraine be fully independent. Eventually, the leaders agreed on a loose commonwealth model, akin to the British Commonwealth. Together, they represented three of the four republics that had created the USSR; the fourth, the Transcaucasian Republic, had been dissolved in 1936. On December 8, they decided to dissolve the union that their predecessors had established.[42]

By the end of the month, the USSR was no more, but Russian resentment, territorial claims, and outrage at the very idea of having lost Crimea, the Donbas, and Ukraine as a whole—territories that Russians were long accustomed to viewing as theirs—did not go away. No longer matters for internal Soviet discussion, these issues simply slid into post-Soviet Russian politics and escalated to the international arena, because Russia and Ukraine were now fully separate—legally, if not mentally.

CHAPTER 7

PHANTOM PAINS

New Year's Eve is the most important holiday in Russia, and the evening gala broadcast on state TV is traditionally a joyful event, packed with celebrity appearances, jokes, songs, and lots of champagne. As 2013 became 2014, one of the two hosts of this televised celebration was a smiling, energetic comedian named Volodymyr Zelensky. Zelensky was born and grew up in Ukraine, but Vova, as he was referred to on the show, was a native Russian speaker and no stranger to Russian prime-time TV. Indeed, Zelensky had spent a large part of his career in Moscow. The tone was cheerful, but the jokes, unlike in previous years, centered on war: the "advance" of the New Year, fireworks as artillery support, "capturing" delicacies, negotiating with the enemy while drunk. Nobody knew it yet, but war between Russia and Zelensky's native Ukraine was just around the corner. For over two decades, Russia and Ukraine had coexisted in relative peace, but tensions—present from the last days of the USSR—were building up, ready to erupt.[1]

After the Soviet Union collapsed, Russia and Ukraine became separate countries, but few Russians viewed Ukraine as a real state. Most parts of Ukraine, and above all Crimea, were perceived as indistinguishable from—indeed extensions of—Russia, separated from their true motherland only by a freak accident of history. For Moscow liberals, who governed Russia's nascent democracy in the early 1990s, independent Ukraine was a curiosity that with time might come to its senses and rejoin democratic, prosperous Russia. The nationalist right and the Communists, on the other hand, wished to destroy Ukraine for ideological and identity reasons. Ukraine had to be incorporated into a reincarnation of the Russian Empire or the USSR. For Putin, who came to power in 2000 and soon turned Russia into a dictatorship, the intent was originally not to destroy but to control Ukraine, primarily to protect his autocratic rule. If Ukrainians could have meaningful elections and replace their leaders, the fear went, then the presumably fraternal Russians might as well. Therefore, to protect the Kremlin, Ukraine had to be dominated by Russia.

As time passed, however, Putin increasingly staked the legitimacy of his autocratic rule on nostalgia and confrontation with the West, and his policies converged with those of the nationalist right. January 1, 2014, was the last New Year's celebration when Russians and Ukrainians would laugh together about military matters.

The birth of independent Russia in 1991–1992 was an unhappy affair. The economy was in shambles and, like in 1917, food shortages were a major concern. "Virginally empty stores. Women, thrashing about in search for any products . . . a uniform expectation of a catastrophe," recalled Yegor Gaidar, Russia's de facto prime minister at the time and the architect of the country's economic reforms. For Gaidar, his government's task was to save the country from famine and collapse. His colleague Andrei Kozyrev, then minister of foreign affairs, was in the meantime busy establishing Russia's international relations. Things were comparatively easy outside of the now-defunct USSR, where Soviet embassies simply became Russian ones overnight, but establishing a relationship with Ukraine was a challenge. "In the USSR, expertise on the Soviet republics was in the economic planning bodies and the KGB. We in the Ministry of Foreign Affairs did not have any experts on Ukraine," Kozyrev admitted."[2]

While liberals spent their energies on trying to pull Russia out of the economic abyss, for many Russians the struggle to survive went hand in hand with lamenting the loss of Soviet power. Titans of Russian culture also joined the rhetorical fight against the loss of Ukraine. Aleksandr Solzhenitsyn, the Nobel Prize winner who resented Ukraine's independence and viewed its borders as illegitimate, complained that Russia "lost 12 million Russians and 23 million more Russian speakers." That these twelve million Russians might wish to be citizens of independent Ukraine or that the twenty-three million Russian speakers were mostly ethnic Ukrainians played no role for Solzhenitsyn. Russia, Ukraine, and Belarus, potentially together with Kazakhstan, the writer argued, should form a single new state, and if that was not possible, Ukraine ought only to exist within its unspecified "real ethnic borders, without conquering Russian" lands such as Crimea and eastern and southern Ukraine.[3]

Joseph Brodsky, another Nobel Prize winner, went even further. His poem "On the Independence of Ukraine" is full of venom, uses ethnic slurs, and predicts that on their deathbeds Ukrainians will come to repudiate "the lies of Taras [Shevchenko]" and return to their true Russian selves, represented by Pushkin. Indeed, for many Russian liberals, Ukrainian independence was a step too far. Anatolii Sobchak, mayor of Saint Petersburg and Putin's mentor, viewed Ukrainian statehood as a catastrophe. For Gleb Pavlovsky, a Soviet-era dissident who would later emerge as Putin's political strategist, "Russian history came to an end" with the loss of Ukraine.[4]

The British historian Geoffrey Hosking observed that Britain *had* an empire whereas Russia *was* one, and this difference was crucial for both countries' postimperial trajectories. The United Kingdom could shed its colonies and largely move on, but if Russia wanted to move on without its Soviet empire, it needed to reinvent itself from scratch.[5]

The USSR was, on paper, a confederation in which each major national group had a republic of its own, but in practice ethnic Russians saw the entire union, not just the Russian republic, as their home and birthright. After 1992, the choice thus was between stubbornly clinging to the old Soviet identity—where the rightful borders of Russia differed from those of the actual, current Russian state—or coming up with a completely new understanding of what Russia was and where it belonged. The majority of Russian citizens regretted the collapse of the Soviet state but also accepted the new post-Soviet reality. Yet there were also those who were determined to bring the lost territories back into the fold.[6]

Those dissatisfied with Russia's post-Soviet borders spanned a broad arc of beliefs and ideologies. Dubbed the "red-brown" coalition after the red of Communism and the brown of fascism, this group was in fact broader: it encompassed Communists, nationalists, National Bolsheviks, conservatives, monarchists, radicals, neo-Nazis, and adherents of various other esoteric teachings. They disagreed on most things, but they were united in rejecting Russia's post-Soviet borders, seeing independent Ukraine as illegitimate, and hating democracy.

The Communists predictably wished to restore the USSR, a goal that required reversing the independence of the post-Soviet states and bringing them back under Moscow's control. Yet in the 1990s Russian Communists also began increasingly embracing nationalist ideas, which saw Ukraine and Belarus as special targets of their restorationist zeal. From 1992, the Communist-controlled Russian parliament, elected in Soviet times, adopted resolutions that invalidated the Belovezha Accords, declared Sevastopol to be Russian, and annulled the 1954 transfer of Crimea from Russia to Ukraine. These were legally nonbinding declarations, but they alarmed Ukraine, poisoned relations between Kyiv and Moscow, and signaled the prevailing mood among large segments of the Russian political class. Kozyrev and his boss, President Yeltsin, did their best to limit the damage, but such declarations, Kozyrev told me, "were definitely not just a background noise" in Russia-Ukraine relations.

The late-Soviet-era Russian territorial claims had focused on Crimea and the Donbas, but in the wake of independence and industrial collapse the Donbas lost its status and appeal. Crimea did not, and red-browns were obsessed with the peninsula and Sevastopol. Their reasons for Crimea's innate Russianness ranged from the deeply mystical, invoking Prince Volodymyr's baptism of Rus', to the ridiculous: unlike Ukraine, the argument went, Russia was a cold, northern country and needed a warm region for recreation. For Solzhenitsyn, Crimea was Russia's "natural southern border." Yet most proffered justifications boiled down to ethnicity—the majority of Crimea's population were ethnic Russians—and simple nostalgia. For the nationalists and many others, Crimea was Russia's paradise: an exotic land with Greek town names and Turkic-sounding landmarks, stunning cliffs, and beautiful beaches. The Russian view of Crimea blended imperial glory, youthful romantic summer retreats, summer camps, and dull but guaranteed Soviet state-funded vacations for the middle-aged. Losing Sevastopol was even more painful because the city boasted a mythical status as "the holy-of-holies of Russian imperialism" and military valor.[7]

Now, in the wake of Ukrainian independence, this paradise and shrine to past glory was simultaneously lost and still present, a recipe for trauma. Imperial triumph was long gone, the welfare system collapsed, seaside romances faded into memory, yet Crimea was still there: Russian speaking and beautiful as ever, but now under a foreign flag, just out of reach, and presumably looking to Russia for salvation. The Russian Black Sea Fleet—which Russia and Ukraine agreed to divide—remained in Sevastopol, its base leased from Ukraine, but the city itself was now Ukrainian, which made those phantom pains unbearable.

In the 1990s and early 2000s, the desire to control Crimea was identity-based. Even among the remaining cold warriors, few thought of the peninsula in the context of Russian security or NATO expansion. And it was not only the nationalists who lamented the loss of Crimea and wanted it back. The feeling was widespread, but most Russians were simply too busy making ends meet to demand that Crimea's return be a policy priority in Moscow.

In 1998, Yuri Luzhkov, mayor of Moscow and one of Russia's leading politicians, signed an agreement with Crimean authorities to build a bridge connecting the peninsula to Russia. The Ukrainian government, which had not been consulted on this cross-border project, vetoed the initiative. Unfazed, Luzhkov changed tack to constructing buildings throughout Sevastopol, opening a local branch of Moscow State University, and starting various welfare projects in the city. The Kremlin, according to Luzhkov, had abandoned the people of Crimea, and Moscow city hall had no choice but to step in. Luzhkov's activities were not restricted to infrastructure and charity; he also publicly called for the return of Crimea to Russia, a statement that made him persona non grata in Ukraine.[8]

While Luzhkov might have been satisfied with retaking Crimea only, for most nationalists it was just the first step. They wanted all of Ukraine—except for Galicia, which they saw as teeming with violent, nationalist Banderites and thus truly foreign. They also wished to reclaim other parts of the former USSR, such as Belarus and northern Kazakhstan, but Ukraine was always the top prize. Nationalists took for granted the idea that Russians and Ukrainians were the same nation and that all the former Kyivan Rus' should rightfully belong to the Russian state. Some explicitly argued that Russia should adopt territorial expansion as state ideology.[9]

Even more radical were the members of the National Bolsheviks (*Natsboly*), a party that combined Communist and Nazi symbols and ideas and believed in imperial territorial conquest abroad supplemented by Communism at home. Led by the eccentric best-selling writer Eduard Limonov, who was especially proud of his brief service with the Serb forces during the war in Bosnia, Natsboly advocated anti-government violence, and their organization was outlawed in Russia. For Limonov, imperial expansion had to start with Crimea. On Ukraine's Independence Day in 1999, a group of National Bolsheviks led by Limonov broke into the Sailors Club in Sevastopol, barricaded themselves inside, and raised a banner reading "Sevastopol—Crimea—Russia" on the club's tower.

The most famous of the Russian nationalist ideologues, Alexander Dugin, was originally an anti-Soviet dissident with mystical proclivities, as well as a onetime associate of Limonov. In the early 1990s, Dugin emerged as a prominent nationalist publicist who combined the foreign policy ideas of twentieth-century geopolitical strategists with the anti-liberal, xenophobic, and autocratic domestic visions of the European extreme right. His most important treatise, *The Foundations of Geopolitics*, was commissioned by the Russian Ministry of Defense and published in 1997. The book presents all of world history and international relations as a struggle between the "Sea," now led by the United States, and the Eurasian "Heartland," epitomized by Russia. To win this global struggle, Russia needed to secure Eurasia and protect itself from relentless American threats. Of the various axes of potential American attack, Ukraine was among the most important. For Russia to be secure, Ukraine had to be controlled by Moscow or dismembered. Dugin even produced a map of a partitioned Ukraine, which revived the tsarist term "Novorossiya" for the southern part of the country. Dugin's ideas quickly took hold among the Russian security establishment. *Foundations* was included in the curriculum of the Russian General Staff Academy, and Dugin started teaching there. In 2008, Dugin also became the head of the newly established Center for Conservative Studies at the Moscow State University and began advising high-ranking Russian politicians.[10]

These ideas and arguments tapped into Russians' sense of loss, disorientation, and resentment that stemmed from the profound post-Soviet political and economic transformations. They offered different solutions to Russia's problems, but each red-brown identity project envisioned a future in which Ukraine would be either swallowed up or dismembered. What was the liberal response to this challenge?

Unfortunately, Russian liberals failed to develop a coherent alternative vision of Russian identity, and thus share at least part of the blame for the disaster that followed. Yeltsin instinctively understood that Russia "had to rid itself of the imperial mission," but it was less clear how this change could be achieved and made to last. He even formed a special commission to articulate the new "Russian idea," but it accomplished little.[11]

Ukraine became the litmus test for postimperial attitudes, and many Russian liberals failed it. Vladimir Lukin, now the chair of the parliament's foreign relations committee and later the Russian ambassador to the United States, kept advocating for the return of Crimea as he did in 1991. Few Russian democrats perceived Ukraine as a real or legitimate state, and some were convinced that it would soon collapse on its own under the weight of economic hardship, corruption, and regional tensions between the Ukrainian-speaking west and the Russian-speaking east. Some Russian officials even advised Western colleagues not to bother building embassies in Kyiv, because the country would soon reunite with Russia anyway. But Russian liberals also supported democracy at home, did not wish for war, and mostly rejected territorial annexation. Still, they failed to offer a coherent political vision and ceded the development of post-1991 Russian identity to the nationalists.[12]

Democratic Russia, the country's main liberal party of the early 1990s, ignored the question of national identity altogether and instead focused its attention on economic and institutional reforms. This was a grave mistake. By staking their fate on the results of reforms alone, the democrats doomed the chances of liberal, postimperial Russia. When the reforms inflicted misery, most Russians simply could not find any reason to support democracy *despite* the economic woes. Democrats lost public support, and the neo-imperial, autocratic vision emerged dominant in the formation of Russian identity. Over time, this neo-imperialism became so ingrained that even some democrats began advocating building a "liberal Empire."[13]

In the absence of alternative visions for national identity, Russian public opinion embraced neo-imperial, revanchist views (though not necessarily the willingness to act upon them). In December 1995, four years after Ukraine became independent, 53 percent of Russians believed that the two countries should be unified. A different poll revealed that 78 percent of Russians thought Sevastopol should be Russian. Among the Russian elites, support for unification was at 65 percent. More than a decade after the Soviet Union was gone, only 29 percent of Russians were satisfied with the country's borders and just 17 percent believed that Ukraine and Russia were different nations.[14]

The situation in Ukraine was very different. While for Russians the collapse of the USSR was the end of their empire, for many Ukrainians (though not all of them) it was the beginning of genuinely welcome independence. Support for Ukrainian statehood varied across regions. In areas where statehood was seen mostly as a way to escape Soviet economic mismanagement, the crisis that followed the USSR's collapse quickly eroded support for independence. But many Ukrainians wanted independence for political and identity-based reasons, and their allegiance to independent Ukraine was therefore not contingent on the economy. A poll conducted in 1993 revealed that while 44 percent of Ukrainians refused to suffer economic hardship in exchange for the country's independence, 19 percent, most of them from the country's western regions, were willing to suffer as long and as much as needed.[15]

Ukraine's regional polarization—simplistically presented as a struggle between the Ukrainian-speaking, Western-oriented Galicia and the Russian-speaking, Moscow-oriented Donbas—was often bemoaned as a key source of the country's problems, but the reality was more complicated. The vision of a European Galicia versus a thoroughly pro-Kremlin Donbas was a caricature. There was much in and about Galicia that was anti-European and anti-democratic, whereas the Donbas was not simply an appendage of Russia. In fact, each side represented a different vision of Ukraine, but neither was strong enough to impose it on the rest of the country, thus producing "pluralism by default." This, unlike Russia's hegemonic, authoritarian neo-imperialism, protected Ukraine from sliding too deep into autocracy.[16] Between the poles of Galicia and the Donbas lay the rest of Ukraine, and it was the voices of the central and southern regions that chiefly determined the country's direction.

States need legitimacy, a justification for their existence. Russia's source of legitimacy was being the successor to the Soviet Union and, before that, the Russian Empire. For Ukraine, establishing legitimacy required demonstrating a difference from Russia in language, culture, behavior, and, later, regime type. Ukraine could not survive as a sovereign state if it was simply Little Russia, and therefore from the very beginning of the country's independence the government invested heavily in developing a distinct national identity. Ivan Dziuba, the author of the Soviet-era

Internationalism or Russification? pamphlet and one of the founders of the Rukh, served from 1992 to 1994 as the minister of culture and promoted many of these identity-building initiatives.

Ukrainian was adopted as the sole state language, dual citizenship was not allowed, and Moscow-inflicted historical tragedies such as the Holodomor became prominent topics in education and for commemoration. These efforts were cheered on in western Ukraine and resisted by many in the Donbas, but even there, attitudes gradually shifted. It was in the center and the south and among younger people such as Volodymyr Zelensky—fourteen years old when Ukraine became independent—that the focus on Ukrainian statehood, culture, and identity made the most impact. If in early elections the center and the south voted with the Donbas, as the years passed, their political preferences shifted closer to the west, but without adoption of the most radical nationalist ideas that circulated in Galicia. And as Russia turned increasingly authoritarian and expansionist, younger Ukrainians became more supportive of their country's independence.[17]

A key component of Soviet inheritance was its nuclear arsenal. When the Soviet Union fractured, Ukraine, Belarus, and Kazakhstan all had nuclear weapons on their territory. Ukraine hosted the world's third largest nuclear arsenal, bigger than that of China, the United Kingdom, and France combined, though it did not have full control over these weapons. The trauma of Chernobyl initially prompted Ukraine's national democrats to strongly oppose nuclear weapons; in post-Chernobyl Ukraine, being antinuclear was synonymous with being anti-Soviet. Ukraine thus joined Belarus and Kazakhstan in committing to give up the weapons on its territory, first the "tactical" short-range weapons, followed by the "strategic" long-range missiles.[18]

But as Russian Communists and nationalists unleashed a stream of declarations and demands targeting Ukraine's territory and sovereignty, more and more voices in Kyiv warmed to the idea of keeping nuclear weapons as insurance against Russian threats and potential attack. Some in the West agreed. John Mearsheimer, a University of Chicago international relations scholar, published an article in the influential *Foreign Affairs* journal in June 1993 in which he promoted the idea of a Ukrainian nuclear deterrent against Russia. Thus, throughout 1993, Ukraine's nuclear disarmament became increasingly uncertain, and policymakers and strategists in Moscow and Washington grew alarmed.[19]

Russia and the United States teamed up to disarm Ukraine. For Russia, the legal and political successor of the USSR, exclusive ownership of the ex-Soviet nuclear arsenal was a marker of status, not just security. Kozyrev, increasingly worried about militant voices in Russian politics, feared a potential Yugoslavia-style conflict, but with nukes on both sides. The Yeltsin government, he believed, was a responsible actor and would not give in to the bellicose nationalists and Communists. According to him, in the early 1990s, Russia could also more effectively ensure the security of nuclear weapons and thus should have had control over the entire ex-Soviet arsenal.[20]

Washington concurred. In a manner reminiscent of Arnold Margolin's laments at the Paris Peace Conference after World War I, the United States cared little about Ukraine, dismissed Ukrainian concerns, and interpreted the situation through a purely Russian lens. That Ukraine had only a small, young, and often inexperienced foreign service also harmed its international position vis-à-vis Russia, which inherited the massive and well-oiled Soviet diplomatic machine.

For both the Republican president George H. W. Bush and, from 1993, his Democratic successor Bill Clinton, building and maintaining a close partnership with Moscow was a cornerstone of US policy. In the worldview of Western politicians, journalists, and even many regional experts, Russia and the USSR were effectively interchangeable, and thus the continued focus on Russia at the expense of other Soviet republics, and later post-Soviet states, was only natural.[21]

Some American policymakers were aware that the former USSR was not identical to Russia, but they still made a conscious choice to prioritize Moscow. "Political disputes between Russia, Ukraine and Kazakhstan were real, we definitely did not want to see states with these kinds of conflicts end up in uneasy nuclear standoff," wrote Bush's secretary of state James Baker. This meant that US policy was to ensure that if violence erupted in the region, only Russia would have access to nukes. The Kremlin could not have asked for more.

When the Clinton administration came to power, the president appointed his friend Strobe Talbott to lead US policy in the region. Talbott was considered an expert on post-Soviet states, but in practice this mainly meant knowledge of Russia and fluency in Russian. Talbott eventually developed some doubts about the US approach, but his superiors remained steadfast. The new administration's policies were explicitly Russo-centric and prioritized Moscow.[22]

Even if Ukraine truly wished to keep its inherited nuclear weapons, it did not stand a chance against combined American and Russian pressure. Instead, alarmed by Moscow's rhetoric, Kyiv sought to trade the weapons for meaningful security guarantees that would protect Ukraine from Russian aggression, but the United States was reluctant to accept any new obligations. For some in Washington, the very demand appeared superfluous, and Ukrainians were perceived as "whiners." "Ukraine's security problem will be solved once Ukraine gives up its nuclear arsenal," claimed Graham Allison, a Harvard University international security scholar who at the time served as an assistant secretary of defense.[23]

Yet Kyiv's insistence on security guarantees could not be completely brushed aside. The solution was to offer Ukraine a set of assurances that recycled the language of existing agreements, such as the Nuclear Non-Proliferation Treaty, and thus offered nothing new or specific. Ukrainian president Kravchuk complained bitterly that he understood the sources of "Russia's nastiness . . . but Americans are even worse—they do not listen to our arguments." Talbott concurred and admitted that US leaders ensured Ukraine's compliance by "roughing [Kravchuk] up." Kyiv was dismayed but, at that point, out of options.[24]

Keeping the weapons risked a clash with the world's only superpower and would have deprived Ukraine of crucial Western economic support amid a deep crisis. It would have also provoked a major confrontation with Russia. In practical terms, control, upkeep, and monitoring of the weapons would also have required major investment and new structures at a time when Ukraine had very few resources.[25]

On June 26, 1994, Ukrainians went to the polls to vote in snap elections. The incumbent president Kravchuk, the Communist from western Ukraine who helped to destroy the Soviet Union, had reinvented himself as a promoter of Ukrainian identity. His economic record, however, was disastrous, and Kravchuk lost the election to Leonid Kuchma. Kuchma, the head of a missile factory in the country's east and a former prime minister, advocated for closer relations with Russia and centered his campaign on fixing the economy, which by 1994 was in free fall. The subsequent peaceful transfer of power was an achievement for Ukraine's democracy, and now it fell to Kuchma to complete the disarmament process.

The Budapest Memorandum, signed on December 5, 1994, finalized Ukraine's commitment to give up nuclear weapons in exchange for very soft assurances from Russia, the United States, and the United Kingdom "to respect the independence and sovereignty and the existing borders of Ukraine." This meant little. "If tomorrow Russia goes into the Crimea, no one will even raise an eyebrow," Kravchuk admitted bitterly.[26]

By mid-1996, there were no more nuclear weapons in Ukraine. In April 2023, Clinton publicly expressed regret at having pushed Ukraine to give up the nuclear weapons despite being aware of Kyiv's fears of Russia. This mea culpa was both long overdue and misplaced. The United States and the West were indeed at fault for not taking Ukraine's security seriously—prioritizing Moscow despite many early warning signs about the direction of Russian politics and failing to offer Ukraine real security guarantees—but in the mid-1990s a nuclear Ukraine was not a viable solution, politically or practically.[27]

After Russia and Ukraine divided the Black Sea Fleet and finalized Ukraine's nuclear disarmament, the two countries signed the 1997 Treaty on Friendship, Cooperation, and Partnership, which recognized the existing borders between the two states. Yeltsin "concluded that an independent and friendly Ukraine was essential to an environment in which Russian democracy and reforms had a chance of succeeding" and was committed to preserving peace, though even he was not immune to using economic pressure to strong-arm Ukraine when it suited him. But Yeltsin's personal commitment to Ukraine's independence did little to change Russian public opinion and the desire of Russian nationalists and conservatives to subjugate, absorb, or split Ukraine. At the end of 1999, Yeltsin resigned. His hand-picked successor, Vladimir Putin, would adopt a very different approach.[28]

Putin was born in Leningrad in 1952 to a working-class family. He studied law at Leningrad State University and joined the KGB in 1975. At the agency, the future Russian president had an unremarkable career culminating in an assignment to the Soviet satellite state of East Germany, hardly a plum posting. In 1990, Putin returned to Leningrad and resigned from the KGB, having attained the rank of lieutenant colonel. When his former professor Anatolii Sobchak became the mayor of Saint Petersburg—Leningrad returned to its pre–World War I name in 1991—Putin started working at the city government, where he was in charge of foreign economic relations. Putin also allegedly had ties to organized crime, and the deals in which he became involved as part of his job jump-started the business careers of his friends, who later became Russia's top oligarchs.[29]

In 1996, Sobchak lost a reelection bid and Putin moved to Moscow to work for Yeltsin. In 1998, Putin was appointed head of the FSB, the KGB's successor agency for domestic security. By August 1999, he was already Russia's prime minister, and after Yeltsin's resignation on December 31, 1999, took over as acting president. On March 26, 2000, Putin won his first presidential election and has ruled Russia since, either as president or as prime minister during the presidency of his sidekick Dmitry Medvedev from 2008 to 2012.

Unlike many members of the Russian elite, Putin had no personal or professional connection to Ukraine before coming to power. *First Person*, Putin's first official biography, mentions Ukraine just once (in the context of his skiing hobby), and in other biographies Ukraine typically appears on the scene only after Putin is already in power. Yet even though Ukraine was not high on Putin's agenda before 2000, his background in the security services, Soviet nostalgia, and worship of a strong state suggest that Putin's views on Ukraine, Crimea, and Sevastopol were likely always at least as restorationist as those of most other Russians.

Putin's first task as president was to rebuild a strong federal government and cement his authority. He immediately launched a second war against Chechnya—the first having seen Russian troops beaten by local forces fighting for independence between 1994 and 1996—solidified control over the media, jailed or forced into exile the most powerful and politically active oligarchs, and severely limited the power and independence of regional governors. In several short years, Putin dismantled what remained of Russia's limited and flawed democratic institutions and turned the country into a dictatorship. In the process of rebuilding a strong state, Putin also promoted to top positions the *siloviki*—people with security service backgrounds and, typically, conservative, anti-Western, and neo-imperialist views. Putin's rise to power fortuitously coincided with a surge in global prices for oil and gas, Russia's chief export commodities. The resulting windfall replenished the government's coffers, raised living standards, and boosted the popularity of the president and the authoritarian system he created.

Soviet symbols, banished under Yeltsin, also made a comeback in Russian public life. The new national anthem, introduced in 2000, retained the music of the Soviet one and had words written by the very same lyricist. The Soviet victory in World War II, which had lost its public prominence under Yeltsin, came back with gusto and quickly became the state's most important and cherished historical myth, thus reinforcing the militaristic and revanchist attitudes.

Building a more assertive Russia also meant increasing efforts to dominate the post-Soviet region, both through economic means and by positioning Moscow as the protector of Russian-speaking communities. The concept of the Russian World (*Russkii Mir*) encompassed all Russian speakers regardless of their ethnicity or citizenship and linked them to the Russian state through educational programs, cultural initiatives, and pathways to citizenship. But at its core, the Russian World was first and foremost intended as a community of Russians, Ukrainians, and Belorussians. At the same time, Putin also tried to build close relations with the United States and even floated the idea of Russia joining NATO. The desire to place Sevastopol, Crimea, and potentially all of Ukraine under Moscow's control was there, but it was in the background, neither a salient political issue nor an immediate policy concern.[30]

Ukraine, in the meantime, was muddling through. Its economy was struggling, governance suffered from pervasive corruption at all levels, and politics was dominated by a succession of inept governments, criminal prime ministers, and parties with names and ideological labels that meant little and stood for nothing except their own enrichment. Kuchma came to power touting his managerial experience but turned out to be an unpopular leader who failed to solve Ukraine's deep economic crisis and root out corruption.

Despite his pro-Russian image, Kuchma—aiming to preserve the legitimacy of Ukraine as an independent state and his personal legitimacy as the country's president—continued to implement the many cultural, language, educational, and foreign policies advocated by his rivals in the nationalist camp. Ukrainian remained the sole state language, and the president even authored a book with the telling title *Ukraine Is Not Russia*. November 22 became Holodomor Remembrance Day, and Kuchma's approach to history was cautious, refraining from antagonizing the supporters of the OUN and UPA. Over time, the rhetorical emphasis on Ukraine's European ideals, origins, and orientation, especially prominent in the Galician nostalgia for the Austrian past, created expectations of tangible change. Ukrainians, especially the younger generation and the middle class, wanted European reality, not just rhetoric.

In 2004, Ukraine elected a new president. Kuchma was term limited and could not run again, so the contest became a choice between two Viktors: Yushchenko and Yanukovych. Both were products of Ukraine's post-Soviet elite: Yushchenko had been prime minister from 1999 to 2001; Yanukovych was the incumbent prime minister at the time of the election.

But this was the extent of their similarities. Yushchenko, a capable technocrat, represented the pro-Western view. He spoke flawless Ukrainian, had been educated in western Ukraine, and had deep connections in the EU and the United States. His spouse was a Ukrainian American who had previously worked at the US State Department.

Yanukovych, Kuchma's handpicked successor, came from the Donbas. His rough youth included two incarcerations in Soviet prison for robbery and assault, but he eventually settled on a career in transportation and trucking before entering regional administration. He rose to become the governor of Donetsk and, in 2002, the prime minister. Yanukovych was uncouth, barely spoke the state's official language, and—despite holding a doctorate from a diploma mill and the title of professor—misspelled his own credentials, listing himself as a "proffesor." But he was also shrewd, ruthless, determined, and notoriously corrupt. Because of his Donbas origins, Yanukovych was widely viewed as pro-Russian, but he was above all pro-Yanukovych. Everything about him was an affront to the idea of a European Ukraine.

By the time of the Ukrainian elections, relations between Russia and the West had worsened considerably. The West bemoaned Russia's ongoing slide toward autocracy and feared the Kremlin's mix of newfound assertiveness, politics of grievance, and imperial nostalgia. Putin regularly railed against US foreign policy—especially the invasion of Iraq, but also the intervention in the war between Serbia and the Albanians of Kosovo and the admission into NATO of ex-Communist states. The Kremlin felt deceived and argued that the United States violated its earlier promise not to expand NATO, though Washington never formally made such a promise.[31]

US policies, Putin believed, challenged Russia's status as a major power that possessed a natural right to dominate its neighborhood. More ominously for Putin, popular protests overthrew budding autocrats in Serbia in 2000 and Georgia in 2003. The Kremlin, prone to conspiratorial thinking, suspected sinister Central Intelligence Agency (CIA) plots and feared that Russia might be the ultimate target. Ukrainian elections, therefore, became for Moscow a crucial battle that it could not afford to lose.

Putin disliked the boorish Yanukovych, but once Kuchma made his choice of protégé, the Kremlin threw its weight behind the presumably pro-Russian candidate. Russian spin doctors working for the Kremlin moved to Kyiv and took over the running of the Yanukovych campaign. Yanukovych promised closer relations with Moscow, recognition of dual citizenship, and the enshrining of Russian as a state language.

Putin, who was popular with many Ukrainians, visited the country multiple times during the campaign to show his support for Yanukovych. A more sinister and secret part of the strategy was to foment conflict (both within Ukraine and with its neighbors), destabilize the country, create insecurity, and falsely paint Yushchenko as some kind of dangerous nationalist. Russian media, which was widely watched in Ukraine, constantly juxtaposed the good Ukrainians, who were pro-Russian and true to the brotherhood of the two people, and the "bad," pro-Western, dangerous, and violent pro-Yushchenko Banderites who were determined to harm Russian speakers.

Yet despite the massive Russian effort to discredit him, Yushchenko remained popular. This popularity threatened the Kremlin's hopes for an easy win and endangered Putin's strategy for controlling Kyiv. On September 5, 2004, Yushchenko was poisoned, most likely at a meeting with the heads of Ukraine's security services. He survived, just barely, and the poison left his face disfigured.[32]

The first round of the election took place on October 31. As expected, Yushchenko and Yanukovych received the most votes and advanced to the runoff, scheduled for November 21. The Yanukovych camp was certain of their ultimate triumph. Relying on the support of loyal government officials, they used creative tricks, clever schemes, and blatant fraud to pad their candidate's vote totals, especially in the east. In Donetsk, the turnout spiked to 96.7 percent and busloads of Yanukovych supporters were driven from one polling station to another to vote multiple times each. The Yanukovych campaign also had access to the computers of the Central Election Commission and could manipulate the official results practically at will. Unsurprisingly, Yanukovych was declared the winner with a reported 49.5 percent of the vote. But the official numbers differed widely from the independent exit polls, and evidence of the massive fraud was quickly uncovered by independent media.

Outraged, Kyivites poured into the city's downtown Independence Square (*Maidan Nezalezhnosti*), commonly known as simply the Maidan, to protest the stolen election. By the second day, the number of protesters had skyrocketed to up to three hundred thousand and kept growing by the hour. The protesters erected a tent city and organized kitchens, field clinics, and cultural activities. They were determined to stay for as long as it took, in the brutal cold of winter, to fight against the stolen election. Smaller sister demonstrations took place all over Ukraine.[33]

On December 3, 2004, Ukraine's Supreme Court invalidated the results of the runoff and ordered a new round to be held on December 26. Yushchenko won the rerun with a convincing 52 percent, versus 44.2 percent for Yanukovych. The successful mass protests that led to Yushchenko's victory quickly became known as the Orange Revolution, after his campaign's color.

Local leaders in the country's east raised the specter of secession or, at the very least, federalization. They even held a congress to discuss the idea, but the initiative quickly died down, in large part because of lack of popular support. Importantly, despite the clear evidence of fraud, neither Yanukovych nor most of his supporters and allies faced any serious consequences. They kept their seats in parliament and remained in control of local authorities in eastern Ukraine; they retreated, regrouped, and waited for the next opportunity.

Moscow, on the other hand, was apoplectic and one Putin advisor even described the Orange Revolution as Russia's 9/11. Few, if any, of the slogans on the Maidan were openly anti-Russian, but the movement was still an explicit rejection of everything Yanukovych and Putin's Russia stood for. For the Kremlin, Ukrainians' rejection of a corrupt aspiring autocrat was thus transformed into an existential geopolitical standoff. Rather than admit the unpopularity of the message they were promoting, the deep flaws of their candidate, and the failure to successfully export Russian electoral manipulation methods, the Kremlin found it more comforting to see the Orange Revolution as a nefarious Western plot. Putin, the argument went, did not lose to Yushchenko and many thousands of ordinary Ukrainians; he lost to the powerful United States and its agents. But this excuse had alarming domestic implications. Putin's second term was due to end in 2008, and he was term limited and could not run again consecutively. In the minds of Kremlin strategists, if Russians and Ukrainians were the same people, and the CIA could engineer a revolution in Kyiv, what would prevent this determined foe from doing the same in Moscow, especially when it now had Ukraine as a base from which to operate?[34]

To protect its hold on power, the Kremlin cracked down on anything and everything that might lead to Ukraine-style regime change. One of the first steps Putin took after the Orange Revolution was to reduce the role and independence of Russian civil society organizations. He also clamped down on the political opposition, to prevent them from posing any real threat to the regime. The electoral threshold for a party to enter parliament was raised from 5 percent to 7 percent, and all single-member districts were eliminated, which deprived the pro-democracy opposition of any real chance of gaining representation in the Duma. The number of parties represented in the Duma shrank from more than a dozen to just four. The Kremlin also began building pro-regime youth movements such as Marching Together and, later, Ours (*Nashi*), which would take to the streets to support and protect the regime should mass protests break out. Nashi invoked both Soviet and tsarist symbols and ideology and was explicitly, violently anti-Western.

Finally, the Kremlin set out to articulate a new state ideology, centered on the idea of sovereignty. This process had started even before the Orange Revolution, but the events in Kyiv imbued the ideological struggle against the West with a new urgency. In May 2004, Valery Zor'kin, chief justice of Russia's Constitutional Court, published an article titled "In Defense of the Westphalian System." In it, Zor'kin argued for the importance of the international system of sovereign states established after the 1648 Peace of Westphalia, which ended the Thirty Years' War. Foreign support for pro-democracy nongovernmental organizations and any intervention in states' internal affairs to promote democracy, human rights, and self-determination, he complained, undermined state sovereignty. States subject to these external interventions are not fully sovereign, and this erosion of sovereignty is liable to cause chaos and destroy the international system.

The idea of the Orange Revolution as a threat to Russian sovereignty and security was further developed by the Kremlin's chief ideologue, Vladislav Surkov. In 2006, Surkov introduced the idea of "sovereign democracy" as Russia's new national ideology. Russia, Surkov claimed, is not and cannot be a Western-style liberal democracy that prioritizes individual rights. Instead, Russians value collective rights and a strong state that protects the nation from foreign interference.

This shift in thinking had profound implications for the Russian approach to Ukraine. With the Orange Revolution now cast as the main threat to Putin's regime, Ukraine became the archenemy. According to Kremlin propaganda, Ukraine's government was merely a product of a foreign plot and, therefore, illegitimate. The country itself, originally created by Moscow and now subject to Western dominance, was not a real state. In Kyiv, the Russian propaganda argued, Western embassies and foreign governments dictated policy. In Crimea, armed Tatar Wahhabis were gearing up to unleash Islamic terror on the region's Slavs. To protect the Kremlin, Ukraine had to be brought back under Russian influence.

Imperial, expansionist dreams were also now on the agenda, and not just among the fringes. *The Third Empire: The Russia that Ought to Be*, a 2006 futuristic novel authored by Mikhail Iur'ev, a former Vice Speaker of the Duma, presents mid-twenty-first-century Russia as a proudly autocratic superpower, a status that Russia gains after defeating the United States in a nuclear war. Russia's expansion and rise to global prominence, according to the book, starts with Ukraine, "which especially irritated [Russia] by the very fact of its existence." A deep political crisis in Kyiv, according to Iur'ev's vision, leads to a mass uprising in eastern and southern Ukraine. The Kremlin dispatches Russian troops to intervene in the conflict and threatens to use nuclear weapons to prevent NATO involvement. Following a referendum, eastern Ukraine is absorbed by Russia. *The Third Empire* captivated Russian elites and reinforced their perception of the coming global struggle and the centrality of Ukraine for Russia's future greatness.[35]

In 2008, Putin chose his longtime aide and deputy prime minister Dmitry Medvedev to be his successor and, despite the Kremlin's fears of mass protests, the transition went off without a hitch. The Orange Revolution never materialized in Moscow, but the fear of it left a potent legacy. Ideas and arguments that the Kremlin would use in 2014 and 2022 to justify its invasions of Ukraine have their origin in the post–Orange Revolution efforts to protect Putin from domestic protests and the specter of democracy.

While the Kremlin was busy defending itself from the Orange threat, the new government in Kyiv struggled, and the leaders of the revolution began turning on each other. Citizens demanded fast improvements, but the country's structural problems, economic woes, and deeply ingrained corruption could not be fixed overnight. Yushchenko, though a competent technocrat, turned out to be a lackluster political leader. And though the Ukrainian government was committed to joining the EU, the EU had no interest in letting Ukraine in. The country was too large, too poor, too corrupt, and, from Western Europe's perspective, too Russian. In 2005, I asked a senior EU official when he thought Ukraine could join the bloc. "If it were only western Ukraine," he replied, "it would be already in the EU. If it were just western and central Ukraine, maybe in twenty years. In the existing borders, with the east, never."

Ukraine's effort to join NATO was equally unsuccessful. In 2008, Ukraine, together with Georgia, applied to join the alliance. But some NATO members, especially Germany, worried about how Russia would react and objected. At a summit in Bucharest that year, NATO declined to offer the two states Membership Action Plans but, crucially, promised that they would eventually be allowed to join the alliance. This was the worst outcome imaginable; it outraged Russia without providing Ukraine with any extra protection or assistance. Reportedly, Putin told US president

George W. Bush in 2008 that Ukraine was not even a real country. The statement and the sentiment were not surprising given the prevalent mood in Russia, but it was also yet another warning signal that was ignored in the West.

Yushchenko failed to achieve quick economic growth and was given the cold shoulder by Brussels. His domestic popularity plummeted. In response, he leaned into identity politics, an area in which he could achieve quick results and where his actions would resonate with a substantial chunk of his supporters. Yushchenko and his advisors believed that history is too important to be left to historians and that the state has a duty to shape the country's historical narrative. They were not unique in this belief; many post-Communist governments practiced such "historical policy." In 2006, the Ukrainian parliament adopted a law that recognized the Holodomor as genocide. The year 2008 was officially declared the "Holodomor Victims' Remembrance Year," and a huge monument to the victims of the famine was erected in Kyiv. These efforts had an impact. In 2003, only 40 percent of Ukrainian citizens viewed the Holodomor as genocide and 13 percent had never heard of the famine. In 2007, 72.4 percent believed that the famine had been deliberately organized and over 63 percent supported its recognition as genocide.[36]

Kyiv's efforts to promote domestic and international recognition of the Holodomor as genocide enraged Russia, which by now had proudly adopted many Soviet symbols and began rehabilitating Stalin as a great statesman. Commemoration of the Holodomor was perceived by the Russian government not as a charge against Stalin but as an attack on Russia itself. The "provocative cry about 'genocide'" took shape "inside spiteful, anti-Russian, chauvinistic minds," complained writer Aleksandr Solzhenitsyn. Russian scholars, think tanks, and official archives responded to Ukrainian claims by churning out numerous articles, books, and document collections that denied the genocidal nature of the famine. Some were overly racist and mocked the Ukrainian "starving identity," while others viewed the recognition of the Holodomor as genocide as being the first step toward a worldwide rehabilitation of Nazism. When Ukraine invited Medvedev to attend the commemorations of the Holodomor on its seventy-fifth anniversary, the Russian president refused and accused Ukraine of rewriting history by presenting the "so-called Holodomor" as genocide.[37]

The commemoration of the Holodomor as genocide may have offended Russia, but it was supported by most Ukrainians. Much more controversial was Yushchenko's decision to award the title of Hero of Ukraine to Roman Shukhevych (commander of the UPA) in 2007 and to Stepan Bandera in 2010. Until then, the legacy of UPA and OUN and especially their involvement in the Holocaust were not a topic of national-level political debate, but Yushchenko's move catapulted history to the forefront. The awards divided Ukrainians and—particularly in the case of Bandera—were widely criticized abroad, even among Ukraine's close partners.

The turn to identity politics failed to revive Yushchenko's political fortunes. The Orange camp fractured, and its leaders focused more on devouring each other than on fixing Ukraine. This infighting created an opening for Yanukovych, and in 2006 he returned as prime minister, this time under Yushchenko's presidency. No longer a disgraced loser who tried and failed to steal an election, Yanukovych now positioned himself as a respectable politician in preparation for the next presidential election.

Yanukovych's triumph finally came in early 2010. On January 17, Ukrainians went to the polls to choose a new president. Yushchenko ran for reelection but came in fifth with a meager 5.45 percent of the vote. Most Orange camp votes went to Yushchenko's former ally and prime minister Yulia Tymoshenko, who advanced to the runoff against Yanukovych. Many of those who had supported Yushchenko in 2004 had grown disappointed with both him and Tymoshenko and consequently stayed home or voted "against all." On February 7, Yanukovych won the second round with 48.95 percent of the vote against Tymoshenko's 45.5 percent. From the Kremlin's perspective, this was an ideal outcome that did not even require much Russian effort. Ukraine, Russian elites thought, was returning to its rightful place as Russia's little sibling.

Yanukovych quietly reversed some of Yushchenko's most controversial policies, and an administrative court in Donetsk invalidated the nationalist leaders' Hero of Ukraine awards. The new president also shelved Ukraine's bid for NATO membership, elevated the status of the Russian language, and extended Russia's lease on the Black Sea Fleet base in Sevastopol. Exceptionally corrupt and heavy-handed, Yanukovych jailed Tymoshenko and steered the country in an increasingly authoritarian and kleptocratic direction. He siphoned fortunes from the state budget to the businesses of family members and friends and, according to a popular joke, police were busy snatching homeless people from the streets of the Donbas—Yanukovych's home region—and appointing them to government offices throughout the country. But Yanukovych also preferred being president of Ukraine to being a governor of a Russian province. He therefore had to pay lip service to the country's independence and European aspirations and demonstrate progress toward their achievement.

In 2012, Putin returned to the Russian presidency. Medvedev stepped back and did not challenge his former boss, but many Muscovites did protest. For Putin, this was confirmation of a Western plot to depose him in an Orange Revolution–style uprising. He became convinced that American leaders, especially then secretary of state Hillary Clinton, were behind the protests as they sought to prevent Russia's resurgence as a global power. To protect his rule from this imagined threat, Putin turned Russia into a full-blown, repressive autocracy. Putin now saw himself as locked in confrontation with the West, and in this confrontation, he could not afford to lose Ukraine. By that time, Putin's view of Ukraine's very existence had also shifted. Relations with Ukraine were never about security alone, but as Russia and Putin became more nationalist, identity and historical myths became paramount. "We are, without a doubt, one people," Putin declared in Kyiv in June 2013. Whether Ukrainians agreed was irrelevant.[38]

In November 2013, Ukraine and the EU were scheduled to sign an Association Agreement that would, among other things, establish a free trade zone between the two. This clashed with Putin's desire to create a competing, Russia-led trade bloc, which in 2013 centered on the Customs Union of Russia, Belarus, and Kazakhstan and eventually became the Eurasian Economic Union (EEU). Completion of the Association Agreement with Brussels would have shut the door on Ukraine joining the EEU, and Putin, like Gorbachev and Yeltsin before him, was certain that without Ukraine no meaningful reincarnation of the USSR would ever be possible. If the EEU was to become more than just a geopolitical fiction, Ukraine had to be brought under Moscow's umbrella. Luckily for Putin, the Yanukovych government was exceptionally corrupt and incompetent at everything other than enriching its officials. This mismanagement and greed produced an economic crisis, making the Ukrainian president vulnerable and desperate for financial assistance—ideally one that would not threaten corruption or require meaningful reforms.

A combination of financial enticements, economic pressure, and direct threats from Putin made Yanukovych relent and pull out of the EU deal a week before the signing ceremony. Instead, Ukraine would place itself under Kremlin dominance in exchange for favorable energy prices and a $15 billion loan. For those who grew up in independent Ukraine, this meant not just a shift in the country's geopolitical orientation but the end of any hopes for a European future. Integration with Russia meant the continuation of Yanukovych's corrupt and widely despised rule, a slide toward autocracy, and the return of control from Moscow. Such a monumental change could not be brought in unopposed.

CHAPTER 8

UKRAINIAN WINTER, RUSSIAN SPRING

In April 2015, journalist Elena Racheva accompanied Russian volunteers returning home from the war in the Donbas on their fifty-two-hour train ride from Rostov-on-Don in southern Russia to Yekaterinburg in the Urals. Many of the volunteers were bitter. They had been mistreated by commanders, resented by the Donbas locals, and not given the resources they were promised. Worst of all, they barely saw any combat. But despite everything, only half of the Ural volunteers who went to the Donbas returned to Russia; the rest decided to stay, some simply because they could not afford a train ticket back home. Why had they come to the Donbas from faraway Yekaterinburg? Some went in search of adventure, or to give meaning to their otherwise predictable and empty lives. But many came to save members of the Russian World from the Ukrainian atrocities they had learned about from Russian state media, or to fight for Russia and push the *ukropy* (a derogatory term for Ukrainians) behind the Dnipro River. The person who organized this volunteer unit dreamed of staging a victory parade in Kyiv on May 9, the day on which Russia celebrates the Soviet victory over Germany in World War II. He was a nationalist, a monarchist, and an anti-Semite on a mission to unite all ancient Rus' lands.[1]

The Russian annexation of Crimea and the war in the Donbas changed Russia, Ukraine, and the relations between them forever. The Russian invasion of Ukraine started in 2014, not 2022. It was a dizzying, disorienting affair accompanied by heavy doses of disinformation and propaganda. It was also much more ambiguous than the Russian attack in 2022, and quite a few of those living in the areas that Russia and its proxies conquered supported Moscow. This was a civil war between Ukrainians, the Kremlin insisted, yet more proof of Ukraine being an unviable and artificial entity. And indeed, in this war, Ukrainians fought on both sides, but those who started and sustained it were Russians—government officials, security services, and nationalist intellectuals—dreaming of past glory, the USSR, and the empire, which could not rise again as long as Ukraine existed.

In Ukraine, the shock of the war changed society, led to new reforms, and made Ukrainians rally behind their state like never before. But Ukrainians also wanted peace and elected those who, they believed, could find a compromise with Russia. Yet even a Russian-speaking president from the country's south such as Volodymyr Zelensky could not achieve a treaty. Ukrainians wanted peace, while the Kremlin, its agents, and the nationalists they mobilized and sent to Donbas sought Ukraine.

On November 21, 2013, when President Yanukovych reneged on the Association Agreement with the EU, Mustafa Nayem, a Ukrainian journalist of Afghan descent, published a Facebook post in Russian. "Who is ready tonight before midnight to come to the Maidan?" Nayem asked. It was a call to action, and thousands—mostly students who saw Ukraine's European future slipping away before their eyes—answered it. The next day, the "Euromaidan" name, a portmanteau of Europe and Maidan, was first used to describe the protests, though in Ukraine the events are more widely known as the Revolution of Dignity.[2]

Originally, the protests were indeed about European dreams, and had the government simply waited, the demonstrations would likely have fizzled out after the EU summit at which the agreement was scheduled to be signed had ended. But in the early morning of November 30, the government dispatched riot police to remove the protesters, ostensibly to make way for a Christmas tree. Demonstrating students were viciously beaten, and the nature of the protests changed. Police violence against peaceful students blatantly violated accepted social norms, and the next day thousands, young and old alike, showed up on the Maidan. The target of their anger was the nature of the Yanukovych regime as such—its violence, corruption, and slide toward autocracy—rather than any specific foreign policy decision. Barricades went up, and, despite the freezing cold, the protesters erected a tent city. A newly organized group of right-wing radicals that called itself the Right Sector occupied the nearby mayor's office and the Trade Unions building.[3]

Even after all this, Yanukovych would have likely survived in office had he done nothing. But the Ukrainian president believed that he had lost his bid for power in 2004 because the government did not repress the Orange Revolution, and he was determined to not repeat this mistake. On December 11, the *Berkut* (Golden Eagle), a feared riot-police unit, tried to clear the barricades, but the protesters repelled the attack and the standoff continued. In addition to being motivated by his own fears, Yanukovych was under pressure from Moscow to quickly resolve the crisis, by force if necessary. On January 16, 2014, the Ukrainian parliament, the Verkhovna Rada, adopted a package of eleven "dictatorship laws" that effectively eliminated freedom of speech, media, and assembly; allowed criminal trial in absentia; and shielded law enforcement from prosecution for violence committed against protesters.

On January 19, in response to the new laws, the protesters tried to storm the parliament building. Clashes with police continued for several days and spread to other cities. The protests also turned deadly. The protests' heroes and victims epitomized Ukraine's diversity: an Afghan Ukrainian sparked the movement, and its first martyrs were Ukrainians of Armenian and Belorussian heritage.

On February 7, 2014, the Winter Olympic Games opened in Sochi in southern Russia. The games were a pet project for Putin and were meant to showcase his revival of Russia, but the violence in Kyiv spoiled the celebrations. On February 18–19, the Berkut once again stormed the Maidan encampment, but the protesters fought back; several dozen people were killed, with many more wounded. The radical, far-right Svoboda Party and the Right Sector were a minority on the Maidan, but they were more organized, motivated, and willing to use violence than the rest. Many members of these groups also had years of paramilitary training and soccer hooligan violence under their belt. This violence by an extreme minority raised the stakes of repression for the regime and for the riot police, who had suffered casualties and now had to decide whether they supported the government enough to put their bodies on the line. At the same time, the nonviolence of the majority of protesters appealed to the international community.[4]

France, Germany, and Poland sent their top diplomats to Kyiv to help mediate between Yanukovych and opposition leaders. Putin dispatched Vladimir Lukin, the former Russian ambassador to Washington who in the 1990s had advocated the return of Crimea to Russia. On February 20, while politicians negotiated, the Maidan became the scene of a bloodbath, with over seventy protesters killed by the Berkut. Svoboda and the Right Sector also escalated, their weapons of choice shifting from batons and pipes to bricks and small firearms.

Eventually, representatives of opposition parties and the government reached a deal. Yanukovych agreed to a package of constitutional reforms that curtailed his powers and to early elections in December 2014. But unlike the Orange Revolution, Euromaidan was neither led by nor associated with any political party. It was a loose coalition and, incensed by the massacre, the protesters rejected the agreement negotiated by politicians. During the night of February 21–22, Yanukovych fled Kyiv, possibly on direct orders from Moscow. He flew to Kharkiv, then to Donetsk, from there to Crimea, and eventually, on February 25, into exile in Russia. The Berkut, without a government to protect, also left. Many of the officers were from Donbas- and Crimea-based units and returned home seething, feeling betrayed and nursing a burning hatred of Euromaidan. On February 22, the Rada voted to remove Yanukovych from office. Oleksandr Turchynov, an opposition politician, Baptist minister, and former head of the Security Service of Ukraine, became acting president.[5]

The Kremlin immediately labeled the change of power an illegitimate coup and the new government a "junta." Even before large-scale violence had broken out, Svoboda and the Right Sector had become favorite topics of Russian propaganda and evidence of Euromaidan's inherent neo-Nazi nature, Western origins, and commitment to exterminating Ukraine's Russian-speaking population. But the Russian propaganda did not limit its attacks to the radicals. Everyone in Ukraine who objected to Russia's plans was now labeled a neo-Nazi or a Western puppet or both. Bellicose rhetoric and references to War World II skyrocketed in the Russian media, where content is determined and tightly controlled by the government. Collision was inevitable.

On February 22, 2014, when Yanukovych was still in Ukraine, Putin held a fateful all-night meeting with his closest advisors. Incensed by the events in Kyiv, the Russian president in the early morning of February 23 ordered the takeover of Crimea. Some chronicles date the decision to a slightly earlier date, February 20, when Yanukovych was still in power in Kyiv. The key supporting evidence for this claim is that this date is listed on the Russian military medal awarded to those who took part in the annexation, but most accounts point to the February 22–23 night meeting as the event at which the Russian annexation of Crimea had begun.

As long as Russian archives remain closed, we will not have a definitive picture of the process that led to the decision to annex Crimea, but the decision itself was almost certainly driven by nationalist and identity-based considerations, rather than national security concerns. Some Western commentators argue that post–Cold War NATO expansion pushed Russia into a corner, heightened the Kremlin's fears, and provoked Putin to attack. The annexation and the war that followed, they maintain, are therefore the fault of the West, especially the United States. There is scant evidence to support this interpretation. The annexation of Crimea had little to do with genuine security considerations. Putin's goal was "to bring Crimea home," no matter the consequences.[6]

The notion that Crimea is a Russian land, unjustly taken away in 1954 on Khrushchev's whim, was deeply ingrained among most Russians, but not many actively advocated returning Crimea by force prior to 2014. If Ukraine was under Moscow's thumb, there was simply no need; Yanukovych's promises to pursue close integration with Russia would have turned the entire country, not just Crimea, into a Kremlin client state. But for some in the Russian elite, the return of Crimea became an obsession. The Russian Institute for Strategic Studies, the Kremlin's in-house think tank, bombarded the government with memos arguing that Russia needed to undo the mistakes of history and retake lost territories. Others pushed for annexation for financial reasons, because it would create a windfall for businesses they owned. Another group saw Ukraine's westward lurch as a betrayal of its true geopolitical destiny as Little Russia, and the Euromaidan as an insult to Russian honor that had to be punished. Ukraine's audacity was a bigger affront to the Kremlin than NATO bases. Whatever the reason, in February 2014 it was now or never.[7]

Unlike the Orange Revolution, Euromaidan, from the Kremlin's perspective, meant a complete and irreversible rupture with Russia by Ukraine. Whereas the Orange Revolution was above all about one stolen election, Euromaidan was triggered by Yanukovych's decision to align Ukraine with Moscow. After the Orange Revolution, the pro-Russian camp remained a formidable force in Ukrainian politics, but now Yanukovych was impeached and his camp scattered. The Kremlin realized it had lost Ukraine, possibly forever. But this was also an opportunity. The rupture had happened, and so the Kremlin no longer had to restrain its expansionist impulses. Ukraine was in turmoil, weak, and disoriented. This represented a rare chance to strike while the other side was distracted, but the window of opportunity was closing fast. Nikolai Patrushev, the powerful, ultra-hawkish chairman of Russia's Security Council, pushed for immediate action and predicted that Ukraine would not fight back if

Russia moved fast enough. Eventually, Putin decided it was time to take Crimea. Russian special forces received an order to invade the peninsula.

By February 26, protests and scuffles between pro-Russian activists and supporters of the new government in Kyiv spilled over into the Crimean parliament building, where the two factions barricaded themselves in different wings. The next day, people in uniforms—disciplined, well organized, armed with modern weapons but without insignia or other identifying marks—appeared on Crimea's streets. They took over railroad stations and airports, blockaded Ukrainian army bases, and refused to reveal their identity. Soon, they became known as "polite people" or "little green men." They were quickly recognized as Russian soldiers, but Putin stubbornly denied any involvement by Moscow and claimed that they must be local militias and self-defense groups. Later, after the annexation, Putin dropped the pretense and confirmed what everyone already knew.

Militias, volunteers, and patriotic biker gangs were also there, a mixture of locals and Russian citizens, mostly nationalists and veterans. Some Russians were ordered there by the government, while others arrived on their own, driven by ideology, boredom, or a desire not to miss such a monumental event. Unlike the little green men, these militias were chatty, undisciplined, armed with any weapons they could find, and dressed in a dazzling variety of old uniforms and civilian attire. Some patrolled the streets and suppressed anti-Russian protests, while others took over public buildings. Leaders of Russia's Tatarstan region were tasked with convincing Crimean Tatars to switch sides, but most remained loyal to Ukraine.[8]

As the Russian government had predicted, the Ukrainian army did not fight back. The United States, as surprised as everyone else, also pressured the new government in Kyiv to avoid direct military confrontation. The Russian takeover of Crimea was not peaceful; there was violence, but the number of casualties was small and barely noticed amid the general upheaval.

The Kremlin orchestrated the removal of the existing regional Crimean leadership and installed Sergey Aksenov, head of the marginal Russian Unity Party, as the peninsula's new leader. Aksenov, who according to multiple sources also went by the criminal nickname "Goblin" and was previously affiliated with two notorious gangs, promptly announced a referendum on whether Crimea should join Russia, to be held on March 16. According to official results, over 95 percent favored joining Russia. The referendum at gunpoint was a sham. There were people in Crimea who genuinely wished to join Russia, but even during Euromaidan—when Russian propaganda bombarded Crimeans with messages about an imminent neo-Nazi attack—they were only about 40 percent of the population. Before 2014, just a minority of Crimea's Russian speakers complained about discrimination, and few wished to obtain a Russian passport. Crimean Tatars, most of whom had returned to the homeland from exile in Central Asia only after 1989, were overwhelmingly pro-Ukrainian.[9]

The Russian government wished to showcase local support for its actions, but when push came to shove, local attitudes in Crimea were irrelevant. The Kremlin, and Russians more broadly, believed that Crimea was Russia and nothing else mattered. "Literally everything in Crimea is suffused with our history and pride," claimed Putin. On March 18, Crimea was formally annexed to Russia.[10]

Russian actions stunned the West. From Western capitals, this resurgent Russia looked ruthless, creative, and like it would stop at nothing to achieve its goals. Western analysts began discussing, with a mix of admiration and fear, Russia's new way of war: "Hybrid warfare" and the "Gerasimov doctrine," named after Valery Gerasimov, chief of the General Staff of the Russian Armed Forces. In fact, the Gerasimov doctrine never existed and there was little new about Russian tactics, but Crimea created in the West an illusion of the Kremlin's menacing invincibility. The Russians—many commentators, analysts, and security experts argued—are coming, and resistance by smaller states like Ukraine is futile. Western countries, led by the United States and the European Union, introduced sanctions against Russia, but beyond their symbolic effect the sanctions were mild and their impact limited.[11]

The annexation also stunned the Russian public. The dream of recovering Crimea had suddenly been realized, seemingly with little effort.

What had been unimaginable became reality overnight, and Putin's approval rating skyrocketed to over 80 percent. Even many liberals struggled to speak out against the euphoric refrain of "Crimea is ours." Alexei Navalny, Russia's most prominent opposition leader, conceded that Crimea had been seized illegally but argued that it would remain Russian and that everyone, including Ukrainians, had better get used to the new reality. Western reaction also allowed the Kremlin to boost jingoism and introduce previously unthinkable restrictions. Thus, in response to sanctions, Russia banned Western food from the country. This gave the Kremlin the opportunity to promote domestic food production, which was now shielded from competition and improved Russia's readiness for a long conflict against the West. Ordinary Russians were forced to spend more money on lower quality food, but most viewed it as a small price to pay for the return of Crimea.[12]

Integrating the peninsula into Russia was expected to be a financially and logistically complicated endeavor, and thus Putin might have preferred to take a tactical pause, but others were just getting started. By annexing Crimea, the Kremlin let the neo-imperial genie out of the bottle and set in motion the process that would culminate in the invasion of Ukraine in February 2022. For many nationalists who flocked to Crimea in February and March 2014 and their backers in Moscow, this was only the beginning—the first step in resurrecting Russia's past glory. Their next target was the Donbas, and after that, all of Ukraine.

In March–April 2014, the Ukrainian state seemed on the verge of collapse. Every day brought new pro-Russian protests and attempts to occupy government buildings in the east and south of the country. Some were organized exclusively by local activists, but many, if not most, were coordinated and financed by Russian citizens, including people with high-ranking positions in the Kremlin and the security services, such as Sergey Glazyev, Putin's economic advisor. In most places these protests eventually died down or were suppressed by the government. In Odesa, a violent standoff between pro-Russian activists and their opponents ended in the death of forty-eight people, almost all of them pro-Russian protesters who suffocated when the Trade Unions building in which they had barricaded themselves was ignited by a Molotov cocktail thrown by one of the opposing sides.[13]

The Donbas—Yanukovych's home region—became the epicenter of anti-government activism. The remnants of Yanukovych's Party of Regions fought to keep what was left of their previous dominance, and even though few Donbas residents liked or respected Yanukovych personally, many did resent the ousting of their home team from the presidency. Still, most protesters, even the nominally pro-Russian ones, wanted a different kind of Ukraine, not direct rule from Moscow. But there were also Russian nationalists who dreamed of the Donbas joining Russia and called on Putin to annex it. The Kyiv government's authority was weak in the region, and Berkut officers who had shot protesters on the Maidan now feared prosecution and were unwilling to protect the new regime.

As early as February 2014, local activists began organizing the Donbas People's Militia, financed and led by Pavel Gubarev, a local entrepreneur and extreme Russian nationalist. On March 1, Gubarev, previously a marginal figure, declared himself the People's Governor of Donetsk. More ominously, anti-government protesters began attacking police stations and seizing weapons caches. But on March 6, Gubarev was arrested and taken to Kyiv. Weak though they were, the new Ukrainian authorities were able, for the moment, to deal with this domestic threat simply because, unlike in Crimea, the Russian military was not yet in the Donbas. War would not have happened if the Russians had not brought it to eastern Ukraine.

Among the people the Kremlin sent to Crimea to organize the propaganda side of the annexation was public relations specialist Alexander Borodai, the son of prominent nationalist writer Yurii Borodai. The younger Borodai was also a die-hard nationalist and in 1993 had joined a brief, ill-fated red-brown uprising against Yeltsin. From his new base in Crimea, Borodai used his PR skills and funding from the nationalist, ultraconservative oligarch Konstantin Malofeev to foment unrest in eastern Ukraine, but by early April this campaign had begun to falter. A friend and colleague of Borodai's, Igor Girkin, who came to Crimea to command a group of Russian volunteers, chose a more radical approach.

Girkin, who went by the nom de guerre *Strelkov* (Shooter), was a nationalist like Borodai but with more combat experience. He fought with the Serbs in Bosnia, joined the Russian army, moved to the FSB, fought in Chechnya, and retired in 2013 with the rank of colonel. Girkin was also an avid Russian military reenactor and, after retirement from the FSB, worked for Malofeev as the oligarch's chief of security. Ukraine, Girkin and his comrades believed, was artificial, weak, and bound to disintegrate if pushed. Buoyed by the ease with which Russia had occupied Crimea, Girkin and his allies decided to lead this push. After receiving funding and procuring weapons, Girkin organized a group of volunteers who crossed the border into Ukraine to start a war and create a new Russian state: Novorossiya.[14]

On April 12, 2014, led by Girkin, a group of fifty-two armed men, almost all of them Russian citizens, occupied government buildings in Slovyansk, a midsize town in the Donetsk region. Slovyansk was a strategically located transportation hub, and its name—the town of Slavs—could not be more symbolic. The war in the Donbas had begun. Girkin's actions might not have been part of Putin's grand plan to split Ukraine, and we do not yet know if the Russian president approved or was even aware of this initiative. But the recently retired FSB colonel was not acting alone either. Behind Girkin was a powerful nationalist faction within the Kremlin and the security services, which also boasted allied oligarchs, propagandists, religious figures, and right-wing intellectuals. The annexation of Crimea energized this group, mobilized them for action, and proved to them that Russian territorial expansion was possible. Girkin's raid, they believed, would make Putin act. The little green men would return, and Novorossiya would replace eastern and southern Ukraine. Then it would be Kyiv's turn.[15]

War was brought to Ukraine by Russian nationalist artists, writers, and intellectuals. Borodai, who became the prime minister of the Donetsk People's Republic (DNR)—as the Russian-controlled part of the Donetsk region was now called—was a native of Moscow and a philosopher by training. Girkin was also a Muscovite and a historian. Zakhar Prilepin—a veteran of Chechnya, a Stalin admirer, and one of Russia's most popular writers—joined the government of the Luhansk People's Republic (LNR), the DNR's twin, and later used his writing honoraria to equip and lead an entire DNR battalion. For these people, the Crimean annexation and the Novorossiya project represented a Russian Spring. This awakening, they believed, would bring Russia closer to reclaiming its glorious past and rightful superpower status. The rise of Novorossiya also required destroying Ukraine.

"Kill! Kill! Kill! There can be no other discussion. This is my opinion as a professor," Alexander Dugin urged the rebels. Ukraine, Dugin argued, was a poisonous fiction; these were simply west Russian lands. Eduard Limonov, too old to join the war, published texts with titles like "Kiev Kaput" and "Kiev Needs to Be Annihilated." The nationalist ideologue Yegor Kholmogorov argued that Ukraine was by definition an anti-Russian project, and thus there could be no point in trying to make it a friendly country; Ukraine needed to be dismembered and destroyed.[16]

Putin might not have personally started the Novorossiya project, but people around him did. The nationalists were not the Kremlin, but they had supporters in the security services, allies in the government, and an outsize presence in the state-controlled media, the primary information source for most Russians. They inspired, financed, and led Russian units in the Donbas; taught generals; advised politicians; and spread their message far and wide across Russia. Public support for Novorossiya was genuine and widespread.

Novorossiya was also an opportunity to further weaken Ukraine in the wake of the Euromaidan protests. In 2014, the Kremlin was not interested in annexing the Donbas, but it also did not wish to see Novorossiya fall. While Ukraine and the international community were preoccupied with Novorossiya, Russia could quietly digest Crimea.

Yet despite seeing Novorossiya as primordial Russian land, the nationalists, in typical colonial fashion, also thought of it as a virginal place that would serve as a model for Russia's broader spiritual regeneration. Their desire was to build a chunk of the Russian state that would somehow be free of Russia's vices: corruption, poor governance, powerful oligarchs, unchecked development, and environmental degradation. Autocracy and repression were, of course, welcomed. In their imagination, this New Russia would be ruled by upright leaders and managed by transparent, capable bureaucrats. They were silent on exactly how Russia would create something so vastly out of character, and completely ignored existing realities and relations in the Donbas, but were wholly unbothered by this. For geopolitical strategists and nationalist daydreamers, Novorossiya was as much an abstract utopia as a real territory full of people who would bear the brunt of the war they had unleashed.

The Russian leaders of Novorossiya were right-wing intellectuals, but the rank and file were more diverse. Many were Russian nationalists and members of far-right groups who flocked across the border to join the fight. For others, the driving force was nostalgia for Soviet times. Still others cared little for ideology: veterans of Russia's previous wars unable to adjust to civilian life, adventurers, petty criminals, and middle-aged men trying to escape quotidian tedium all came to fight Ukraine. Zakhar Prilepin's short story *"Rabotiagi"* ("Hard Workers") centers on a DNR militia officer, a reflection of Prilepin himself, who finally returns home to Russia after a long spell fighting in the Donbas and invites four of his comrades for a reunion. Of the five men, two are veterans of Russia's previous wars, two are drug users, one served time in jail, and another had to flee Donetsk because he had "disappeared" someone and was under criminal investigation. They are also a mix of Russian citizens and Donbas natives.

Novorossiya was not purely a Russian project. Many of its soldiers and leaders were Ukrainian citizens, locals who joined for ideological reasons, former Berkut officers who fought against the Euromaidan and now feared prosecution, or simply those whom the war had left without any other job prospects. Novorossiya was concocted in Russia, but it could not survive without local, Ukrainian collaboration. By late fall 2014, Borodai, Girkin, and many other leading Russians had returned home, and Donbas natives—technically still Ukrainian citizens of both Russian and Ukrainian heritage—took over key positions, though always under Moscow's watchful eye. Russian volunteers continued to come to kill and die for the Russian World in Ukraine, but the participation of many Donbas residents in the fighting allowed the Kremlin to paint the conflict as a civil war, even though it would have neither started nor persisted without Russian involvement.

After Girkin's band occupied Slovyansk, Ukraine's acting president, Oleksandr Turchynov, launched a military response, officially named the Anti-Terrorist Operation. Ukraine had not fought for Crimea, but the Donbas was where the line had to be drawn if the country was to survive. The Ukrainian army—still disoriented by the revolution and plagued by two decades of corruption and neglect—failed to suppress the Donetsk and Luhansk People's Republics and restore order. The territory of Novorossiya expanded, and residents of Donetsk and Luhansk who supported Ukraine were beaten, tortured, and murdered.

In the early days of the war, it was the volunteer battalions, made up of recent civilians and equipped through online fundraising campaigns, that held the line on the Ukrainian side. Many of these volunteers had taken part in Euromaidan, and some units had far-right origins and political extremists in their ranks. They were motivated but unprofessional, violent, and unruly. Yet they gave the Ukrainian military enough relief to regroup, and once it did, the volunteer formations became less prominent.

In July 2014, Ukraine recaptured Slovyansk, and the end seemed near for Novorossiya. The Kremlin responded by escalating the war—both propaganda and actual. Russian media was already filled with stories about atrocities purportedly perpetrated by Ukrainian neo-Nazis against Russian speakers. The Ukrainian army was described as *karateli* (executioners or persecutors), a term that typically referred to the World War II German perpetrators, and there were constant references to World War II in the Russian media after Euromaidan. Girkin and his supporters also appropriated World War II imagery to mobilize Russian supporters for the fight against "Ukrainian Nazis." But now even that was not enough, and the anti-Ukrainian rhetoric became hysterical.[17]

Russian reporters were instructed by the Kremlin to make their stories "more hellish," and the media duly obliged. When no real Ukrainian violence against civilians was to be found, it had to be invented, and later some Russian propagandists admitted that the alleged victims or witnesses they interviewed had been paid actors. On July 12, 2014, Russian state TV recounted an especially hideous atrocity: in Lenin Square in Slovyansk, Ukrainian soldiers crucified a three-year-old boy. The description of the event resembled ritual murder plots such as that of the Beilis trial and invoked the same tropes and imagery. The story quickly fell apart. Slovyansk had no Lenin Square, there were no other eyewitnesses, and the story itself was likely lifted from Dugin's Facebook account. The crucifixion may have been fake news, but its impact was real. In 2015, Elena Racheva asked Russians returning from the LNR why they had gone to the Donbas, and some volunteers explicitly cited the crucifixion story. Racheva explained to the volunteers that the story was a fabrication, but it made no difference. *This* case might not have happened, they conceded, but it surely represented a broader truth.[18]

Alongside the stream of volunteers enraged by atrocities that never happened, the war gave rise to state-sanctioned private military companies (PMCs) that also appeared on the front lines in the Donbas. The most notorious was the Wagner Group. Wagner was owned by Yevgeny Prigozhin, a Leningrad-born former criminal who, after the Soviet collapse, became a retailer and restaurateur. By 2014, his business empire included everything from construction to catering for Russia's Ministry of Defense and Moscow city government to internet troll farms. Later, Prigozhin's Internet Research Agency would become deeply involved in Russia's efforts to influence the 2016 US presidential election.

Heavily dependent on state contracts, Prigozhin was tasked with organizing a mercenary force. The PMC was named after the German composer Richard Wagner because its military commander, Dmitry Utkin, a former lieutenant colonel in the Russian special forces, was obsessed with the Third Reich, sported Nazi tattoos, and used "Wagner" as his call sign. That a unit taking part in what Russian propaganda described as a continuation of the World War II fight against Banderite "neo-Nazis" was named after Hitler's favorite artist never bothered the Kremlin.

During the early days of the Wagner Group's operations, it attracted many men who were well acquainted with violence but had few other ways to make ends meet. Marat Gabidullin typified this group. A junior officer when the Soviet Union collapsed, he left military service, went into business, became involved in crime, served time in prison and, after release, had trouble making enough money to support his family. Gabidullin's decision to join Wagner was purely pragmatic, but the PMC also attracted extreme right activists, drifters, adventurers eager for adrenaline, and bored alcoholics.[19]

And, of course, there was also the regular Russian army. As in Crimea, Putin denied any involvement, claiming that the Novorossiya fighters' heavy weaponry had simply been purchased on the market or seized from Ukrainian army depots—even weapons that were unique to the Russian military. At most, the Kremlin conceded that some Russian servicemen were using their annual leave to volunteer to defend the Russian World in eastern Ukraine.

Yet the Russian army was not just arming the DNR and the LNR; it was actively fighting for Novorossiya. When the Ukrainian military was on the cusp of defeating the Girkin-led formations, units of the Russian army crossed the border and soon drove back and crushed the unprepared and ill-equipped Ukrainian forces. This debacle forced the newly elected Ukrainian president, Petro Poroshenko, to negotiate an armistice. The Minsk Protocol, signed on September 5, 2014, declared a cease-fire and outlined the next steps of resolving the conflict. Yet the agreement soon collapsed, fighting resumed, and the DNR and LNR held elections in violation of the agreement. The war escalated in January 2015, with Russian and DNR forces capturing the last sections of the Donetsk airport still held by Ukrainian troops and Debaltseve, a strategically important railroad junction.

Contrary to nationalists' dreams, Putin did not annex Novorossiya, but he was still committed to preventing its fall, and the Ukrainian army was simply too weak to defeat the Russians with the weapons it had. Western aid eventually began arriving in Ukraine, but not nearly enough. Kyiv most needed weapons, but the United States was initially only willing to provide nonlethal matériel, such as military rations and uniforms. For US president Barack Obama, the chief goal was to avoid escalation between the United States and Russia, but this approach only emboldened Putin and frustrated Ukraine and its allies. The Ukrainians, fighting "to free themselves of Russian dominance and build a European democracy . . . deserve more than Spam in a can," argued Senator John Barrasso, Republican of Wyoming. "Blankets are important . . . [but] one cannot win a war with a blanket," complained Poroshenko.[20]

Germany and France stepped in to broker a new agreement: Minsk II (February 12, 2015). Besides a cease-fire, Minsk II set out the foundations for future peace. The DNR and LNR would be reintegrated into Ukraine but given special status and unspecified-but-substantial powers. Russian nationalists were predictably incensed at the very thought of returning the Russian-controlled parts of the Donbas to Ukraine, but for Putin the deal was a potential win. If the LNR and DNR returned to Ukraine with special privileges, this might have granted the Kremlin an effective veto over all major decisions made in Kyiv. Subjugating Ukraine was cheaper than occupying it. Neither Minsk agreement addressed the status of Crimea, and Moscow had reason to believe that its hold on the peninsula was now secure.

Yet neither the Donetsk and Luhansk warlords nor their Russian nationalist allies had any intention of honoring the Minsk agreements and reintegrating with Ukraine. Kyiv was also not keen on de facto submitting to Putin's authority by granting special powers to warlords beholden to Moscow. The conflict became semi-frozen; fighting ebbed in intensity though never wholly went away. Before Russia's attack in February 2022, the war had taken the lives of about 13,000 people on both sides, among them 3,400 civilians. Close to 10 percent of civilians killed as a result of the war were not even Ukrainians but the passengers and crew of Malaysia Airlines flight MH17, shot down by the DNR on July 17, 2014, with a missile provided by the Russian army. In 2021, the year that preceded the full-scale Russian invasion, the conflict led to the deaths of twenty-five civilians, the lowest annual count since 2014.

With the war in stasis, the DNR and LNR's leaders refocused on internal repression. The statelets became increasingly violent, lawless, and totalitarian entities where politicians and military commanders were often assassinated, the distinction between government and organized crime disappeared, the economy collapsed, incomes plummeted, the death penalty made a comeback, and prison camps, secret jails, and torture chambers proliferated widely. The ideologues of Novorossiya dreamed of it as a fairy-tale Russia, and many locals who supported them pined for the return of the pre-Gorbachev USSR, but in reality the DNR and LNR became poor, grim, and violent nationalist-criminal fiefdoms.[21]

The self-proclaimed republics, corrupt and economically unviable, became fully reliant on Moscow for support, both military and economic. The statelets' residents grew increasingly Russian not just in language but also by citizenship. The Kremlin began distributing Russian passports in the DNR and LNR, and in 2019–2022 alone over 650,000 people became Russian citizens. In Crimea, Russian rule meant repression and wider, better-organized Russian government corruption that displaced the weaker local networks. The Crimean Tatars, most of whom remained loyal to Ukraine, became the target of especially brutal Russian repression that mixed political animosity with xenophobic prejudice against this Muslim minority community. In Russia itself, Ukrainian identity came under severe pressure. In 2011, ethnic Ukrainians were the third largest group in Russia, after Russians and Tatars. In the 2021 census, the number of Ukrainians in the country decreased by a half, most likely because people became too scared to self-identify as Ukrainians or because the census takers refused to record them as such. Russian authorities shut down Ukrainian diaspora organizations and in 2018 closed the Ukrainian library in Moscow.[22]

Ukraine was also changing. The annexation of Crimea and the loss of substantial parts of the Donbas convinced Ukrainians that the country had to reform if it wanted to survive, let alone recover lost lands.

Euromaidan had divided Ukraine, but the annexation of Crimea and the war in the east, destructive though it was, helped to reduce tensions within government-controlled Ukraine. Regional divisions were declining even before 2014, but with the onset of Russian aggression they decreased even further. Contrary to the narrative of Russian propaganda, the cleavages in Ukraine were primarily political, not ethnic, and the Russian invasion changed politics. The country remained diverse but gradually ceased to be highly polarized, though this remained unnoticed by many observers in Russia and the West.[23]

Even before 2014, only a small minority of Ukrainians wished to join Russia, but many of those who did lived in Crimea and the Donbas. Now that group was cut off from the Ukrainian public sphere and could not influence it. The more radical pro-Russian politicians were also gone, either into Russia or the occupied territories. Furthermore, Russia's actions shifted the attitudes of those in Ukraine who had wished merely to build closer relations with their neighbor. The annexation, the violence, and the Kremlin's blatant lies deeply offended many Ukrainians and bred animosity. "If you have a conflict in your family, it is not an excuse for your neighbor to steal the apartment," a mayor from Ukraine's east told me, referring to Russian opportunism after Euromaidan and the sense of betrayal it produced. Russian repression in Crimea and the destruction in the Donbas were a live demonstration of the future that awaited Ukrainians in the Russian World. Even in the Donbas, many of those who were originally pro-Russian changed their minds and fled to government-controlled areas. The share of Ukrainians who viewed Russia positively dropped precipitously. In Melitopol, a rather typical southern Ukrainian town, before 2014 about 60 percent of residents had been pro-Russian. By 2021, this had dropped to about 10 percent.[24]

In response to Russia's self-proclaimed mission of protecting the Russian World, Russian-speaking Ukrainian citizens were increasingly "shedding Russianness" by adopting Ukrainian as their primary language and starting to self-identify as Ukrainians. In the process, they slowly changed the meaning of being "Ukrainian" from a predominantly ethnic concept to a more civic, national one. National identity also became substantially more salient than regional or local identity in Ukraine.[25]

The war mobilization meant that all regions and communities—east, center, west, Russian speakers, Ukrainian speakers, Orthodox, Uniates, Muslims, and Jews—were contributing to a common struggle, and they observed members of other groups working, fighting, and sacrificing their lives toward a shared goal. Societal cleavages did not disappear, and all regions were convinced that others contributed less than they themselves did, but Ukrainian society overall became more committed to Ukrainian statehood. This defensive consolidation quickly spread to the ballot box. In the snap presidential election scheduled for May 25, 2014, Petro Poroshenko—a tycoon often referred to as "Ukraine's chocolate king," one of the leaders of the Orange Revolution, and a former minister of foreign affairs—received 54.7 percent of the vote, winning almost all districts.[26]

Poroshenko's politics since 2014 could be summed up in three words: army, (Ukrainian) language, and faith. But he was not just an identity warrior. Poroshenko and his government set about reforming Ukraine's military, health care, education, local governance, banking system, law enforcement, and judiciary. It was an ambitious agenda and not all reforms were completed or ended in success, but many did.

Effective military command required centralized control over volunteer battalions, which had become symbols of heroism while also raising domestic and international concerns due to their far-right connections, politicization, and occasional lack of discipline. The battalions became the favorite bugbear of Russian propaganda but also alarmed many supporters of Ukraine and complicated Kyiv's efforts to gain foreign political, financial, and military assistance. The volunteers resented, and some resisted, government attempts to assume control, but eventually these units were professionalized and depoliticized. Other military reforms reorganized the army, encouraged initiative, and gave more power to ground-level commanders. The character of the military also changed, as more well-educated and motivated people signed up, driven by patriotism or civic duty.

Identity and symbolism were another focus for Poroshenko's government. Among the first things Poroshenko did was to reverse Yanukovych's policies and fully commit to Ukraine's pro-Western orientation, with NATO membership as the key foreign policy goal. Domestically, the de-Communization laws, adopted in 2015, mandated the removal of Soviet statues and the change of Communist-linked street and town names. By late August 2016, 987 localities had been renamed, often returning to their pre-Soviet roots. In fact, the removal of Communist-era symbols—especially those associated with Lenin, known as the *Leninopad* (Lenin fall)—had started even earlier, but the new legislation went beyond Lenin. It was divisive, repressive, and raised questions about freedom of speech, but it helped Ukraine to break away from the symbolism and identity that Russia invoked to justify its attack on the country. In Odesa, a massive statue of Lenin was replaced with one of Darth Vader, which quickly became a local landmark. Approval of the OUN and UPA also increased. They were now viewed predominantly as fighters for Ukrainian statehood and against Moscow's rule, but this part of their legacy could not be neatly separated from the OUN's ideology, collaboration with Nazi Germany, and mass violence against civilians. The legacy of Bandera and his followers remained contentious and provided ammunition for Russian propaganda, which equated Ukrainian nationalism with neo-Nazism.[27]

The most successful of all post-2014 reforms was that of local government. Small municipalities were merged to form larger ones, allowing them to benefit from economies of scale, raise more taxes, and provide better public services; these restructured local authorities now also retained 60 percent of all locally raised personal income taxes. Communities were granted more freedom to decide how and on what to spend money and could do so more effectively. The number of local councils in Ukraine dropped from 10,961 to 1,470, while the efficiency and responsiveness of local authorities improved. Trust between citizens and their elected leaders went up, and Ukrainians became more involved in local politics and their communities. In eastern and southern Ukraine, the results of this devolution were especially impressive.[28]

Poroshenko's platform was ambitious, but he failed in his most important task: to either win the war or negotiate a peace. Fighting continued, soldiers kept dying, and the displaced began to lose hope of ever returning home. Ukrainians were tired of war and increasingly willing to compromise. Meanwhile, Poroshenko's identity politics were divisive and too nationalist for many Ukrainians, economic growth was slow, and corruption remained widespread.

Volodymyr Zelensky—a popular actor, comic, and show-business executive—emerged as a surprising alternative to Poroshenko. Zelensky, a Russian-speaking Jew from southern Ukraine who had spent much of his career in Moscow, was an improbable potential president for a country at war. His only qualification for the job was playing the role of a history teacher who suddenly becomes Ukraine's president in the widely popular TV comedy series *Servant of the People*. But he was also young and likable, had name recognition, and could scarcely be further from the macabre image of a Nazi-infested Ukraine that Russian propaganda was eagerly promoting. In fact, his native Russian and time spent in Moscow were seen as potential advantages in reaching a deal with Putin. Besides, after almost thirty years of independence, Ukrainians were so tired of failed professional politicians that a comedian as the country's leader seemed like a breath of fresh air. In the presidential elections in March 2019, Zelensky triumphed, receiving 73 percent of votes versus Poroshenko's 24.5 percent and easily winning every region besides Lviv. In the parliamentary elections held later that year, Zelensky's Servant of the People Party won a majority in the Rada, with 254 of 450 seats. The far right, the Kremlin's favorite bogeyman, won just a single seat.

But even an expert communicator like Zelensky failed to achieve a breakthrough with Putin. The Russian president did not take the young, inexperienced Ukrainian leader seriously and believed he could easily strong-arm him, but Ukraine held firm. The issue was structural, not personal: no politician committed to a truly independent Ukraine could concede to Putin's goal of controlling the country through his Donbas proxies. The peace process outlined in the Minsk agreements reached a dead end.

Zelensky, meanwhile, never an efficient administrator, struggled to govern. His term was overshadowed by scandals and crises. Some—like COVID-19 or US president Donald Trump's request that Ukraine criminally investigate the son of his rival Joe Biden, who was affiliated with a Ukrainian energy company—were not Zelensky's fault. But others were self-inflicted, products of impatience, inexperience, bad choices, arrogance, and, according to critics, autocratic impulses. The economy struggled, and Zelensky's approval rate nose-dived to just 33 percent by early 2022.[29]

Ukraine's preoccupation with internal reforms and domestic politics also meant that the country effectively gave up on trying to return the lost territories in the Donbas and de facto, though not de jure, reconciled itself to the prolonged, possibly even permanent Russian occupation of Crimea. The conflict continued, but the Ukrainian army was neither interested in nor preparing for an offensive. The war in the Donbas also effectively dashed any hopes for NATO membership. NATO would have never admitted a country that had an ongoing territorial conflict with nuclear Russia, and no Ukrainian politician could relinquish the claim to lost lands. Contrary to Russian propaganda, by 2022 Ukraine was neither on the cusp of joining NATO nor preparing an independent offensive. For Kyiv, the status quo was painful, but no viable alternative existed.

Among Zelensky's most controversial actions was the decision in February 2021 to shutter three TV channels owned by oligarch Viktor Medvedchuk. These channels, security services claimed, spread Russian propaganda and undermined the state. Zelensky's critics complained of censorship, but the decision was implemented and no other similar restrictions on the media followed. The channels had been neither very popular nor influential, but their owner was no ordinary oligarch. Medvedchuk was the most prominent of Ukraine's remaining pro-Kremlin politicians. He had also been Leonid Kuchma's powerful head of the presidential administration (an equivalent to the White House chief of staff in the United States) and a close confidant and personal friend of

Putin. According to many reports, Medvedchuk was Putin's principal source of information on Ukraine, and the Russian president was the godfather of Medvedchuk's daughter. The attack on Medvedchuk was, intentionally or not, an insult to Putin. In April 2021, Russian troops began amassing on Ukraine's borders.

CHAPTER 9

TO KILL UKRAINE

In spring 2022, soon after the start of the Russian invasion, I overheard a conversation in the street between Ukrainian women, most likely refugees. "You finally need to understand," one of them explained animatedly in Ukrainian-accented Russian, "Russians want us to return to the Soviet Union and make everything as it was in the USSR." Whereas now, even after more than two years of war, some Western pundits still believe that the invasion was driven by Russian security concerns and fear of NATO expansion, this woman grasped the Kremlin's intentions from the very beginning. In February 2022, the Soviet Union—not its Communist veneer but the Russian imperial-nationalist core—made its latest attempt to rise from the dead. This attempted comeback, like all previous efforts to build or maintain a Russian-led empire, necessitated the subjugation and, if necessary, destruction of Ukraine.

In 2022, the Kremlin—driven by a belief in its historical right to dominate Ukraine—wanted to execute a quick, decisive incursion that would decapitate the Ukrainian government and bring the country back under Moscow's control. This did not happen. Fierce and successful Ukrainian resistance foiled Putin's plans, but in the process, Russia obliterated entire cities, killed and maimed hundreds of thousands, and forced millions to flee. Ukraine survived, but areas that came under Russian occupation turned into sites of massive destruction—physical, political, cultural. An invasion that began as an attempt to subjugate the state of Ukraine quickly morphed into a deliberate campaign to physically destroy Ukrainians as a group and Ukrainian statehood and identity as an idea. Invasion became genocide.

The full-scale invasion was thus a logical, if shocking, continuation of Russia's past policies: the extensive efforts to dominate Ukraine, the annexation of Crimea, and the war in the Donbas. The genocide, however, represented a radical shift in the Kremlin's approach. Despite all the previous violence, before February 2022 Putin did not seek to target Ukrainian civilians as such and emphasized the shared identity and origin of Russians and Ukrainians. The violence of this war also differed from all earlier instances of Russian repression. Even Stalin's Holodomor targeted predominantly (though not exclusively) the ethnically Ukrainian countryside and spared the Russian-speaking cities, in line with the time-tested "divide and repress" strategy. Now, everyone in Ukraine was a potential victim regardless of ethnicity or language. Ukraine was to be destroyed as a state, and Ukrainians as a national group.

Violence—murder, rape, torture, kidnapping, imprisonment—against Ukraine's political and intellectual elites, and eventually anyone suspected of supporting Ukraine's independence, became the key pillar of Russian actions. In addition to targeting people, the Russian state set out to eradicate Ukrainian language, history, culture, and symbols thereof. Instead—just as the Ukrainian lady that I overheard had predicted during the early days of the war—the Kremlin brought back Soviet and Russian flags, books, myths, street names, and monuments. Ukraine was to become, once again, Little Russia.

In September 2020, I received an email from a former student—Victor Muller Ferreira, a Brazilian of German heritage—asking for a recommendation letter. Muller Ferreira was applying for a position at the International Criminal Court, an institution tasked with prosecuting perpetrators of genocide, crimes against humanity, war crimes, and, since 2018, the crime of aggression. Muller Ferreira was a good, intelligent student, so I immediately agreed. The hiring process took a while but eventually he got the job and, in April 2022, arrived in the Netherlands to begin work. He never made it to The Hague.

Muller Ferreira was not Brazilian. His real name was Sergei Cherkasov, and he was an undercover Russian military intelligence officer. Cherkasov was uncovered by the Dutch security services, deported to Brazil, and sentenced to fifteen years in prison. Was the GRU trying to infiltrate the ICC in 2020 because Moscow was already planning a full-scale invasion of Ukraine, or at least strongly considering it?

Why, when, and how Putin decided on the February 2022 invasion continues to be the subject of speculation and debate. The decision was likely born of multiple motivations; foreign policy moves are rarely driven by a single cause. Most likely, Putin decided to invade Ukraine in February–March 2021, though the Kremlin might have started preparing for such an eventuality even earlier. The immediate catalyst seems to be Zelensky's decision to close the TV channels that belonged to Putin's Ukrainian confidant Viktor Medvedchuk. Putin took the move against Medvedchuk as a personal slight, but more crucially, the channels were seen as Russia's last remaining tools to influence Ukrainian public opinion. The peace process that began at Minsk was dead, and little hope remained for a diplomatic solution. A short, victorious military operation would break the impasse, and Putin's security services assured him that Russian soldiers would be greeted by Ukrainians as liberators.[1]

The attack on Medvedchuk might have been the trigger, but the causes of the invasion ran much deeper, and the idea had germinated in Putin's mind for several years at least. Putin had always seen Ukraine as artificial, but long isolation during the COVID-19 pandemic radicalized him and provided an opportunity to articulate these views. The Russian president became obsessed with history and spent hours reading manuscripts about

Russia and Ukraine. It is unclear what exactly he read or how much of it he understood, but the product of his historical inquiries—a July 2021 article entitled "On the Historical Unity of Russians and Ukrainians"—differed little from the arguments of the early twentieth-century Kyiv-based Club of Russian Nationalists or the writings of the Russian nationalists of the 1990s and early 2000s. "Every one of the statements that in Dugin's mouth seemed so radical in 2012 would by 2021 be adopted—often word for word—by Putin himself," observed British journalist Owen Matthews.[2]

It was not just Ukrainian history that bothered Putin but also his own. The president was almost seventy years old and thinking of his legacy and place in history. Ruling Russia for more than twenty years and annexing Crimea were significant achievements indeed, but Putin aimed higher. He looked up to tsars who had transformed and expanded Russia. Bringing Ukraine back under Moscow's control would be an achievement worthy of Russia's greatest leaders. Putin "has three advisors," Russia's foreign minister Sergei Lavrov reportedly admitted, "Ivan the Terrible. Peter the Great. And Catherine the Great."[3]

The COVID-induced isolation also insulated Putin from dissenting views or contradictory information. His residence became an echo chamber. Anyone wishing to meet him in person had to first undergo a fourteen-day quarantine, and few officials were willing or able to do so. According to multiple reports, the only influential person constantly by Putin's side during the pandemic was his friend Yurii Kovalchuk: a deeply mystical oligarch committed to restoring Russia's past greatness. By early 2021, Putin had become ever more obsessive, nationalist, anti-Western, misinformed, and committed to regaining the Kremlin's control over Ukraine.[4]

The year 2021 was also a good time to plan a war. The West appeared weak, divided, and preoccupied with its own problems. The United States was reeling from its disastrous and chaotic retreat from Afghanistan, while the United Kingdom was in constant turmoil after Brexit. In continental Europe, longtime German chancellor Angela Merkel was about to retire, and her successor would have neither the experience nor the clout that Merkel accrued. The West, Putin believed, would be outraged but do little.

In 2014, the annexation of Crimea was met with relatively gentle sanctions, and Putin's assumption was that this time things would be no different.

Preparation for a major attack could not go unnoticed. When, in April 2021, Russia began gathering troops near its border with Ukraine, Kyiv and the West became seriously concerned, but after some time most Russian units departed. Some, however, stayed put, and slowly a new buildup began. By October, the US intelligence community was convinced that Putin had resolved to invade. It was more than just troop movements that convinced Washington; one senior US diplomat was confident that Moscow had given up on negotiations because she had never before heard Russian officials directing such derogatory language toward Ukraine or anyone else.[5]

But Zelensky and his team were skeptical. They had lived through several seemingly threatening Russian military buildups and came to see them as exercises in coercive diplomacy. A major conventional war in Europe in 2022 was simply inconceivable, and the Ukrainian government, until the very last moment, refused to believe that invasion was imminent. This skepticism hampered preparations and likely cost Ukraine dearly on the battlefield.

American, German, French, and British leaders all searched for a diplomatic solution that would prevent war, but Moscow seemed uninterested. The Kremlin's most detailed proposal to defuse the crisis not only envisioned a block on any future NATO enlargement but also required the alliance to effectively pull out of post-1991 member states such as Poland and Bulgaria. This was a clear nonstarter; the Russian plan was built to fail. Putin was determined to fight.[6]

In its pursuit of Ukraine, the Kremlin was driven by concerns of identity, not national security. On January 10, 2022, Russian deputy minister of international affairs Sergei Ryabkov met with his American counterpart, deputy secretary of state Wendy Sherman. Western diplomats had always considered Ryabkov serious, measured, and professional, but in that meeting the Russian stunned everyone by shouting, "We need Ukraine! We will not return home without Ukraine!" On January 21, 2022, in a last-ditch attempt to prevent war, US secretary of state Antony Blinken negotiated with Lavrov. "Sergei, tell me, what it is you're really trying to do?" Blinken asked at the end of their meeting. "Was this all really about the security concerns Russia had raised again and again—about NATO's 'encroachment' toward Russia and a perceived military threat? Or was it about Putin's almost theological belief that Ukraine was and always had been an integral part of Mother Russia?" This was a softball question, but instead of quickly blaming NATO and the United States for the crisis, Lavrov simply got up and left the room without answering. Diplomacy could not achieve a solution to the crisis. It was Ukraine's very existence as an independent state that offended Putin, not this or that specific policy it had pursued.[7]

On February 21, 2022, Putin recognized the independence of the Donetsk and Luhansk People's Republics, and even the most cautious observers became convinced that something significant was afoot. But what exactly? A limited military operation in the Donbas? An invasion to secure a land bridge connecting the DNR to Crimea? An all-out war? Outside a tiny circle of confidants, not even Russian elites knew what Putin was planning.

In Russia, February 23 is Defender of the Fatherland Day. Despite the name, in practice the celebration encompasses all males, even draft dodgers. Families gather, friends go out and drink, men receive gifts, and, in the evening, there are fireworks. The invasion of Ukraine began just hours after the celebration of Russia's defenders ended, in the early hours of February 24. At 2 a.m., Russia issued a warning to all civilian aircraft to leave Ukrainian airspace. At almost 4 a.m., Russian troops—this time in full uniform, unlike in 2014, and adorned with mysterious Z, O, and V markings—crossed the Ukrainian border.[8]

At 4:50 a.m., the Kremlin released a prerecorded address in which Putin announced the beginning of a "special military operation." The Russian president complained about security threats emanating from the West, NATO expansion, and disdain shown to Russia. Yet the core of the problem was not Ukraine's desire to join NATO but the Soviet collapse and Russia's resulting weakness, which had ushered in oppressive Western global hegemony. The West was hypocritical; it lied and had wrought destruction in Iraq, Libya, and Syria. According to Putin, he had tried to negotiate with the West to prevent the bloodshed, but the other side had shown no interest. Instead, in Russia's "own historical territory" of Ukraine, the West was busy establishing an externally controlled "anti-Russia." The Ukrainian government had come to power in a coup, Putin maintained, and had been subjecting the residents of the Donbas to "bullying and genocide" since 2014. The time had come for Moscow to intervene. Ukraine's borders were artificial and had been determined arbitrarily, Putin continued, but Russia had no intention of occupying the country. The president then called on the Ukrainian military to surrender and not to fight for the "neo-Nazi" junta ruling their state. At 5 a.m., Russian missiles struck Ukrainian cities and produced the first civilian casualties of the war.

The Russian army invaded northern Ukraine from Belarus toward Kyiv; from Crimea toward Kherson, Zaporizhzhia, and the Azov Sea coast; and from the Donbas and Russia toward Kharkiv and Mariupol. On February 27, Russian special forces reached Kharkiv, Ukraine's second largest city. Their assaults on the city were beaten back, but they captured large swaths of the Kharkiv region. Kherson, a regional capital in southern Ukraine, fell on March 2, and Mariupol was surrounded.

Prior to the invasion, the Russian army had widely been considered the second best in the world. It was large, well funded, confident, and boasted a vast arsenal of slick, modern weapons. After the short war against Georgia in 2008, Russian armed forces were extensively reformed and modernized. Russian troops then gained valuable combat experience in Syria, fighting on behalf of Bashar al-Assad's regime in that country's bloody civil war, and—despite all the Kremlin's denials—in the Donbas. On paper, Russia enjoyed massive superiority over the much smaller and less equipped Ukrainian armed forces. The Ukrainian security services, especially the upper ranks, were also riddled with Russian spies and paid informants. The US intelligence community and military believed

Russia could take Kyiv within three days, and several prominent American experts counseled against sending weapons to Ukraine because they would make no difference in the coming confrontation.[9]

They were wrong. The Russian army turned out not to be nearly as formidable as most observers presumed, Kyiv did not fall, and the weapons the West sent Ukraine made an enormous difference on the battlefield. Behind the Russian military's shiny facade was a rotten, corrupt, and mismanaged force that suffered from ossified strategic thinking, dysfunctional logistics, inept command, poor morale, and lack of discipline. But they did have many soldiers and vast quantities of weapons.

Despite rapidly conquering territory roughly the size of Greece, after several days of fighting the Russian advance was woefully behind schedule. The Kremlin had planned to complete the conquest of all of Ukraine in a matter of weeks, and neither Putin nor his generals expected meaningful resistance. Russian troops were not at all informed about the upcoming campaign and went into battle unprepared. Many, possibly even most, Russian soldiers expected to be welcomed by the presumably oppressed Russian speakers of Ukraine. Some even carried ceremonial dress uniforms for the planned victory parade in Kyiv.

Instead of surrendering and welcoming the Russian troops, Ukrainians, both soldiers and civilians, overcame their initial shock and fought back. Columns of Russian vehicles were ambushed and destroyed, Ukrainian recruitment offices were inundated with more volunteers than they could process, and farmers arrived with tractors to steal Russian tanks and tow them across to the Ukrainian side. In an iconic encounter from the first day of the invasion, the flagship of the Russian Black Sea Fleet, the cruiser *Moskva*, ordered the tiny garrison of Ukraine's Snake Island to surrender, only to be told, "Russian warship, go fuck yourself." This exchange quickly became a potent symbol of Ukrainian defiance, but similar confrontations were taking place wherever the Russians went.

When Russian troops entered a settlement, they were typically met with hostility and protest. Cities where locals would likely have welcomed Russia in 2014, when it annexed Crimea, became sites of dogged resistance in 2022. In some towns, unarmed civilians gathered to block Russian columns with their bodies, confront the heavily armed soldiers, and shout at them to return home to Russia. When, due to Russian repression and violence, open protest became impossible, Ukrainians adopted more subtle forms of resistance, often as simple as graffiti of the letter Ї, which features in the Ukrainian alphabet but not in Russian.

Kyiv was the linchpin of the entire campaign. Russian strategy hinged on quickly capturing the Ukrainian capital, decapitating Ukrainian leadership, and installing a puppet government, likely headed by Yanukovych or Medvedchuk. This plan, if successful, also would not have required prolonged occupation of Ukrainian territory, as Putin had promised on February 24; Ukraine would simply be turned into a compliant Russian protectorate. Elites committed to the preservation of Ukraine were to be physically eliminated. Russian military units were accompanied by security services teams that had specially prepared "kill lists" of local leaders, political activists, teachers, journalists, priests, and state officials, among others. Ukrainian army veterans, especially those who had fought in the Donbas, were also high-priority targets.[10]

The Russian military was much weaker than expected, but it was still a formidable force, and Ukraine's successful defense of the capital was far from assured. Russia's plan to quickly deploy elite airborne units to Kyiv depended on the capture of the crucial airport at Hostomel, just northwest of the city, but following dogged resistance by Ukrainian troops, the runway was rendered unusable. Zelensky's personal bravery and decision to remain in Kyiv despite the danger—he and his family were at the top of Russia's kill list—raised Ukrainian morale. Successful resistance galvanized Ukraine's supporters in the West. Weapons began arriving, and Russia was hit with heavy economic sanctions.

After its initial attack faltered, the Russian army attempted to encircle Kyiv, an effort that required conquest and occupation of the city's suburbs. This plan also failed, and on March 22, Ukraine launched a counteroffensive. By April 1, Russian forces had retreated from northern Ukraine in what Putin claimed was a "gesture of goodwill." The news from liberated towns and villages near Kyiv shocked the world: almost every settlement bore evidence of plunder, sexual violence, and mass murder committed by Russian soldiers.

When Russians realized Ukrainians were not, in fact, oppressed and had no desire to be "liberated," they were equal parts dumbfounded and outraged. Both elites and ordinary people in Russia had overlooked the changes that had taken place in Ukraine since 2014, ignored the deep resentment that Russia's actions in 2014 had unleashed, and were stuck in a pre-Euromaidan perception of Ukraine as a divided country in which the east and the south sympathized with Russia and geography determined allegiances. The conviction that the Revolution of Dignity was an externally imposed coup poisoned Russian judgment and prevented a realistic assessment of the Ukraine of 2022 and the population's will to resist.

There were Ukrainians who welcomed Russia and collaborated with the invading forces. Some did so out of ideological convictions, others because the new regime offered opportunities for career advancement or because they expected that Russian rule was there to stay so adjustment to new realities was prudent. Such collaborators exist in every conflict, but their number was relatively small, and most of Ukraine's population had little interest in the "unity of the Russian and Ukrainian peoples." Ukraine was a separate, sovereign state, and, by 2022, most Ukrainians were willing to support it. For the first time in its history, Ukraine's population went to war free of deep internal divisions. Differences in language, ethnicity, class, and regional identity did not disappear and still had political impact, but they took a back seat to allegiance to Ukraine's independence. This challenged the Kremlin's belief in Russia's natural right to rule Ukraine and threatened Russian elites' foundational worldview. On the ground, it disoriented Russian troops and heralded their deaths.

The Russian response to Ukrainian rejection was apoplectic. "What should Russia do to Ukraine?" asked an article published by the state-owned news agency RIA Novosti on April 3, just two days after Russian troops fully withdrew from the Kyiv area, portending a change in Moscow's policy. The piece outlined a plan to destroy Ukraine as a nation and Ukrainians as a national group. After a Russian victory, it argued, Ukraine would be "impossible as a nation state," and its very name "likely cannot be retained." Kyiv's elite "need to be liquidated, [their] reeducation is impossible." But a "substantial part of the populace" is "also guilty" and would require "reeducation" and "ideological repressions" lasting "at least a generation," which would "inevitably mean de-Ukrainization." The Russian invasion was morphing from a neo-imperial quest for dominance into a genocide: violence carried out with the intent to destroy Ukrainians as a national group.[11]

In a matter of days, similar and ever more violent and radical views began permeating the Russian media—almost all of which is tightly controlled by the Kremlin. In 2014, calls for extreme, large-scale violence against Ukrainians were mostly confined to Russian nationalist and radical circles. They represented the views of the hawkish parts of the Russian political and security elite who enjoyed influence and ready access to the media, but their beliefs were not mainstream. In 2022, genocidal rhetoric took over newspapers, radio, state-owned TV channels, and prime-time talk shows.

The barrage of anti-Ukrainian propaganda was unrelenting and became more violent by the day. Russians were told that the Ukrainian language does not exist, that Ukrainians are not a real nation, and that Ukraine is a fake state that will soon be no more. Vladimir Solovyov, Russia's chief propagandist, promised the viewers of his prime-time TV talk show that "Zelensky is Ukraine's last president because there won't be any Ukraine after that." Ukrainians, it was claimed, are Russians who had forgotten their true language, identity, and history, and Russian troops were therefore duty bound to reintegrate Ukrainians into the Russian World. Those who resisted Russia were simply Nazis of "bestial nature" or insects that should be physically destroyed or sterilized.[12]

In one particularly violent segment, Anton Krasovsky, director of broadcasting at the state-owned channel RT, which targets foreign audiences, declared that Ukraine should be erased from the map, joked about the rape of old Ukrainian women by Russian soldiers, and suggested drowning or burning Ukrainian children who opposed Russia. Following a public outcry, RT suspended Krasovsky, even though his calls for violence were only slightly more extreme than most other rhetoric in state media that went unpunished.[13]

Russian politicians, church officials, and diplomats also joined the chorus. "Wanted to distance yourselves from all things Russian? That's what you get!" wrote Sergei Mironov, leader of the Just Russia Party and former Speaker of the Russian parliament's upper house. Ambassador Mikhail Ulyanov, the Russian representative in Vienna, urged "no mercy for the Ukrainian population!" The Russian Ministry of Defense distributed a pamphlet to soldiers fighting in Ukraine that pledged: "We won't forgive anyone."[14]

Yet the most radical of them all turned out to be former president Dmitry Medvedev, who at the time of the invasion served as the deputy chairman of Russia's Security Council. Despite—or possibly because of—his previous reputation as a relative liberal, Medvedev reinvented himself as a genocidal ultra-hawk. In early April 2022, he was the first prominent government official to claim that Ukrainian ethnicity was fake and should be destroyed by force. "I hate them. . . . And while I'm still alive, I will do everything to make them disappear," he promised on June 7, 2022. Over time, Medvedev's writing became even more violent, mixing ethnic slurs with threats of nuclear annihilation. On August 19, 2023, Medvedev insisted that Russia should not stop fighting until the Ukrainian state is completely "wiped off the face of the earth," even if it takes decades.[15]

Because of Zelensky's Jewish origins, Russian anti-Ukrainian rhetoric also became suffused with anti-Jewish dog whistles and stereotypes, which on multiple occasions crossed the line into explicit anti-Semitism. As in the early twentieth century, the Ukrainian and Jewish questions became intertwined in Russian nationalist thinking, because each, in its own way, interfered with the dream of making Ukraine totally and exclusively Russian.

The Kremlin and its mouthpieces were not alone in cheering for war and genocide. Many Russians, most likely a sizable majority, support the invasion or at least do not object to it. There were some initial protests, but they were quickly suppressed by the government, which also introduced increasingly draconian punishments for anyone publicly opposing the war. Denunciations, widespread during Soviet times and especially under Stalin, have returned to Russian life with gusto; those who oppose the official party line find themselves turned in by colleagues, neighbors, teachers, priests, and even family members.[16]

Hundreds of thousands of Russians, possibly more than a million, left the country in the wake of the invasion, reducing the size of any potential opposition. But among those who remained, genocidal rhetoric directed against a fraternal people failed to spark protests. This was partly because of repression but also because many propaganda narratives tapped into already widespread imperial nostalgia and xenophobia. Even among the internet-savvy younger generation that has been exposed to the West and does not imbibe state-controlled TV as heavily as their parents or grandparents, the Kremlin's prewar investment in nationalist and paramilitary education led many to support the violence.[17]

Enthusiastic jingoists are in the minority, however. Most people simply want to be left alone and do their best to pretend that nothing important is happening. Russians—who for more than two decades have been encouraged by the Kremlin to stay out of politics—get on with their lives, especially if those lives are not directly affected by the war. Even among those who do not support the war, many believe they do not have the power to change anything and that it is therefore better not to try. Whatever the reason for their acquiescence or support for the invasion, war and genocide have become a joint enterprise of the Kremlin and Russian society. The war is Russia's war and the genocide is Russia's genocide, not just Putin's.[18]

Having failed to achieve a quick victory, Russia turned its attention to the parts of the Donbas that were still under Ukrainian control. As losses mounted, the Kremlin also became increasingly reliant on the Wagner Group. The company embarked on a recruiting spree in Russia's prisons, promising convicts amnesty if they fought and survived. To beef up manpower reserves, Putin declared a partial remobilization on September 21,

2022, which placed thousands of poorly trained Russians under arms and triggered a new wave of emigration, as military-age men rushed to escape possible enlistment. Massive call-ups of reserves also meant that many more Russians now had family members or acquaintances fighting in Ukraine. Even among those who had been politically disengaged before the war, hatred of Ukraine and prejudice against Ukrainians—already a widespread phenomenon—thus became more natural. The spouse of a mobilized Russian man who tried and failed to prevent her husband from going to war described how their five-year-old daughter now asks God every night to give her father a good grenade launcher. The mood in more actively prowar families is even more bellicose and anti-Ukrainian.[19]

In late September 2022, the Kremlin decided that if it couldn't control the whole of Ukraine, it would at least take what it could. Moscow announced referenda on formally joining Russia in the LNR, DNR, and the parts of the Kherson and Zaporizhzhia regions that were under Russian control. The annexation drive allowed Putin and the Russian elite to stop pretending that the invasion had nothing to do with territorial expansion. Russia, the argument went, was rectifying past injustices and simply reclaiming what had historically belonged to it. Putin, ever the historian, invoked Peter the Great to justify the land grab: "During the war with Sweden, Peter the Great did not take anything from Sweden, he took back what was ours, even though all of Europe recognized it as Sweden. . . . Looks like now it is our turn to get our lands back," the Russian president stated.[20]

The referenda were a sham, producing predictable, made-up results in favor of joining Russia. On September 30, Putin announced the annexation of the four regions even though Russia did not fully control them. In Zaporizhzhia in particular, only a small part of the region's territory was under Russian occupation. But for the more radical members of the Russian elite, the annexation was still just the first step toward completely destroying Ukraine. Medvedev chimed in to predict that Kyiv's Maidan would soon be renamed Russia Square and even posted an image of the square with the Russian flag photoshopped atop its buildings. On August 15, 2023, he responded to the proposal that Ukraine cede some of its territories to Russia in exchange for NATO membership by stating that Russia claims all of Ukraine besides Galicia. Vladimir Solovyov began talking on his prime-time TV show about the "primordially Russian" town of Chop, Ukraine's westernmost settlement on the border with Hungary and Slovakia.

While Russia was busy annexing lands it did not control and turning convicts into cannon fodder, Ukraine was preparing to retake the territories it had lost. The Ukrainian counteroffensive to free Kherson started on August 29, 2022, and the city—the only regional capital that Russia captured in 2022—was liberated on November 11. Another counteroffensive was launched on September 6 and liberated most of the Kharkiv region and parts of the Donbas. In summer 2023, Ukraine launched a large-scale operation that aimed at retaking all remaining Russian-occupied territories, including Crimea, but it achieved little. At time of writing, large parts of eastern and southern Ukraine and Crimea remain under Russian control.

As the front line stabilized, Russian violence became more systematic, better organized, and fully focused on destroying the Ukrainian national identity. Ukrainian POWs and civilians trying to flee the war were put in what the Russians called "filtration camps." There, detainees were subjected to constant interrogations and violence, sometimes for months on end, as Russian security services tried to uncover or concoct their connections to the Right Sector or former Ukrainian volunteer battalions. Those who passed the filtration could move on. Civilians continued their journey into Russia proper. From there, many moved to the EU, which opened its borders to Ukrainian refugees. Those who stayed in Russia were promised welfare payments, jobs, and housing but often ended up in remote regions and received nothing. Some became so desperate that they returned to occupied Ukraine, even to places that had been devastated by the fighting. Those who did not pass filtration disappeared into a hastily created network of more than one hundred Russian prisons and detention centers, many of them secret. Many Ukrainians were also detained outside the filtration camps. A common practice was arresting civilians for "opposing the Special Military Operation," the Russian official label for the invasion, even though such an offense does not exist in Russia's Criminal Code.[21]

In Russian detention centers—which one former prisoner likened to medieval dungeons—torture, both physical and psychological, and sexual violence were widespread. Among released prisoners interviewed by UN investigators, over 90 percent reported experiencing torture or ill-treatment. In one illustrative case, interrogators attached wires to the nipples of a female detainee from southern Ukraine and administered electric shocks. When the woman was eventually released, she returned to her home to find it looted. After the liberation of Kherson in southern Ukraine, Ukrainian authorities even discovered a special torture chamber for children. In the Zaporizhzhia region, Ukrainian detainees were forced to don Russian military uniforms and dig trenches, thus making them potential targets for Ukrainian forces. Some prisoners were summarily executed, and the fates of many others remain unknown.[22]

During the interrogations, Ukrainians were grilled about their political views and their support for Ukraine and its military, and were pressed for information on neo-Nazis, the Ukrainian radical right, and war crimes committed by Ukrainian forces, regardless of whether they were even in a position to know about such things. A former prisoner interviewed by UN investigators suffered two days of beatings after refusing to declare their support for Russia. Yet another "was forced to stand naked and shout 'glory to Russia' while being beaten, and described beatings as a 'punishment for speaking Ukrainian' and 'not remembering the lyrics of the anthem of the Russian Federation.'"[23]

The primary targets of detention and forced disappearances were Ukrainian political activists, veterans, those on kill lists who had survived or slipped through the cracks of the initial round of post-occupation repression, and anyone else who supported an independent Ukraine. Their relatives, regardless of their occupation or politics, were also often victimized. Even possessing Ukrainian state symbols or "patriotic tattoos" was sufficient cause for arrest. "You know why you are here. Because of your pro-Ukrainian views, you are already in big trouble," a Russian interrogator told a detainee in Kherson. Mayors and local leaders—who after the decentralization reforms had become the embodiment of Ukrainian statehood at the local level—were especially important targets for Russian security services as they tried to destroy the Ukrainian nation.[24]

Ivan Fedorov, mayor of Melitopol, a town of about 150,000 in southern Ukraine, was arrested on March 11, 2022, even before the invasion had turned fully genocidal. I met Fedorov less than two months after his release. Tall and athletic, he wore an olive-colored T-shirt and khaki pants, the unofficial wartime uniform of Ukrainian government personnel, and was glued to a cell phone, constantly speaking or messaging. His ordeal in captivity had made Fedorov famous, and people took selfies with him. When I later interviewed Fedorov, he admitted he had not believed that Russia would invade. Neither the military authorities nor the central government had reckoned that war might be on the horizon, and Melitopol, a strategically important transportation hub, had been unprepared.

When Melitopol was occupied and local citizens began peacefully protesting against Russian rule, FSB officials showed up at Fedorov's office and demanded he stop the demonstrations. Products of Putin's system, these FSB officers were, according to Fedorov, "really zombified" and simply could not believe that protests could be organized without the involvement of city hall. Shortly after that, Fedorov was arrested, blindfolded, and brought to a makeshift FSB prison. There, Russian authorities pressed him to sign a resignation letter and transfer authority to their handpicked collaborator. Fedorov was placed into a cell and, his hands still tied, spent twenty-eight hours alone. "This was the scariest thing," he recalled, "not [to] have any information about what is going on and realize that any moment anyone at this place can shoot you and, at thirty-three, your life is over." After five days, Fedorov was released in a prisoner swap.

Other local leaders were not so lucky. Viktor Marunyak, the head of a village in southern Ukraine, was arrested as well but, unlike Fedorov, was also tortured. When he was finally released from Russian captivity, he had nine broken ribs. Russian authorities could not capture Oleh Buryak, the head of the Zaporizhzhia district administration, so instead they imprisoned his sixteen-year-old son Vladyslav, who spent ninety days in captivity simply because of the family connection.[25]

How widespread these forced detentions and disappearances have been is unknown. The extremely cautious UN Office of the High Commissioner for Human Rights (OHCHR) identified close to a thousand such cases in the period between the launch of Russia's full-scale invasion and May 23, 2023. Given that Russian authorities do not allow the OHCHR access to facilities in which Ukrainian civilians are detained, the real number is certainly much higher.[26]

Russian invasion forces have abducted, tortured, raped, and murdered civilians—a topic that will be discussed in depth in the next chapter—but violence against human beings is just a single component of a broader campaign to destroy Ukraine. Another part of this strategy is to target the country's national identity, language, and culture and the very idea of Ukrainian statehood.

From the early stages of the invasion, Russia has been deliberately targeting cultural monuments, schools, universities, libraries, museums, and landmarks associated with Ukraine's statehood and identity. These attacks have no military purpose and do not contribute to winning on the battlefield but make perfect sense in the broader context of Russia's war goals. During the brief but bloody occupation of Borodyanka near Kyiv, Russian troops shot a monument to Taras Shevchenko, Ukraine's national bard. The poet's bust, peppered with bullet holes, quickly became one of the war's most iconic images and the symbol of the Russian assault on Ukrainian identity. This incident may have been an individual act of vandalism, but other attacks show signs of a systematic plan. On May 6, 2022, a Russian artillery strike destroyed the home and museum of eighteenth-century Ukrainian philosopher and poet Hryhorii Skovoroda in a village near Kharkiv. The museum was situated far from any military installations, railroads, or depots. This could not have been a shell gone astray; the museum itself was the target.[27]

According to data collected by Ukraine's Ministry of Culture, since the beginning of the full-scale invasion, Russian forces have destroyed almost six hundred libraries and eighty-four museums and art galleries. Not all cultural destruction was deliberate, and not every destroyed cultural institution was attacked because of its Ukrainian identity. Yet most of the carnage clearly was an attempt to erase Ukrainian nationhood. Libraries and books were targeted with a special zeal eerily reminiscent of the late-nineteenth-century Romanov empire and the Russian occupation of Galicia during World War I. In the town of Izyum in the Kharkiv region, all Ukrainian textbooks were destroyed. In nearby Kupyansk, Russian occupation authorities destroyed all books published in independent Ukraine, even fairy tales, and brought in Russian books instead. In other parts of Ukraine, Russian authorities burned school libraries and destroyed Ukrainian history textbooks. Publications discussing Euromaidan or the war in the Donbas were targeted with a special zeal. Books on Hetman Mazepa, Petliura, the OUN, the UPA, and anti-Soviet dissidents Vasyl Stus and Viacheslav Chornovil were also confiscated.[28]

The Russians didn't just destroy culture and history; they also stole it. According to multiple reports, the Russian state archival agency, Rosarkhiv, has been busy transferring documents and archival collections, especially those related to Soviet security services, from occupied Ukraine to Moscow. About thirty museums were also stripped of precious art and historical artifacts in what UN experts describe as "the hidden part of the cultural destruction of Ukraine." At the Kherson Regional Art Museum alone, Russian authorities looted over eleven thousand items, including precious fourth-century BC Scythian gold jewelry. Over two thousand pieces of art, including the works of celebrated artists Arkhip Kuindzhi and Ivan Aivazovsky—both natives of southern Ukraine—were plundered from Mariupol museums. And if art was not enough, in one especially bizarre episode Russians stole llamas, a donkey, and several raccoons from the Kherson Zoo and moved them to Crimea.[29]

Mariupol, a city destroyed by Russian forces in a brutal siege, is the clearest example of how Russia envisions its new rule. Mariupol is now on Moscow time, signs use Russian spelling only, and street names have returned to the old Soviet ones, with the city's central avenue predictably named after Lenin. In the few schools that are still open, instruction is in Russian and follows the Russian curriculum. Russian political parties and patriotic movements have opened branches in Mariupol, while the city's Holodomor monument has been dismantled and murals memorializing Russian and DNR attacks on Mariupol have been painted over. Administrators, teachers, police officers, construction workers, and doctors have arrived from Russia to replace the Ukrainians who fled or were killed. Russian authorities try to lure people from Russia to the occupied territories with promises of jobs and higher pay, and ordinary Russians are buying up apartments in Mariupol to fulfill the old Soviet dream of summering by the seaside in southern Ukraine. About forty thousand Russian citizens have moved to Mariupol alone, and similar movement of Russians into Ukraine is observable across all occupied areas.[30]

The Sovietization and Russification of Mariupol might be extreme, but it is not unique. Throughout all occupied Ukrainian territories, Russian authorities change street names, put up monuments with Soviet flags and red stars, change curricula, and dismantle symbols of Ukrainian identity and statehood. In Melitopol, Hrushevsky Street was renamed after Karl Marx, and Hetman Street after Lenin. Gone are Greek and Jewish Streets and, obviously, Ukrainian Street, which became "Soviet." Independence Street is now named after Alexander Zakharchenko, a former head of the DNR, and there is even a street named after Dariia Dugina, far-right activist and daughter of Alexander Dugin who died in a mysterious car bombing on August 20, 2022.[31]

Russian authorities have sought to make the occupation permanent by "forced passportization," making residents in the occupied areas become Russian citizens whether they want to or not. Those who refuse and cling to their Ukrainian passports might lose property rights, access to welfare benefits, and medical care and potentially face deportation. Those who become Russian citizens not only sever their links to Ukraine, which does not recognize dual citizenship, but also risk being drafted and sent to the front line.[32]

In Russia proper, the government has embarked on a campaign to erase any evidence of Ukraine's identity, history, and very existence.

Prosveshchenie (Enlightenment), one of Russia's major textbook publishers, was instructed by the government to remove references to Ukraine and Kyiv from its publications. In the new textbooks, Prince Volodymyr is said to have baptized "the capital" rather than Kyiv, and other publishers went even further by removing "Kyivan" from the name of the Kyivan Rus', which is now simply "ancient Rus'." Among Russians, "Country-404," a reference to the internet's "page not found" error code, has become a popular way to describe Ukraine. For ethnic Ukrainians living in Russia, self-identifying as Ukrainian is simply no longer safe.[33]

This attack on Ukrainian identity has moved beyond the past and the present and seeks to destroy the country's future. Throughout occupied Ukraine, Russian authorities engage in a massive, coordinated effort to deport to Russia and forcibly Russify children, without whom the Ukrainian nation cannot go on. According to Maria Lvova-Belova, Russia's commissioner for children's rights, more than seven hundred thousand minors have been transferred from Ukraine to Russia. Some came as refugees together with their families, but many—as many as half a million, according to some estimates—are in Russia against their will, placed in reeducation facilities or adopted by Russians even if they have families in Ukraine. Forcible transfer of children is explicitly prohibited under the Geneva Conventions and—if done with the intent to destroy a national group, which is clearly the case in Ukraine—constitutes an act of genocide.[34]

The campaign to make Russians out of Ukrainian children is extensive and coordinated by Lvova-Belova with the active support and direct involvement of Putin himself. Abduction of Ukrainian children follows several patterns. Since the beginning of the war, Russian authorities have been removing unaccompanied children from orphanages and hospitals in Ukraine and putting them up for adoption by Russian families, to be raised as Russians. The government has even created a streamlined adoption procedure for such cases, and adopting families receive special financial benefits. Some of these Ukrainian children are orphans without relatives, but others simply became separated from their families amid the fighting or when their parents were detained by Russian security services. The policy is so widespread and well-known that, in the occupied regions of Ukraine, teachers and medical staff began hiding orphans from the Russian authorities out of fear of abduction.[35]

The Mezhevyi family of Mariupol became victims of this adoption campaign. The thirty-nine-year-old Yevhen Mezhevyi, a single father of three, was detained by the Russian military when soldiers discovered he was a Ukrainian army veteran. Mezhevyi spent almost two months in a prison camp, while his children were transferred to a facility near Moscow. Soon after release, Yevhen received a panicked call from his twelve-year-old son: "Dad, you have five days to come and pick us up, or we will be adopted!'" Mezhevyi rushed to retrieve his children and left Russia quickly after.

Sixteen-year-old Liza Galkina from Kherson lived in a dorm at her culinary college. First, Russian authorities took Liza and other students to Crimea without even notifying their parents. Then, she was moved to a different place and offered Russian citizenship. She refused. After eight months, Russian authorities proclaimed Liza an orphan, even though her mother was alive. Eventually Liza returned home, but many other Ukrainians were not so lucky.[36]

Another policy was to put children, with or without parental consent, in reeducation camps inside Russia and refuse to allow them to return home. Researchers have already identified dozens of facilities in which Ukrainian children were forced to become Russians. In these camps, Ukrainian children are subjected to Russian patriotic education and forced to listen to presentations from military officials about Russian successes in Ukraine, make trench candles, and provide emotional support to wounded Russian soldiers. Resistance to these indoctrination efforts is met with violence. Commissioner Lvova-Belova has spoken proudly about Ukrainian kids who eventually became indistinguishable from Russians, or children from Mariupol who initially defiantly sang the Ukrainian anthem but in the end were forced to love Russia.

Lvova-Belova was silent about how exactly Mariupol kids were imbued with such Russian patriotism, but children who returned to Ukraine were more forthcoming. A group of teenagers from Kherson was sent to the *Mechta* (Dream) summer camp in Crimea—originally for ten days, but they spent six months there. The children and their parents were told by camp administrators that they would be adopted and become "children of Russia," and those who had pro-Ukrainian views were locked in the basement, abused, and beaten with a metal rod.[37]

The Russian government never hid its goal to Russify Ukraine's next generation and thus ultimately change the country's identity. The chairman of the Russian parliament's defense committee declared on national TV that Ukrainian children ought to be moved to Russian military boarding schools for reeducation. Lvova-Belova openly discussed with Putin her plan to keep Ukrainian children in Russia permanently. In the occupied areas of Ukraine, parents are being threatened with the abduction of their children if they refuse to send them to Russian schools. If Putin and Lvova-Belova have their way, Ukrainian children will become Russian and Ukrainians will then disappear as a national group, at least in territory occupied by Russia.

Because the Kremlin is so deeply and openly involved with these policies, forcible transfer of children has also become the best chance to hold Putin accountable for his actions. On March 17, 2023, the ICC issued arrest warrants against Lvova-Belova and Putin for war crimes related to the unlawful transfer of children from Ukraine to the Russian Federation.

The Russian invasion was driven by a desire to subjugate Ukraine but quickly transformed into a sustained and deliberate effort to destroy the country outright. In this genocidal campaign, violence against Ukrainian elites, institutions, culture, and identity became Kremlin policy. Yet the mass murder of Ukrainians started even before genocide became Russia's objective, and the two campaigns—state-led genocide and uncoordinated mass murder—went hand in hand. Russian soldiers killed tens of thousands of Ukrainian civilians even before they were directly ordered to do so by their government. Two Ukrainian towns emerged as symbols of this campaign of Russian violence: Bucha and Mariupol.

CHAPTER 10

RUSSIAN ROULETTE

When Russian forces invaded Ukraine on February 24, 2022, children's writer Volodymyr Vakulenko decided to remain in Kapytolivka, his home village in the Kharkiv region. The area was soon occupied by Russian troops, and on March 23 Russian authorities detained Vakulenko. He was interrogated and beaten but released after several hours. The next day, Russian soldiers returned, shoved Vakulenko into a car marked with a Z, the symbol of the invasion, and drove away. This was the last time the writer was seen alive. When Ukrainian troops liberated Kapytolivka, another writer, Victoria Amelina, found Vakulenko's diary, which he had buried before being murdered.

Amelina, a native of Lviv, was long fascinated by how the past and memories of violence—so vivid in our shared hometown—transform identity, language, and emotion. In the wake of Russia's invasion, she became a war crimes researcher, traversing Ukraine's south and east to document violence and destruction. And she kept writing. "Sirens," a poem Amelina wrote in 2022, captured the experience of millions of Ukrainians targeted by indiscriminate bombing and missile strikes:

Air-raid sirens across the country
It feels like everyone is brought out
For execution
But only one person gets targeted
Usually the one at the edge
This time not you; all clear

On June 27, 2023, it was her. A Russian missile struck the Ria Lounge, a popular restaurant in Kramatorsk in the Donbas where Amelina was dining with a group of Latin American journalists and writers. Amelina was critically wounded and died on July 1, one of many Ukrainian civilians killed by the Russian state.[1]

The killings of Amelina and Vakulenko exemplify two different modes of Russian violence: murder from a distance, by the indiscriminate use of artillery or missile strikes against nonmilitary targets, and point-blank executions, which started even before the Russian invasion turned genocidal. In addition to trying to destroy the Ukrainian state, national identity, institutions, and culture, Russian soldiers killed, assaulted, tortured, and raped tens of thousands of Ukrainians, even when not directly ordered to do so by the Kremlin. This violence, in addition to being morally shocking, flies in the face of the Russian official narrative that stresses the historical unity, joint origin, and shared identity of Russians and Ukrainians. This chapter unpacks the logic of Russian mass violence against civilians—Amelina, Vakulenko, and thousands of other Ukrainians. Deliberate targeting of civilians and indifference to noncombatant casualties is deeply rooted in the Russian and Soviet way of war fighting, from Afghanistan to Chechnya to Syria. In Ukraine, however, the murder of civilians was also a punishment for Ukrainians' stubborn resistance, successful defense, repudiation of Putin's vision of "historical unity," and refusal to join the Russian World. At its core, mass murder was revenge for rejection.

Russia's invasion is the largest conventional war in Europe since World War II, and violence against Ukrainian civilians is the defining feature of the conflict. Violence—murder, disappearances, torture, rape, and looting—was integral to Russia's wars in Chechnya (1994–1996, 1999–2009). Indiscriminate targeting of civilians has also become Russian doctrine in Syria, where Moscow supports Bashar al-Assad's regime. At the same time, even though the annexation of Crimea and the war in the Donbas in 2014–2022 also featured violence against civilians, it was significantly less widespread than what Ukraine has experienced since February 2022. Neither Putin's emphasis on the "historical unity" of Russians and Ukrainians nor Russia's insistence that it was saving oppressed members of the Russian World augured mass murder—least of all in eastern and southern Ukraine, where the Russian language was common and many people had voted for Yanukovych. Yet violence, theft, and destruction of property were exactly what Ukrainians experienced when "liberated" by Russia.

Looting began immediately when Russian troops entered a Ukrainian settlement. Stores were emptied and homes ransacked. Everything could be pilfered: jewelry, money, TVs and laptops, cell phones and video games, clothes, even cat food. Bathtubs, kitchen sinks, washing machines, and toilets were in especially high demand and quickly became symbols of Russian pillaging. Some devices could be remotely tracked, and Ukrainian owners would occasionally trace their property to locations deep inside Russia.

This plunder might have been surprising because, prior to the war, Russia enjoyed a much higher per capita GDP than Ukraine: $12,194 versus $4,835. But while richer overall, Russia also had extreme levels of economic inequality. The Russian soldiers who invaded Ukraine came predominantly from poor regions and backgrounds. A military salary, a mere pittance by the standards of Russia's big cities, was respectable elsewhere in the country. Even a modest Ukrainian home was therefore typically richer than the soldiers' own. Looting was also a long-standing practice of the imperial Russian and Soviet militaries. It was considered socially acceptable and rarely prevented, let alone punished, by commanders. The war was an opportunity to make some extra rubles, including through its spoils.

Looting was often accompanied by drinking. Alcohol, weapons, lack of discipline, and a sense of impunity were a deadly mix that cost many Ukrainian civilians their lives. Eyewitness and survivor testimonies are full of stories of Ukrainians of all ages and sexes being murdered by drunken Russian servicemen. A resident of Bohdanivka, a village near Kyiv, described one such encounter: "A machine gun in one hand, a bottle in the other. He'd shoot, then take a swig. And he'd dress for it—he already had someone's red sneakers on." The few Russian servicemen who dared to share their experiences with journalists also confirmed the frequency of wanton, vodka-fueled violence.[2]

In many places, when Russian troops withdrew and residents returned, they found their homes mined and their cars, apartment doors, refrigerators, and cupboards rigged with explosives (usually hand grenades), which the Russians had deliberately left to kill and maim civilians. According to some accounts, retreating Russian soldiers also booby-trapped toys and children's books. Another scheme was to mine a closet and place a live animal—such as the family's cat—inside. When the owners returned and heard the animal crying to be let out, the instinctive reaction was to immediately open the door, leading to an explosion.[3]

Looting, booby-trapping, and destruction of property were just the beginning. Soon, Russian troops began employing large-scale and deadly violence. The mass murder came in two forms. The first was at close range, requiring direct contact between the victims and perpetrators. Russian soldiers knew precisely what they were doing and saw the results of the killing, rape, or torture they committed. The second was murder from a distance by shelling, missiles, and air strikes against civilian targets.

Bucha, a suburb of Kyiv, which before the invasion was home to thirty thousand Ukrainians, became the unfortunate symbol of this first kind of violence. Russian troops, most of them from the country's easternmost regions bordering China and Mongolia, briefly occupied Bucha in late February, were pushed back, and returned on March 3, 2022. A local official I spoke with recalled that Russian soldiers had expected to find throngs of far-right nationalists from western Ukraine oppressing the Russian-speaking population. When they encountered neither neo-Nazis nor a welcome ceremony, they grew confused, irritated, and increasingly violent.[4]

Russian rule in Bucha, which lasted less than a month, was a round-the-clock spree of terror and murder. On March 4, Russian troops killed three volunteers delivering food to an animal shelter. The next day, a Russian machine gunner opened fire on cars full of Ukrainians trying to escape the town; two young children and their mother died on the spot. Russian soldiers moved from house to house, taking residents away and executing them either out on the street or at their unit's makeshift headquarters. A group of Ukrainian volunteers who had previously served in the local Territorial Defense unit were rounded up, taken to the Russian headquarters, beaten, and summarily executed. Only a single person survived, by playing dead.[5]

In Bucha, leaving the house to smoke a cigarette, walk a dog, or buy food was potentially fatal, and even pro-Russian views could not offer protection. The bodies of the murdered civilians lay on the streets because it was too dangerous to hold funerals. In an intercepted phone call, a Russian soldier in Bucha told his mother that he and his comrades simply shot everyone, regardless of sex or age. Another bragged to his wife about how many civilians he had killed and admitted that he was going crazy from all the violence he was committing. Several victims were beheaded, their bodies dismembered and mutilated. Retreating Russian troops also rigged many unburied bodies with mines and grenades, turning later burials into an exceptionally long, agonizing, and potentially deadly process. The number of civilians killed was so large that the town ran out of body bags. Besides murder and disappearances, ordeals such as beatings, rape, and torture became so commonplace that locals, journalists, and even hardened human rights investigators came to describe Bucha as "hell." It is still unclear how many people were killed in the town. The local memorial, unveiled in July 2023, lists 501 names, but it remains incomplete and new bodies are still being found more than a year after liberation.[6]

In August 2022, Daniil Frolkin—a Russian soldier from the Sixty-Fourth Motor Rifle Brigade, which occupied parts of Bucha and the surrounding villages—confessed to the investigative journalist Ekaterina Fomina that he and his comrades had looted and murdered in a village close to Bucha. Frolkin admitted to executing a Ukrainian civilian himself. Russian authorities reacted swiftly. An investigation was opened, and in December 2022 Frolkin was put on trial. The charge: neither murder nor war crimes but spreading "fake news" about the Russian military. He was convicted and received a suspended sentence of five and a half years.[7]

Russian violence in Bucha drew global attention because it was brutal, and because the town was quickly liberated. Proximity to Kyiv made reaching Bucha easy for journalists, Ukrainian government officials, and foreign visitors. But many other Buchas happened all over Ukraine. Some were far from major cities and thus less visited; others remain under Russian control and are therefore inaccessible to the media and investigators. The pattern of Russian violence in these places aligned well with that of Bucha: murder, beatings, rape, and wanton destruction took place all over Russian-occupied Ukraine. Local leaders, activists, state officials, and Ukrainian army veterans were deliberately targeted by the Russian forces, but everyone—families trying to escape the fighting, volunteers helping those who stayed, unfortunate owners of loot that Russian soldiers fancied, anyone looking suspicious or simply unlucky enough to encounter a trigger-happy Russian—was a potential victim, regardless of occupation, social position, or beliefs.

In Yahidne, a village in northern Ukraine, the entire population was imprisoned. Russian troops locked 360 people, including 68 children, in a school basement for four weeks, with limited food and without beds, toilets, or medical care. The soldiers threatened their Ukrainian victims with execution and sexually harassed the women. Ten people died in this makeshift concentration camp. The indiscriminate nature of this early Russian violence clearly differentiated it from the later, more systematic, and better-organized effort to destroy Ukrainians as a national group.[8]

Alongside murder, sexual violence was an important component of Russian soldiers' behavior. Sexual violence is typically grossly underreported because of social stigma and shame, but the evidence that is available strongly suggests that it was widespread across Russian-occupied Ukraine. People of all ages, from young children to octogenarians, suffered assault, rape, and castration.

In March 2022, in a settlement near Kyiv, Russian soldiers entered a home, raped the woman living there, sexually assaulted her husband, and forced the couple to have sex while they watched. Then the couple's four-year-old daughter was forced to perform oral sex on a Russian soldier. In a nearby village, a Russian soldier tried to force a Ukrainian woman to have sex with him at gunpoint. "There are no laws in war!" he shouted. "I can do whatever I want to you—and I won't be punished for it. If you don't go with me right now, I'll shoot!" On that occasion, the woman talked the Russian out of raping her, but the following night, the soldiers raped her neighbor and murdered the neighbor's husband. Sometime later, a different group of Russian servicemen gang-raped another woman in the village. The victim remembered that while two soldiers were raping her, a third was masturbating nearby. Soldiers also tortured and murdered the woman's husband.[9]

In the Chernihiv region, an eighty-three-year-old woman was raped in her home in the presence of her disabled husband. Another elderly woman was found dead, partially undressed and with blood around her vagina. Some victims of such sexual violence could not bear the trauma and considered taking their own lives. The geographic spread of sexual violence shows it to be a common behavior, not attributable to any specific Russian unit gone rogue. Sexual violence was not official Russian army policy, but it was definitely its practice.[10]

Sexual violence also took place on the front line and in POW camps. In July 2022, a video was posted to social media of a Russian soldier adorned with the Z symbol castrating with a box cutter a fully conscious Ukrainian POW. The video went viral but was initially perceived as an isolated, if gruesome, atrocity. Only months later would the true extent of Russian troops' use of castration begin to emerge. Other Ukrainian soldiers who returned from Russian captivity admitted to having been castrated. According to one victim, "Russians performed the castration procedure very skillfully, as if they knew how to do it," suggesting a much broader pattern of abuse.[11]

At other times, Russian violence was especially gratuitous or even extra-lethal, directed at the bodies of the already dead. Videos filmed by Russian soldiers and uploaded to social media depict troops executing a Ukrainian POW for saying "Glory to Ukraine," beheading a captured Ukrainian with a knife, and impaling the severed head of a different serviceman on a pole. Igor Mangushev, a Russian nationalist and army officer who fought in Ukraine, even appeared at a literary festival devoted to Eduard Limonov bearing a skull, which, he claimed, was that of a Ukrainian soldier. Mangushev's speech at the festival centered on the need to destroy Ukraine and Ukrainians, as well as his dream of seeing Kyiv burn. Mangushev was no stranger to extreme violence. According to the journalist Elena Racheva, who encountered Mangushev while reporting from the Donbas in 2015, he was known as the torture expert of the LNR security services and had previously been active in the Russian extreme right.[12]

It is unclear whether the most gratuitous Russian violence, such as castrations and beheadings, was primarily carried out by regular servicemen or by Wagner mercenaries, many of whom are convicts. This distinction has no bearing on the question of overall responsibility—because both convicts turned mercenaries and regular soldiers fight for the Russian state and are part of the Russian military machine—but it is important if we wish to understand the causes of violence.

The Russian invasion from the very beginning targeted Ukraine's political and social elites, local leaders, state officials, and army veterans. Some of these people were among the victims of Russian close-range atrocities in Bucha and elsewhere. Their murder fits into the Russian project of decapitating Ukraine and destroying its national identity. But most Ukrainian civilians murdered by Russian soldiers during the early stages of the invasion, in Bucha and elsewhere, were ordinary people with no prior history of political activism or leadership. They were teachers, farmers, small-business owners, truck drivers, pediatricians, salesclerks, and retirees. Their names did not appear on FSB kill lists, and Russian soldiers rarely asked people about their identity or beliefs before murdering or raping them. These killings were not government policy but independent decisions and actions taken by Russians on the ground.

As it turns out, the massacres were not the gruesome work of hardened criminals, plucked out of jails and sent to kill in Ukraine. Nor were they carried out by volunteer units of the Russian far right, neo-Nazis, and football hooligans, such as the infamous *Rusich* and *Española* groups, which might be especially prone to wanton violence. The perpetrators typically were Russian army troops, professional and presumably well-trained soldiers serving in different branches of the military: airborne troops, motorized infantry, armor, the National Guard, and Chechen units. They came to Ukraine from different parts of Russia, from the border with China in the east to the border with the EU in the northwest, and the official orders they received did not include rape and mass murder. There is evidence that some officers ordered their troops to kill civilians, but most murders occurred because Russian soldiers decided—of their own volition—to kill. Why would they do it? The information we have is still limited, but what we do know so far—coupled with evidence from other, well-researched campaigns of mass violence—allows me to try to reconstruct the logic of Russian violence.[13]

Genocide scholars have long established that rank-and-file perpetrators of mass violence are typically normal people, possessing no special criminal tendencies or proclivity for murder and without major mental health problems. They were generally ordinary Germans during the Holocaust and ordinary Hutu during the genocide in Rwanda. And in Ukraine, the killers are ordinary Russian soldiers.[14]

Every society contains the capacity for mass violence. Individuals, groups, and whole societies are in a constant tug-of-war between factors pushing for escalation and those promoting restraint. Most of the time, the forces of restraint are much stronger than the forces of escalation, ensuring peace. But when sources of escalation overpower those of restraint, the risk of mass violence goes up.[15]

In Russian-occupied Ukraine, multiple factors promoted escalation and thus violence against civilians among Russian soldiers. The first major factor was the war itself. Russia's preparations for war were so secretive that very few people in the country were aware of the imminence of conflict. Russian soldiers who would soon be sent to kill and die in Ukraine were also kept in the dark. When the Kremlin began amassing troops on Ukraine's borders, soldiers were told that they were being sent to take part in exercises. They spent months in field camps, during winter, doing little but waiting, often without proper clothing or equipment. Boredom and lack of purpose or information about the future increased tensions and undermined already poor discipline, which is the Russian army's traditional weak point.

Closer to the start of the invasion, the Russian army understood that action was imminent, but instead of all-out war, soldiers were promised a limited operation in or near the Donbas. According to one former serviceman, Russian troops were told that they would "go in, scare the folks a bit, everyone would run away, and they would come back home." Multiple additional testimonies and intercepted phone calls from Russian soldiers in Ukraine confirm this general expectation: a Crimea-style, geographically limited, brief, and not very dangerous operation.[16]

In other words, Russian soldiers were not aware they were going to a large-scale war and were not mentally prepared for it. Among the regular Russian troops who were soon occupying Bucha and other Ukrainian towns and villages, few had combat experience. In the junior ranks, most were simply too young to have taken part in the wars in Chechnya or against Georgia in 2008. Russian units had fought in the Donbas, but their numbers were limited, and large-scale fighting died down after 2015. In Syria, Russian military involvement was largely limited to the air force, airborne units, special operations forces, and mercenaries, not the regular infantry or mechanized troops who would be tasked with most of the ground fighting in Ukraine and who would maintain the occupation regime. According to multiple reports, some Russian soldiers who invaded Ukraine were recent conscripts, forced to sign professional service contracts on the eve of the invasion. According to Russian law, conscripts are not allowed to be deployed outside of Russia in peacetime, and because the Kremlin insisted that the invasion was a "special military operation," not a war, officers had to use coercion to keep units at full strength. All this combined to ensure low morale and resentment among soldiers sent to fight Ukraine.[17]

Problems with morale and discipline alone, however, do not explain why Russian soldiers killed, raped, and tortured civilians. Had Russian troops quickly conquered Kyiv, Ukraine would have likely been subjugated. There would certainly have been looting, murder of those on kill lists, and a generally repressive regime afterward, but the war would not have escalated into an orgy of uncoordinated mass murder.

Russian soldiers went to war unprepared, expecting to be greeted as liberators and not to meet massive resistance. When Ukraine resisted stubbornly and Russian units suffered their first, unexpected losses, a toxic mix of factors led to slaughter of civilians: mental and physical unpreparedness; resentment toward commanders who had lied about an easy, bloodless campaign and failed to provide necessary equipment; the shock of fighting; a profound sense of danger; the trauma of losing comrades; and anger at hostile Ukrainian civilians.

The desire to avenge lost comrades was a powerful motivator to kill. Pavel Filatyev is currently the only Russian serviceman who has defected to the West and published an extensive account of the war in Ukraine from the perspective of a Russian soldier. Filatyev, a former paratrooper, is not a hero. His memoir is blatantly self-exculpatory, and the organization that helped Filatyev escape Russia later accused him of not disclosing information about war crimes committed by his unit. Yet, flawed as it is, the memoir helps us understand the motivations of a regular Russian soldier. Filatyev's deep patriotism and pride in being a paratrooper overshadow all other considerations, but he is no brainwashed, ideological killing machine. He shares the same prejudices and myths as other Russians, but his primary motivation for enlisting was making a living. He is fully aware of how deeply corrupt the Russian military is, but he still partook in the system and was willing to die fighting for it (that is, until he was not). Filatyev's main loyalty was to his branch, his unit, and especially his immediate comrades. And when they started dying, the soldiers' mood changed. Filatyev is older than most of his comrades and even served a tour in Chechnya, but nothing prepared him for full-scale war. "When losses started, brutality and desire for revenge have risen in people," he testified. The first victim of this thirst for revenge was a Ukrainian POW captured by his unit. After being injured, Filatyev left the war zone, but while he was gone, those Russian soldiers who stayed in Ukraine sought to avenge lost comrades.[18]

The situation was especially grave for Russian units near Kyiv. Skillful Ukrainian resistance stalled the Russian drive toward the city and inflicted heavy losses. Instead of marching into Ukraine's capital, holding a victory parade, getting a hefty bonus and medals, and returning home with the loot, Russian soldiers found themselves stuck behind the frontline in places like Bucha. They were frustrated and burning for revenge, but only limited fighting was going on and there were few military targets on which to exercise this desire. Ukrainian prisoners of war were too few, but someone still had to pay the price for the Russians' losses and frustrations. Unable to destroy Ukraine, Russian troops settled for killing Ukrainians.

The Russian troops who invaded Ukraine expected to be greeted by civilians as their saviors from neo-Nazi, Banderite, western-Ukrainian oppression. This expectation made sense against the background of an almost sixteen-year-long Russian propaganda campaign. The portrayal of Ukraine as a place where Bandera-worshipping Galician neo-Nazis oppress the Russian-speaking majority (all of whom dream of joining the Russian World) became a staple of Russian media after the Orange Revolution. But after Euromaidan, it grew into an obsession. The silencing of dissenting voices in major media outlets also meant that Russians would need to make an extra effort to access alternative information, and few of those in the army had the time, the means, or the desire to do so. Even if soldiers were not heavily influenced by state media, they still could not have escaped the barrage of propaganda messaging about Ukraine.

Unfortunately, there is no polling data available on the attitudes of Russian soldiers, and there are only a handful of testimonies and memoirs. This does not mean that Russian soldiers in Ukraine are silent, however.

Wall Evidence (*Nastinni Dokazy*) is a Ukrainian project that collects messages and graffiti left by troops in occupied Ukraine. The more than four hundred pieces of graffiti that the project generously shared with me offer a glimpse into what Russian soldiers care about and wish to communicate.

The most common graffiti message is an assertion of Russian dominance, typically via the Latin letters *Z* and *V*, which are Russia's semiofficial symbols of the invasion. Some graffiti are apologetic, though without accepting responsibility: "Please forgive us, we were forced" or "It's not us, it is the war." But a very large number reproduce the slogans, prejudices, and statements of Russian state propaganda, such as "Ukraine! Why do you need NATO???" in Bucha, "Bandiera [*sic*] is toast" in nearby Borodyanka, and "Ukraine is a fraternal Nation of Russia, and we will protect it from fascism and Banderite scum" in Hostomel. Also common are pejorative terms for Ukrainians such as *Ukry* and *khokhly*.

Some, though not many, Russian soldiers openly acknowledge the impact of propaganda on their motivation to take up arms. One serviceman admitted that he had wanted to go and fight in Ukraine to avenge the alleged Ukrainian atrocities in the Donbas, and that he expected to see real Nazis in Ukraine. To his credit, once actually there, he quickly realized that reality differed greatly from what Russian propaganda had taught him and resigned from the military, but this case is an exception. The majority took for granted that Ukrainian patriots were neo-Nazis and Russians were liberators.[19]

When Russian forces entered Ukraine, the negative reactions of civilians were thus psychologically even more unsettling than the stiff resistance of the Ukrainian armed forces. The behavior of Ukrainian soldiers might have been rationalized as simply following orders or the armed forces being brainwashed. Losing comrades demanded revenge, but at least the situation made sense. The openly hostile behavior of civilians—most of whom spoke flawless Russian and, from the soldiers' perspective, were members of the Russian World—was much harder to accept.

One possibility was for the Russian troops to admit that the civilians they came to liberate were not oppressed, did not seek protection, and that the Russians themselves were invaders and oppressors, not liberators. But this would have meant accepting that the cause for which these soldiers were risking their lives was unjust; that they were consistently and deliberately deceived by their commanders, the media, and Putin himself; and that all the sacrifices they and their comrades had made were meaningless. Such things would have been extremely painful and difficult to admit. We know that some Russian soldiers did come to this realization, but even among this group, many likely stayed silent.

An alternative path was to reaffirm the justness of Russia's cause and conduct, and to blame Ukrainian civilians themselves for their refusal to welcome the invading troops. According to this explanation, the population of Bucha and other Ukrainian towns had refused to welcome the Russian armies because they themselves had become neo-Nazis just like the Ukrainian army. While people from western Ukraine were expected to be nationalist enemies of Russia, those from the Kyiv region were not. These people were worse than enemies; they were traitors. Thus, the perception of Russian-Ukrainian unity that should have restrained violence was transformed into outrage at Ukrainians' rejection and perceived treachery, and a key source of escalation.

This view reinforced the already strong security fears of the Russian military and elevated them to paranoia. On their way to Kyiv, Russian columns and convoys were frequently ambushed, and the Russians were certain that locals were providing Ukrainian troops with reconnaissance information. This suspicion was not unfounded; some civilians did spy on the Russian troops and relay intelligence to Ukrainian authorities. But in an environment in which all Ukrainian citizens were coming to be perceived as enemies and traitors, everyone—no matter their actions, age, gender, ethnicity, or social status—became a suspect and potential target.

Other factors also contributed to the unfolding mass murder. Alcohol, which Russian soldiers plundered from Ukrainian homes and stores and drank in large volumes, clouded judgment, inflamed emotions, and reduced the threshold for deadly violence. The fear and resentment of rejection that could have been controlled while sober encouraged violence among drunk, heavily armed soldiers.

Ukrainian civilians under total Russian control were no longer perceived as people worthy of support and protection, and perpetrators
became increasingly likely to dehumanize their victims. In a notable
encounter in Bucha, a Russian officer told local resident Lucy Moskalenko
that people who had just been executed and whose bodies were lying on the
road were "not humans. They are absolute dirt. Dirt. They are not human.
They are beasts." Such dehumanizing language would become standard in
the Russian media only weeks later, but on the ground in Ukraine it was
already exacting its toll, even without state propaganda taking the lead.[20]

Evidence from other conflicts also shows that violence conducted
in groups—especially gang rape, an immense but also shared moral
transgression—serves as a powerful bonding mechanism among troops who
must rely on each other for survival. Finally, against the backdrop of a stalled
Russian offensive and mounting casualties, violence against civilians—who,
in Russian minds, became indistinguishable from the Ukrainian army—gave
Russian troops a rare sense of victory over the enemy.[21]

Whereas multiple factors—widespread Ukrainian rejection of the
Russian belief in historical unity, fear, dehumanization, propaganda,
desire for revenge, losses, and alcohol—fueled the escalation of Russian
violence, those factors that encouraged restraint became too weak to
make a difference. The perception of Ukrainian civilians as compatriots
of the Russians quickly disappeared. Nor were Russian soldiers bearing
a strong cultural rejection of extreme violence, which could have helped
to protect civilians in occupied Ukraine. Even prior to the invasion
of Ukraine, violence ran "through the whole of Russian society, from
the family and school to state institutions." In 2021, Russia's homicide
rate was 6.8 per 100,000 inhabitants, almost the same as the US rate,
but much higher than Ukraine's (3.8), and almost six times that of the
United Kingdom (1.2).[22]

The most important sources of restraint among soldiers are, of course,
military discipline, commanders' control over their troops, and accountability for wrongdoing. Discipline, however, had historically been weak in
the Russian and Soviet militaries. This lack of discipline had manifested

itself long before the war in Ukraine in the massive plunder of occupied territories, pogroms as long as there were Jews to beat, large-scale rape inflicted on women in territories liberated from Nazi rule by the USSR (predominantly, but not only, in Germany), and brutal hazing of conscripts—the infamous *dedovshchina*.

Without a large, professional corps of noncommissioned officers, as is common in Western militaries, Russian commanders had only limited control over their troops; during wartime, it declined still further. In the Sixty-Fourth Motor Rifle Brigade, soldiers complained that instead of leading or taking care of the troops, their commanders passed the time plundering Ukrainian stores and warehouses on an industrial scale and sending entire trucks of loot back to Russia. On social media, Russian soldiers in Ukraine have recorded dozens of collective complaints about their officers because they see no other way to raise their concerns. In Bucha and elsewhere, Russian soldiers were essentially on their own, without meaningful control by officers to prevent violence against civilians.[23]

Russian soldiers also quickly realized that violence against Ukrainian noncombatants, no matter how gruesome, had no consequences. Most Russian crimes were never recorded, let alone reported, and Russian troops were confident in their total impunity. In the very rare cases in which civilians complained to Russian occupation authorities, it typically achieved nothing.

When Russian troops withdrew from Bucha and the extent of Russian mass murder became clear to the world, Putin dismissed the massacre as a "provocation," while Foreign Minister Sergei Lavrov said it had been staged by the West. To this day, the Russian government steadfastly refuses to acknowledge the violence its troops carried out. On the contrary, Putin later decorated the Sixty-Fourth Motor Rifle Brigade with the prestigious "Guards" designation. If Russian soldiers needed any further confirmation that killing Ukrainian civilians was acceptable, even encouraged, they could not have received it more pointedly.[24]

These problems were not new, and the propensity of Russian soldiers to target innocent people in war is well known and well documented. Historically, when the Russian (and, previously, Soviet) army interacted with civilian populations, violence was common. Neither the intervention in Syria nor the brief war against Georgia in 2008 featured extensive Russian control over populated areas, but in both Chechen wars, journalists and human rights investigators documented numerous cases of violence against civilians committed by Russian troops. In most incidents, the number of victims was relatively small, but there were also large-scale massacres, such as the "cleansing operation" in Samashki on April 7–8, 1995, in which over one hundred Chechens—almost all of them civilians—were shot or burned by Russian internal troops.

The Soviet war in Afghanistan also saw violence against civilians that strongly resembled the carnage in Ukraine four decades later. Soviet troops killed civilians in revenge for losses, burned people alive, booby-trapped bodies, threw grenades into rooms full of deliberately assembled women and children, and shot at passing civilian vehicles for amusement. A recent study of Soviet anti-civilian violence in Afghanistan identified its main causes as "inadequate training, hazing and substance abuse, and a lack of punishment for crimes. . . . The military also purposely misinformed recruits about their mission."[25]

It is therefore hardly surprising that when so many factors pushed toward the escalation of violence against civilians and no meaningful restraints opposed it, Russian soldiers massacred Ukrainians on a massive scale and with total impunity. Even before it was declared Russian policy to kill Ukraine, murdering Ukrainians became Russian practice. The two campaigns—state-mandated genocide and uncoordinated mass murder—went hand in hand.

The second type of Russian violence was indiscriminate bombardment from a distance: air strikes, shelling by artillery, and the use of short- and long-range missiles against civilian targets. No region of Ukraine was spared this discriminate violence, but Kyiv, Kharkiv, and southern and eastern Ukraine were targeted more frequently than regions farther from the front line. And nowhere in the east and the south was the destruction as extensive as in Mariupol, which became the embodiment of indiscriminate devastation wrought by Russia.

Since 2014, Mariupol, a city of half a million people in the Donbas, had become a key target for Russia. Besides the city's strategic importance as a port on the Azov Sea, an industrial center, and key to the land bridge the Kremlin wished to establish between the Donbas and Crimea, Mariupol was also a symbol. The DNR had captured Mariupol in 2014 but lost it after two months. Thanks to extensive Ukrainian government investment, Mariupol emerged as a thriving alternative to the violent and decaying Donetsk, just one hundred kilometers (sixty-two miles) away. Mariupol was the embodiment of what the Ukrainian Donbas could become. That the majority of Mariupol's residents were primarily Russian speaking but still embraced Ukrainian national identity flew in the face of the Novorossiya project and the Russian obsession with the supposed persecution of Russophones in Ukraine.

Even more crucially, Mariupol was the birthplace and center of operations of the post-Euromaidan volunteer unit the Azov Battalion, which the Kremlin saw as the prime example of "Ukrainian neo-Nazism." While the Azov Battalion did have far-right origins and many of its early fighters were known for their political extremism and lack of discipline, by 2022 the unit, now a brigade-size formation of Ukraine's National Guard, had been thoroughly professionalized and de-radicalized. Its soldiers came from different ethnic and religious backgrounds, and many Azov servicemen spoke Russian as their first language. Mariupol was home to very few actual neo-Nazis, but from the Kremlin's perspective, the city had to be "de-Nazified," no matter the cost.[26]

Vadym Boychenko, the mayor of Mariupol, hailed from a Russian-speaking family. Like many others in Ukraine, he was unprepared for the war. "The day before the invasion . . . we had a meeting of the city council and the only topics we talked about were economic development, construction, and our bright future," he told me. Up until the very start of the fighting, Mariupol authorities did not allow Azov to erect new defensive positions or dig trenches in the city.[27]

The mayor had also not anticipated the direction of the Russian assault. Since 2014, the main threat to Mariupol had been from the DNR to the north and east, and the city was well defended on those approaches. This time, the Russians advanced from Crimea in the southwest, where defenses were minimal. In just four days, Russian troops, determined to crush any resistance and wipe out the hated Azov Brigade, encircled the city. Within a week, all of Mariupol's critical infrastructure, besides the gas supply, had been rendered inoperable. On March 6, the gas was also gone. Without heating, temperatures in homes plunged to five degrees Celsius (forty degrees Fahrenheit). People melted snow in outdoor fires to get water.[28]

The Mariupol garrison—the Azov Brigade, a detachment of Marines, some border guards, and a motley crew of soldiers from other units— fought neighborhood by neighborhood and eventually retreated to the sprawling Azovstal steelworks complex and its many underground tunnels. There, they continued to resist until May 17, when the last pockets of Mariupol's defenders surrendered to Russian forces.

The siege of Mariupol featured the most brutal urban warfare that Europe has seen since 1945. Most of the destruction came from indiscriminate Russian artillery fire and air strikes that obliterated entire city blocks. According to UN estimates, up to 90 percent of apartment buildings and 60 percent of houses in the city were destroyed or damaged. Courtyards were turned into makeshift cemeteries; holding funerals was impossible and the number of dead was too large to handle. Many bodies could not be identified, and neighborhood chat groups in Mariupol became a constant stream of messages about where and when someone had been killed or might be buried. A channel on the Telegram messaging app devoted exclusively to identifying civilians killed in Mariupol had over twenty-five thousand subscribers searching for their disappeared loved ones.[29]

Yevhen Sosnovsky, a local photographer, recalled that on the morning of March 20 he emerged from his apartment block to discover that four out of the six nine-story buildings in his courtyard were burned out. When Russian soldiers—he identified them as *Kadyrovtsy*, Chechen troops loyal to the Kremlin-installed strongman Ramzan Kadyrov—arrived on the scene, they expelled Sosnovsky, his wife, and wounded relatives they were sheltering from their apartment and did not let them take any food. They had to move to the basement of a nearby building, where they remained for the next two weeks. In the basement there was no food, and death was everywhere. Only on their fourth attempt did Sosnovsky and his wife manage to finally escape what remained of their hometown.[30]

Iegor Kravtsov—Sosnovsky's great-nephew, who was also sheltering during those two weeks in the basement—later recalled his experiences and drew pictures of angels, representing those he had lost in the war.

[April 3, Sunday]. I slept well, woke up, smiled. . . . Also, my grandpa died on [March] the 26th. I have a wound on my back and ripped skin. My sister has a head injury. Mom has flesh ripped out and a hole in her leg.

[April 4, Monday]. I woke up, smiled like yesterday etc. . . . By the way, my birthday is coming up. . . . I lost two dogs, Grandma Galia and my beloved city Mariupol during the time since [Thursday, February] 24th.[31]

But among the general carnage, there was also very deliberate targeting of schools, government buildings, and cultural institutions, all of which had become shelters for masses of homeless and trapped civilians. The drama theater building became a refuge for more than a thousand civilians, who marked the plaza outside with the word "children" written in Russian in large, clearly visible letters. On March 1, the theater was destroyed by Russian planes and up to six hundred people sheltering inside were killed. On March 9, another Russian air strike destroyed the city's maternity hospital. Multiple school buildings were also destroyed in targeted attacks. In February 2023, Maria Ponomarenko, a Russian journalist who publicized the details of the attacks, was convicted of "spreading fake news" and sentenced to six years' imprisonment.[32]

The scale of the devastation in Mariupol is enormous, and we might never know the true extent of the casualties. Official Ukrainian sources put the number of civilians identified as having been killed in the siege at over twenty-two thousand, but they also openly acknowledge that this is a gross underestimation. Thousands of unidentified dead bodies were thrown into hastily dug mass graves, and many who died in their apartments were never found after the buildings were demolished by Russian authorities. Russian-operated mobile crematoria disposed of the dead without leaving a trace. The destruction of the municipal water system represented a major health hazard, and some residents remaining in the city went to work removing debris in exchange for drinkable water, the supply of which Mariupol's new rulers controlled tightly and used to ensure compliance. Ukrainian Mariupol was no more, its buildings and factories destroyed, most residents dead or displaced.[33]

Was this destruction a deliberate policy, an aberration, or the unintended yet inevitable collateral damage of siege warfare? The civilian death toll in Mariupol was high even by the standards of typically brutal Russian warfare, but Mariupol was not an exception. Mariupol was the largest Ukrainian city that the Russian army turned into rubble, but not the only one. Bakhmut, Volnovakha, Sievierodonetsk, and several smaller towns in the Donbas were also extensively targeted and almost completely destroyed by the Russian armed forces. From the beginning of the war, Russia also subjected many other Ukrainian cities to a constant barrage of missile and suicide-drone attacks that killed many civilians. The feeling of being brought out for execution when the air-raid sirens sound, which Victoria Amelina described in her poem, is widespread among Ukrainians. More than fifty civilians died in Kramatorsk on April 8, 2022, when a Russian missile hit the railway station. Twenty-one Ukrainian civilians were killed when another missile hit a shopping mall in Kremenchuk in eastern Ukraine on June 27, 2022. On July 14, 2022, two missiles targeted the city center of Vinnytsia in central Ukraine, killing twenty-seven. On October 5, 2023, a Russian missile hit a funeral reception in Hroza, a small village in the Kharkiv region. Fifty-nine people, more than 10 percent of the village population, died in the strike. Smaller but still deadly attacks occur on an almost daily basis. These attacks are indiscriminate, and none of the civilians killed or injured are a specific target that Russia seeks to eliminate. But the killing of civilians in such a random manner is also not unintended collateral damage.

"We will do to the rest of Ukraine what we did to Mariupol," one Russian soldier told Boychenko when the mayor tried to pass a checkpoint and leave the city. Many other refugees recall hearing similar sentiments among the Russian troops they encountered. Killing civilians is not always the goal, but it is a tool. Beyond the immediate death toll, such indiscriminate violence destroys infrastructure, inflicts psychological damage on the population, causes disruptive flows of refugees, and makes the postwar return of those who escaped the fighting less likely. Conquest of destroyed cities is also easier for Russian forces; the number of civilians who might affect the course of the fighting is lower, and the defenders have fewer places to hide and fight from or infrastructure to support them. But indiscriminate targeting is also not always about military expediency. A well-known study analyzing the impact of indiscriminate violence on insurgency during Russia's war in Chechnya found that, on occasion, Russian artillery would simply get drunk and start firing at random rather than targeting places from which they were previously attacked.[34]

Like many other Russian policies, indiscriminate violence in Ukraine is also a product of history. This is how Russia fights. Before flattening Mariupol, Russia did the same to Grozny in Chechnya, and it heavily bombarded cities controlled by anti-government forces in Syria, such as Aleppo. In one notable example, on October 21, 1999, Russian forces targeted the center of Grozny with two missiles, which exploded above the city's central market and close to other civilian targets, including a maternity hospital. More than a hundred civilians lost their lives. When Russia stormed Grozny, it made extensive use of highly destructive weapons such as thermobaric rockets, "each of which could bring down a whole apartment building." At the end of the Russian siege, the UN declared Grozny the most devastated city on the planet. Other settlements in Chechnya were also pummeled; Komsomolskoye, the site of a large engagement between Russian and Chechen forces, was completely destroyed. Beginning in 2015, Russian intervention in the Syrian civil war would follow much the same pattern. Unsurprisingly, the Russian commander of the siege of Mariupol, General Mikhail Mizintsev, had also served with the Russian army in Syria.[35]

In a cruel twist of history, in August 2023 Grozny and Mariupol—both destroyed and then conquered by Russia—were declared twin cities, if not under direct orders from the Kremlin, then certainly with its approval.

Destroying Ukraine and killing Ukrainians were two initially separate, but intertwined, strategies of Russian violence. These actions—killings, plunder, abductions, and destruction of culture and identity—echo policies adopted by the Russian Empire and the USSR during and after both world wars. Yet it is unlikely that the Kremlin is consciously using the past as a template. More plausibly, the policies are similar simply because Putin's attitude toward Ukraine and the Russian military's willingness to abuse or kill civilians are in line with those of their Romanov and Soviet predecessors. Ukrainian culture, language, and desire for independence are as much a threat to Russia's nationalist identity and vision of history in 2022–2024 as they were a century earlier, and thus prompt a similar Kremlin reaction. In Moscow's efforts to control and kill Ukraine, history neither rhymes nor repeats itself, it simply continues, save brief interruptions such as the Ukrainianization campaigns of the 1920s and the 1990s. Can it ever stop?

CONCLUSION

S ince February 2022, the Russian invasion has spawned a range of slogans, memes, and images that went viral, became iconic, and continue to shape public perceptions of the war. There is the ominous Russian Z, a Ukrainian tractor towing a Russian tank, the call to "be brave like Ukraine," and a Ukrainian soldier giving the middle finger to a sinking Russian warship. Among the lesser-known memes is one based on a song that says, in Ukrainian, "Our national idea: leave us the fuck alone." In fact, Ukrainians do not really want to be left alone, quite the opposite. Since the outbreak of the war, support for joining NATO and the EU has reached near consensus in Ukraine. As of March 2023, 83 percent of Ukrainians support joining NATO, and over 90 percent seek EU membership.[1]

What most Ukrainians want, passionately, is to be left alone *by Russia*. They do not want to be considered Russians, they do not want to be brought back under Moscow's rule, they do not want to "rediscover," at gunpoint, what the Kremlin believes is Ukrainians' true identity. Instead, they wish to be treated as a nation that has the right to an independent existence. Most importantly, Ukrainians do not want to be invaded, annexed, displaced, murdered, plundered, tortured, abducted, and raped in the name of the mythical "historical unity" and "East Slavic brotherhood" that shape Putin's thinking and impact the attitudes of many Russians. But is coexistence between the two nations even possible, given the intensity of Russian feelings toward Ukraine, the long-standing, hegemonic Russian belief in the unity of the two nations, and Russia's insistence on ownership over the Kyivan Rus' patrimony?

During the final years of my doctoral studies at the University of Wisconsin, I worked as a research assistant to one of my dissertation supervisors, Nadav Shelef. My task was to identify irredentist governments, parties, and political movements: those who believed that parts of their homeland were controlled by a foreign state and sought to reclaim them. There were partitioned homelands I already knew much about, such as Israel and Palestine, Crimea, Taiwan, Kashmir, the territories lost by Hungary post–World War I, Northern Ireland, and Serbia and Kosovo. But there were also many cases that even I, a PhD candidate specializing in conflict and violence, had heard only vaguely about or not at all. Indeed, Professor Shelef's key insight was that "there are many, often unnoticed instances of once-voluble claims to lost homeland territory, melting away." Few Germans still desire East Prussia and Königsberg, now Russian Kaliningrad; Poles reconciled themselves to the loss of Lviv, a city for which they doggedly fought in 1918; and Italians have given up on retaking the northern Adriatic coast, the very demand that gave birth to the term "irredenta."[2]

There is no reason why in the future Russian desire to control or conquer Ukraine cannot be added to the list of once-voluble claims now melting away. Indeed, something along these lines happened before. In 1914, the Russian imperial government considered Galicia historically Russian land, which needed to be reunited with the rest of the empire. In 1939, the Soviet Union invaded Poland on the pretext of unifying the Ukrainians of Galicia and Volhynia with their Moscow-ruled homeland. But now, except for those dreaming of a continent-wide Russia, even the most radical Russian nationalists typically do not wish to rule western Ukraine. It will be exceptionally hard to change Russian attitudes toward and perceptions of Ukraine, but not impossible. This task is essential if we—Ukrainians, anti-war Russians, the world—want the invasion and genocide that started in 2022 to be the last Russian attempt to destroy Ukraine.

As the preceding chapters have shown, the Russian obsession with Ukraine is driven by two factors: identity and security, both national security and the security of the autocratic regime that rules Russia. Thus, to ensure that future Russian rulers do not intend to destroy Ukraine, both Ukraine's centrality to the Russian national identity and its importance for the Kremlin's security perceptions will have to change first. This is not an easy task. A lot will depend on how the current war ends, but even a total defeat might not change Russian attitudes toward Ukraine. Just like after the Orange Revolution, the Kremlin will be tempted to embrace the soothing delusion that Russia lost not to the strength of Ukraine but rather to NATO, and the Kremlin might try again when the West seems weak or distracted by crises elsewhere. Remarkably, even now there are voices in Russia who explain the failure to conquer Ukraine by insisting that Ukrainians are such excellent soldiers because they are, in fact, Russians. These excuses, ridiculous as they may sound, do not bode well for Ukrainians' desire to be left alone.

To fundamentally change the nature of Russian-Ukrainian relations, to go from neo-imperial, genocidal expansion to durable coexistence, longer-term reforms will be more important than ground-level developments in the war. Liberation of territories currently under occupation is crucial to save Ukrainian lives, but an equally important long-term goal is ensuring that, in the future, Russia will be neither willing nor able to destroy Ukraine or kill Ukrainians.

Russia, despite the hopes of decolonization advocates, is unlikely to collapse, even after a painful loss to Ukraine. Even if the Russian Federation did splinter, Ukraine will still have to live with some kind of Russian state, even a different one, across its border, and there will also be attempts to resurrect the lost empire, just like the Bolsheviks in the past and Putin now. Geography is a hard fact that cannot be altered at will, and Ukraine will still have to deal with Russia.

Security is a more technical issue than identity and therefore arguably easier to address. This is why, since 2014, politicians, academics, and policy analysts have preferred to focus on the geopolitical and security dimension of the conflict. Over the years, they have put forward several schemes to halt the violence in the Donbas and later the full-scale war by deciding which alliances Ukraine should or should not belong to, which weapons it might or might not possess, and how Kyiv ought to carry out its defense policies.

One of the most popular proposals is to reduce Russia's threat perception by enshrining Ukraine's neutrality. Ukraine, the argument goes, should not be allowed to join NATO or any other alliance the Kremlin views as hostile. The logic behind this idea is straightforward: the conflict in the Donbas, the annexation of Crimea, and the February 2022 invasion were presumably all caused by Ukrainian attempts to join NATO and the security concerns that such a move elicited in Moscow. NATO bases in Ukraine, just across the border, would pose a threat that no Russian leader could stomach. It was Russia that attacked, but NATO and Ukraine are ultimately responsible for the violence. Thus, if Ukraine abandons its desire to join NATO—or if NATO declares that Ukraine would never be admitted—this would alleviate Russia's fears and guarantee peace.[3]

A slightly different proposal suggests providing Ukraine with security guarantees in exchange for Kyiv agreeing to drop its NATO membership bid. Such guarantees would ideally be stronger and more legally binding than the soft "assurances" given in the 1994 Budapest Memorandum while also not threatening Russia, because Ukraine would not be part of NATO. The list of countries expected to guarantee Ukraine's security varies from one proposal to the next, sometimes including France, Germany, Israel, Poland, Turkey, the United States, the United Kingdom, and even Russia itself.

Regardless of external guarantees, Kyiv also recognizes the need to protect Ukraine from future invasion by investing in domestic defense industries, arms production, and military capabilities. Zelensky himself floated the idea of Ukraine becoming a "big Israel": a heavily militarized society, constantly on alert and ready for war. The "Israel on the Dnipro" metaphor quickly became popular in discussions about Ukraine's postwar

security, but it is unclear whether the Israeli model would require possession of nuclear weapons and a strategic partnership with the United States,
both of which Israel enjoys.[4]

Finally, another argument maintains that NATO membership for
Ukraine *is* the best and easiest way to address the security fears of both
Kyiv and Moscow. At the time of writing, it is still uncertain if, let alone
when, Ukraine might join the alliance. The final communiqué of the June
2023 NATO summit in Vilnius stated that NATO "will be in a position
to extend an invitation to Ukraine to join the Alliance when Allies agree
and conditions are met." If Ukraine joins NATO, the argument goes, this
would not only protect Ukraine but also provide Russian leaders with an
excuse to ignore nationalist demands for irredentist expansion and thus
help direct the Kremlin's energy elsewhere.

Each of these arguments has merit, but none offers a viable long-term
solution that would ensure the peaceful and respectful coexistence of
Ukraine and Russia. As previous chapters demonstrated, identity, not
security or the fear of NATO, has historically been the main driver of Russian aggression. The suggestions of what Ukraine should or should not do
and which organization it can or cannot join ignore the core of the conflict. The sticking point is not Ukrainian policy but Russian perceptions of
Ukraine and its right to exist as a sovereign state. Without addressing this,
security arrangements alone cannot effect lasting change. Even NATO
membership for Ukraine might not suffice. The alliance's protection might
prevent a future Russian invasion, but it would do little to stop the Kremlin from trying to gain control over Ukraine. Russia might continue to
destabilize or split Ukraine through nonmilitary means such as electoral
interference, support for corrupt politicians, economic pressure, or disinformation campaigns. As long as the Kremlin wants to control Ukraine, it
will find the means to try, and no nuclear weapons, security guarantees, or
collective defense arrangements can prevent that.

The obsession with security arrangements and the Kremlin's security
concerns, real or imagined, overlooks the basic fact that Ukraine—even
if it does join NATO—cannot really imperil Russia, and that Russian

elites understand security differently from their counterparts in the West. Despite its failure to conquer Ukraine, Russia remains a vast country boasting significant resources and a large military. Most crucially, Russia has nuclear weapons, which remain the ultimate guarantor of the country's territorial integrity. Ukraine—a much smaller, weaker, nonnuclear state—never threatened Russia and has never sought to conquer its territory. Even if Ukraine were to join NATO, it would not be Russia's first neighbor to do so. Norway, one of NATO's founding members; Poland, which joined NATO in 1999; and Estonia, Latvia, and Lithuania, which joined in 2004, all share land borders with Russia. When, in the aftermath of the 2022 Russian invasion of Ukraine, Sweden and Finland also decided to join NATO, the Kremlin's reaction was restrained and nonconfrontational, even though the Russia-Finland border stretches for 1,340 kilometers (830 miles). Ukraine's desire to join NATO was met with such outrage in the Kremlin not because the move endangered Russia, but because Kyiv sought to break free from Russian dominance and had the chutzpah to ask NATO for protection.

All this, of course, does not mean that security issues should be overlooked. I am convinced that Ukraine joining NATO is the best of the available alternatives. Even if Ukraine's NATO membership cannot and would not prevent Russia from trying to divide, destabilize, and control the country, it would most likely prevent Russia from physically destroying it. Russian leaders, all their saber-rattling and borderline-apocalyptic rhetoric aside, are expansionist but not suicidal. They want to control Ukraine, but not at the cost of destroying Russia or their own rule, palaces, and yachts. The threat of a war against NATO is the most effective deterrent against a future Russian invasion.

Ukraine's NATO membership would restrain not only Moscow but also Kyiv. Without allies or meaningful security guarantees, Ukraine will inevitably seek to beef up its own defense capabilities and potentially seek nuclear weapons. A large, well-educated country with industrial capacity and scientific expertise, Ukraine can develop nuclear capabilities, and the existential threat it faces might easily push Kyiv in that direction. The common belief that Russia would not have dared to invade had Ukraine kept the nuclear weapons it inherited from the USSR and not exchanged them for the empty "security assurances" of the Budapest Memorandum only reinforces the argument for nuclear weapons. NATO's existing security umbrella would prevent a nuclear race in the center of Europe and remove the possibility of Ukraine developing its own weapons and becoming "Israel on the Dnipro." NATO protection will also allow Ukraine to redirect the resources it would otherwise have to spend on defense toward reconstruction, social services, and economic development. Finally, the benefits would go both ways. Ukraine and its large, experienced, and battle-tested military will shore up NATO's capabilities and readiness not just in Europe but everywhere, and Ukraine's government and society will offer allies invaluable expertise in operating under conditions of extreme crisis and war.

The real threat that Ukraine poses is not to Russia's national security but to the stability of its autocratic regime. In this, the Kremlin is a victim of its own deeply held conviction that Russians and Ukrainians are one people. If Ukrainians managed to build a system in which the opposition can win elections and presidents often lose power, Russians, Putin fears, might be capable of doing the same. This fear is exacerbated by conspiratorial thinking, widespread among Russian political and security elites, as well as the conviction that the West (especially the United States) is plotting tirelessly to depose Putin and uses Ukraine as a base to promote such regime change in Moscow.[5]

Unfortunately, the Russian elites have no solution to this problem save subjugating—and, if necessary, destroying—Ukraine. There is nothing that Ukraine can do to ease or put to rest this Russian fear, unless it gives up on its democracy and becomes a dictatorship. Similarly, the United States cannot disabuse the Kremlin of its conviction that there is a long-standing American plot to topple the regime in Moscow, because the basis of this belief is not empirical evidence but conspiratorial thinking that is impervious to logic and facts. The Kremlin also cannot overcome this issue by rejecting its belief in the unity of Russians and Ukrainians, because doing so would destroy the very foundations of the Russian identity and worldview. Once again, concerns of identity shape perceptions of security.

On a more practical level, no security arrangement is currently possible because over the last decade Putin and the Kremlin have violated every major treaty signed between Russia and Ukraine and broken every promise and public assurance to respect Ukrainian sovereignty and territorial integrity. Moscow lied about the Russian army's presence in Crimea, its war in the Donbas, its intentions just prior to the February 2022 invasion, its goals and conduct during the war, and the many atrocities and war crimes committed by Russian troops in that time. In this environment of justified mistrust, it is futile to focus solely on the security aspect of Russia's approach to Ukraine.

A Russian transition to democracy would remove the Kremlin's fear that democratic Ukraine might serve as an example to Russian citizens or as a tool for the West to pursue regime change in Moscow. A democratic Russia might also no longer be an acute threat to democratic Ukraine because, as the "democratic peace" theory argues, while democracies do fight wars, they almost never fight other democracies. Citizens of democratic states presumably hold generally more liberal views and respect the beliefs and identities of others. Democratic institutions and electoral accountability constrain leaders. Thus, in relations between democracies, negotiation, compromise, and abiding by treaties are usually preferable to wars, of which constituents are unlikely to approve.

It is tempting to identify the authoritarian nature of the Russian regime as the key problem and democratization as the solution, but this view is wrong. Blaming the war on the regime alone allows the rest of Russian society—those who believe that Ukraine is not a real nation, who cheered on the annexation of Crimea, and who called for Moscow to protect Russian speakers from nonexistent atrocities—off the hook for a war that was driven by such beliefs. History demonstrates the perils of relying too heavily on formal institutions, which can change or collapse. In the 1990s, Russia was a weak, flawed, and very limited democracy, yet under Yeltsin's rule it neither invaded nor annexed Ukrainian territories. But the government also did nothing to change common perceptions of Ukraine as an illegitimate entity and Crimea and eastern Ukraine as fundamentally Russian. Yeltsin and the liberals failed to stop or effectively counter neo-imperialist politicians pushing for territorial expansion, and they largely ignored the problem despite a plethora of warning signs. When Putin replaced Yeltsin and dismantled the last remnants of democracy, nothing was left to restrain Russian aggression. Democracy in Russia is desirable for multiple reasons, but it alone is unlikely to prevent a future conflict between Russia and Ukraine. Indeed, if most of the Russian population retains its irredentist convictions, democracy could even exacerbate conflict by handing power to jingoists.

To secure lasting peace, neither security arrangements nor democratization alone will suffice. Russian beliefs about Ukraine, national identity, and proper relations between the two countries also must change. The widespread belief in the historical unity and shared origin of Russians and Ukrainians is not a sacred, primordial truth but a relatively recent construct: a product of nineteenth-century writings and activism of Russian nationalist historians and their Little Russian allies. Like every other national myth, it can change over time. This change cannot and will not happen overnight; changing national identity and myths takes decades and generations even when there is the political will to implement the change. But it is not uncharted territory either, and history teaches us how this change in identity can be achieved, if and when the Kremlin decides to do so.

Ukraine's experience under Soviet rule demonstrates the vital role education plays in shaping popular belief. The core of the Ukrainization process of the 1920s was education, especially primary education, which not only introduced children to the core tenets of Communist ideology but also promoted a distinct Ukrainian identity. Indeed, one of the key reasons for Stalin's anti-Ukrainian policies was the success of Ukrainian-language primary education, which challenged the class-based and, later, Russo-centric nature of the USSR. The fight against anti-Semitism is another example of how, over time, education changes attitudes. Anti-Semitism was widespread in early twentieth-century

Ukraine, so when Soviet authorities decided to eradicate anti-Jewish prejudice, they adopted a wide range of policies: from criminalizing xenophobia to propaganda to designing school curricula that promoted ethnic equality and harmony. Less than two decades later, during the Holocaust, younger generations of Soviet Ukrainians were substantially more likely to help Jews than residents of neighboring Moldova, which had not seen similar attempts to eradicate anti-Semitism.[6]

Laying the groundwork for a change in Russian attitudes and future coexistence should therefore start in history textbooks. Instead of being taught that Russians and Ukrainians are the same people, divided by the tragedy of Soviet collapse and nefarious Western machinations, Russian students might learn to respect Ukraine's distinct nationhood and independence. It will take years, possibly even decades, for such ideas to become commonplace, but once they do, this will secure peace more effectively than any externally imposed security guarantee. Similarly, instead of funding films, plays, and exhibitions that promote Russian-Ukrainian historical unity and repudiate Ukraine's independence, the Russian government might support cultural works that reject neo-imperial, expansionist narratives. Financial support for a certain type of popular culture is a political choice, and the Kremlin can change its priorities at will.

Beyond education and culture, the emergence of a Russian post-Soviet identity in the 1990s is vivid proof that liberals and those committed to peaceful and democratic Russia must articulate a clear vision of what Russia is, its history, and its place in the world and not cede the development of a national identity to Communists, nationalists, and the restorationists of failed empires. Russians need to learn, understand, and come to believe that Ukraine is a different country and not a severed limb of Russia, that Ukrainians are not Russians who speak in a funny dialect, and that the Russian World is an invention of politicians seeking resources and prestige. Luckily, this change in identity does not even require Russia to become a democracy and could be accomplished without major investment or institutional reforms; the only thing that is needed is time and a political leadership genuinely committed to changing popular attitudes.

Russia, as a popular saying goes, is a country with an unpredictable past. Such a change of national identity and historical mythology is not at all inconceivable.

The impetus for this change should ultimately come from within Russia, but Ukraine can make it easier for Russians to accept its independence and distinct identity. Over the centuries, Russian control over Ukraine hinged on the existence of large groups within Ukraine who supported, or at least acquiesced to, being ruled from Moscow or Saint Petersburg. These local supporters of Russian rule changed over time, from Cossack elites to Little Russian intellectuals to the Russian-speaking urban working class, Jews, or those nostalgic for the USSR and committed to the Russian World. These people were driven by a variety of motivations, such as religion, ideology, or a simple desire for security and protection. But no matter who they were or what drove them, they provided Moscow or Moscow-affiliated Ukrainian governments with legitimacy, local knowledge, public support, and normative reinforcement of the idea of Russia and Ukraine as part of a larger whole. Without local support, Russian control cannot be maintained and the narrative of unity underlying Russian strategy will eventually collapse.

In 2022, for the first time in its long history, the population of Ukraine was not deeply divided from within, and this cohesion was crucial to the successful defense of the country. Had the people of Mariupol, Kharkiv, Kyiv, and Kherson or soldiers hailing from these areas viewed the Russian army as liberators rather than invaders, Ukraine would have almost certainly lost the war. Indeed, this is exactly what the Kremlin and many Western observers expected. But the Ukraine of 2022 was not the Ukraine of 1917 or 1991.

For Ukraine, the implications of this national cohesion are profound. Internally, a record number of Ukraine's residents are now committed to and value the country's independence, and ever more Ukrainians are switching from speaking Russian or being bilingual to speaking only Ukrainian, because they do not want to use the language of the enemy. The post-2014 laws banned Soviet and Communist symbols and names, but since the beginning of the 2022 war, Ukrainian towns are also removing monuments and place names associated with the pre-1917 Russian Empire, and the push for these changes is coming from below, not from Kyiv. Many Ukrainians have cut off contact with friends and relatives in Russia who support the Kremlin's narrative or who refuse to believe that the Russian army is committing atrocities or bombing civilian targets. Such estrangement is tragic on the personal level, but it reinforces the message that citizens of Russia and Ukraine are, contrary to Putin's claims, members of two distinct—and now hostile—communities.

The outside world, probably for the first time ever, also moved from viewing Ukraine as a troublesome appendage of Russia to treating it as a separate state and nation. In 2022, on the eve of the Russian attack, only a third of Americans could place Ukraine on a map, but now anyone who watches the news or reads a paper knows about Ukraine. The number of foreigners learning Ukrainian has skyrocketed, and museums and cultural institutions across the globe no longer automatically label artists born in what is now Ukraine as "Russian." Following the full-scale Russian invasion, the European Parliament and national legislatures of Brazil, Germany, Italy, the Netherlands, and several other states recognized the Holodomor as genocide.[7]

When, after World War I and in the wake of Soviet collapse, great powers viewed the region and its conflicts predominantly from a Russian viewpoint, this weakened Ukraine and emboldened revanchism in Moscow. Hopefully, this recent shift in foreign attitudes will strengthen both Ukraine and those Russians who advocate restraint and responsible statecraft.

Russian violence helps to solidify Ukraine's inclusive national identity, but this cohesion cannot be taken for granted; identities and attitudes can change, and Ukrainians know this as well as anyone. No national or state-linked identity exists without at least some government interference, but for the peaceful future of Ukraine, it is essential that this interference does not become coercion. This is always a risk in the realm of identity formation, and it is therefore essential for Ukraine to remain a vibrant, inclusive democracy in which minorities and their rights are protected, government actions can be contested, and politicians are held accountable if their nation-building zeal oversteps the bounds of popular support. National unity in as diverse a country as Ukraine can never be maintained by force, and any attempts to do so will be self-defeating. A push by one camp, region, or party to impose its vision on the rest of the country will fracture Ukrainian society, weaken it from within, and invite future external interference.

Ukrainian national identity is still a work in progress, and after the war Ukrainians will have to address painful issues, including the memory of the conflict, future relations with Russia and Russians, what to do with those who collaborated with Russian authorities in occupied areas, and the role in the new national mythology of past violence, the OUN, the UPA, and their leaders. Each of these issues has the potential to cause internal rifts. Some—like the lionization of Stepan Bandera—might become especially contentious not just within Ukraine but also in relations between Ukraine and Poland, Kyiv's key supporter, and between Ukraine and the EU. But the war is also an opportunity to create a pantheon of new heroes who fought for Ukraine's independence but are not politically divisive and who strengthen Ukraine's inclusive identity. The choice of identity and historical narrative is a decision for Ukraine alone, but it will have implications for Russia's willingness to view Ukraine as a separate nation and for the Kremlin's ability to secure local support if it decides to dominate or conquer Ukraine once again.

Importantly, Russian acceptance of Ukrainian independence would mean coexistence but not necessarily reconciliation. Reconciliation between Russia and Ukraine will be much harder to achieve because it will require Russia to accept responsibility for the invasion and the atrocities it committed, demonstrate genuine remorse, and, ideally, punish war criminals and compensate victims. None of this is likely to happen unless Russia is defeated and a new government comes to power in Moscow. Even if Russia apologizes and pays reparations, it will take decades for Ukraine's wounds to heal. Mass violence and genocide affect societies for generations, and violent trauma experienced by parents impacts their offspring, even those born after the violence is over.[8]

For Ukraine, the Israel model might unfortunately mean not just the militarization of public life and investment in defense production but also a society where the memory of war and genocide is the key pillar of national identity that defines relations with the outside world. In this model, each threat and attack could trigger existential fears and drive violent overreactions. A victory in the war might mitigate the effects of victimhood, but they will endure for decades, even after the physical destruction has been repaired and the economy recovered.

The West—while unable to dictate how Russians and Ukrainians should structure their societies, national identities, and foreign relations—can help to contain Russia, shore up Ukrainian democracy, and give the country the tools it needs to protect itself. In addition to the NATO collective defense protection, the EU is another organization crucial for securing Ukraine's future, and at the time of writing Ukraine is finally on track to become a member state. EU membership is not a panacea and cannot prevent economic crisis, mismanagement, corruption, xenophobia, and even autocracy. But it is nonetheless an effective tool to minimize and confront these vices, and the accession process that requires candidate states to meet multiple membership criteria is an important catalyst for reforms. The prize of EU membership is also powerful enough an incentive for society and entrenched interests to tolerate the social and political price of potentially painful changes.

The Orange Revolution and Euromaidan were driven by Ukrainians' dreams of a better, democratic, and prosperous European future. Many citizens of Ukraine were willing to endure cold, police brutality, and repression to keep this dream alive. Since February 2022, Ukrainians are paying the ultimate price for this determination to join the European community instead of the Russian World. EU membership would be a natural and morally just outcome of this process. Closing the EU door, on the other hand, would shatter not just Ukraine's aspirations but also the very foundations of its efforts to build a democratic and free society.

Becoming fully "European" also implies accepting or at least paying lip service to the dominant Western European historical narrative in which Nazi Germany is the ultimate evil and collaboration with the Nazis deserves unqualified condemnation. Yet this narrative creates inevitable complications in places where both Germany and the Soviet Union were foreign occupiers, and where national liberation fighters collaborated with the Nazis against the Soviets and some also became implicated in the Holocaust. It is unlikely that Poland or Germany will suddenly change their perception of the OUN or the UPA and their actions during World War II, nor should they. Therefore, it is possible that eventually Ukrainians will have to choose between Bandera and Brussels. Yet this might also be an opportunity for an honest, nuanced discussion about the darkest events of European history: the impact, legacies, and lessons of the Holocaust and World War II. This discussion should take place not just between Ukraine and the EU but also within Ukraine and within the EU itself, where some member states exhibit increasingly neofascist, far-right, and revisionist tendencies.

On the most fundamental level, the West needs to keep supporting Ukraine's fight for sovereignty and territorial integrity until the liberation of occupied Ukrainian territories or for as long as Ukrainians themselves have the will to keep fighting. Western partners should not pressure Ukraine to make concessions, agree to cease-fires, or freeze the conflict if Russia remains committed to destroying Ukraine. This does not mean that cease-fires, concessions, or compromises are impossible or undesirable, but unless the Kremlin changes its goals, they will just offer Russia the breathing space to regroup, rearm, and attack again. The West should also avoid the trap of going back to business as usual with Russia and hoping that trade and economic engagement alone will suffice to change Russia's behavior and attitudes toward Ukraine and other neighbors. Without deep political and ideological change within Russia, this will just provide the Kremlin with more leverage over the West and money and equipment to build and sustain imperial expansion and anti-Western political and military mobilization.

Having endured repression, invasion, famine, and genocide, Ukrainians justifiably want Russia to finally leave them alone. Whether this will happen depends first and foremost on Russian society and its willingness to respect Ukrainian sovereignty, abandon irredentist dreams, and shed its widespread belief in the unity of the two nations. Neither Ukraine nor any other country can force Russians to change or abandon their perceptions of national identity and history. Only through deep internal change will Russia's intent to destroy Ukraine be consigned to painful history, and never again be policy.

What Ukraine can do is maintain its unity by wholeheartedly embracing democracy and prioritizing a unique, inclusive civic national identity over exclusionary and radical alternatives. Western partners ought to assist Ukraine in this process, but the initiative and the main effort should come from within Ukraine itself. The key lesson of history is that only a strong, united, and democratic Ukraine can meet the challenges of independent statehood and survive, even if there are forces intent on destroying it.

ACKNOWLEDGMENTS

My biggest thanks are to those who over the years dreamed of, fought for, and sought to create a democratic, liberal, and inclusive Ukraine. Many do this as I write these words, and I am grateful for their effort and sacrifices.

I decided to write this book after Dutch and American security services uncovered a former student of mine, Victor Muller Ferreira, as Sergei Cherkasov, a Russian intelligence operative. I do not expect Cherkasov to understand the damage and injustice carried out by the state he serves, even if he ever reads this book. But hopefully this book will help others better grasp the genocidal nature of Russia's policies, and I thank Cherkasov for prompting me to write it. I also hope his superiors in Russian intelligence know the crucial role Cherkasov played in making this book about Russian violence happen.

Writing a book is a collective endeavor, especially when it is written in response to ongoing events yet takes a broad historical view. I benefited from the generosity and wisdom of many colleagues and friends who commented on the text, shared their knowledge, and offered advice and encouragement. I could not have written this book without the help of Maxim Ananyev, Dominique Arel, Janetta Azarieva, Fabian Baumann,

Elissa Bemporad, Yitzhak Brudny, Eliot Cohen, Janine di Giovanni, Bart Drakulich, Volodymyr Dubovyk, Ian Garner, Scott Gehlbach, Mark Gilbert, Anna Hájková, Yoi Herrera, Ellie Knott, Jeff Kopstein, Andrey Kozyrev, Serhiy Kudelia, Mart Kuldkepp, Jared McBride, Danylo Mokryk, Radomyr Mokryk, Dirk Moses, Olga Onuch, Mike Plummer, Oleksandr Polianichev, Peter Pomerantsev, Maria Popova, Elena Racheva, Sergey Radchenko, Luís de Matos Ribeiro, Per Rudling, Steven Seegel, Oxana Shevel, Marci Shore, Kate Tsurkan, John Vsetecka, Polly Zavadivker, and the students in my Russia and Ukraine in Peace and War class. I am grateful to Emma Shercliff and the family of Victoria Amelina for the permission to reproduce her poem "Sirens." There are surely others who should be named as well, and I apologize for the omission. Of course, all mistakes are my responsibility only.

Johns Hopkins SAIS Library staff found every possible book and article that I needed, and I am grateful to Gail Martin, Ludovica Barozzi, Heather Kochevar, and Maria Marcich for their efforts. My students Vanina Morrison, Jack Kennedy, and Georgiy Kent were extraordinary research assistants who helped with data collection, editing, and fact-checking; Louis Martin-Vezian, also a former student, produced the maps.

My agent, Caroline Hardman, took a chance on a hapless academic who has never published a general audience book before, and she and the entire team at Hardman & Swainson did their best to demystify the process of nonacademic publishing. At Basic Books in New York and London, Brian Distelberg, Joe Zigmond, and Michael Kaler were dream editors who asked pointed questions, never compromised on clarity, steered my thinking in the right direction, and made the book so much better as a result. Also at Basic Books, I thank Sarah Caro, Alex Cullina, Kelly Lenkevich, Shena Redmond, Siam Hatzaw, and Caroline Westmore. Liz Dana expertly copyedited the text.

My parents and sister always cared but were careful not to ask too much about how the writing was going, especially when the going got tough. Finally, and most importantly, I am deeply grateful to Julie, my wife, and to our children, who supported me, always, through thick and thin, despite my obsessions with war, violence, and genocide. They did all they could to keep me sane (more or less), tolerated me when I was unbearable, and showered me with love and support, without which I would not have survived the many months of despair, research, and writing round the clock. Thank you for everything.

This book is dedicated to my grandmother, Lina Guler (born 1931). I pray she lives long enough to see her beloved Kyiv—in which she was born, grew up, got married, and gave birth to my mother—at peace again.

Notes

Introduction

1. Serhii Plokhy, *The Gates of Europe: A History of Ukraine* (New York: Basic Books, 2015).

2. Philippe Sands, *East West Street: On the Origins of "Genocide" and "Crimes Against Humanity"* (London: Vintage, 2017).

3. Nadav Shelef, *Homelands: Shifting Borders and Territorial Disputes* (Ithaca, NY: Cornell University Press, 2020).

4. Olga Onuch and Henry Hale, *The Zelensky Effect* (New York: Oxford University Press, 2022); Yitzhak Brudny and Evgeny Finkel, "Why Ukraine Is Not Russia: Hegemonic National Identity and Democracy in Russia and Ukraine," *East European Politics and Societies* 25, no. 4 (2011): 813–833.

5. Eugene Finkel, "What's Happening in Ukraine Is Genocide. Period.," *Washington Post*, April 6, 2022, www.washingtonpost.com/opinions/2022/04/05/russia-is-committing-genocide-in-ukraine/.

6. See, for example, Alex Hinton, "A Year On, We Have Clear Evidence of Genocide in Ukraine," *The Hill*, February 19, 2023, https://thehill.com/opinion/international/3859439-a-year-on-we-have-clear-evidence-of-genocide-in-ukraine/; Kristina Hook, "Why Russia's War in Ukraine Is a Genocide," *Foreign Affairs*, July 28, 2022, www.foreignaffairs.com/ukraine/why-russias-war-ukraine-genocide; Timothy Snyder, "Russia's Genocide Handbook," *Thinking About...* (newsletter), April 8, 2022, https://snyder.substack.com/p/russias-genocide-handbook.

Chapter 1: Deep States

1. Paul Magocsi, *A History of Ukraine* (Toronto: University of Toronto Press, 1996), 196–203.

2. Aleksandr Dugin, *Ukraina: Moia Voina* (Moscow: Tsentrpoligraf, 2015), 34.

3. Jake Epstein and John Haltiwanger, "US Embassy Trolls Russia with Meme After Putin's Revisionist History Rant on Why Ukraine Is Not a Real Country," *Business Insider*, February 22, 2022, www.businessinsider.com/us-embassy-trolls-russia-meme-after -putin-ukraine-history-rant-2022-2.

4. Scott Reynolds Nelson, *Oceans of Grain: How American Wheat Remade the World* (New York: Basic Books, 2022), chap. 2; Plokhy, *The Gates of Europe*, chaps. 3–5.

5. Yohanan Petrovsky-Shtern, "The Art of Shifting Contexts," *Harvard Ukrainian Studies* 34, no. 1/4 (2015): 241–257.

6. Oleksiy Tolochko, *Kievskaya Rus' i Malorossiya v XIX Veke* (Kyiv: Laurus, 2012), 11; Marie Favereau, *The Horde: How the Mongols Changed the World* (Cambridge, MA: Harvard University Press, 2021), chap. 2.

7. Favereau, *The Horde*, epilogue.

8. Geoffrey A. Hosking, *Russia and the Russians: A History* (Cambridge, MA: Harvard University Press, 2001), 5; Favereau, *The Horde*, 302.

9. Serhy Yekelchyk, *Ukraine: Birth of a Modern Nation* (New York: Oxford University Press, 2007), 26–28; Plokhy, *The Gates of Europe*, chap. 8.

10. Geoffrey Parker, *Global Crisis: War, Climate Change and Catastrophe in the Seventeenth Century* (New Haven, CT: Yale University Press, 2013), chap. 6.

11. Magocsi, *A History of Ukraine*, 196–199.

12. Adam Teller, *Rescue the Surviving Souls: The Great Jewish Refugee Crisis of the Seventeenth Century* (Princeton, NJ: Princeton University Press, 2020), chap. 1; Plokhy, *The Gates of Europe*, chap. 10.

13. Nathan Hanover, *Abyss of Despair* (London: Routledge, 2018), 44.

14. Teller, *Rescue the Surviving Souls*, 38, 59, 95, 149, 181, 307.

15. Charles King, *Odessa: Genius and Death in a City of Dreams* (New York: Norton, 2011), 101–102.

16. Plokhy, *The Gates of Europe*, 100–103.

17. Plokhy, *The Gates of Europe*, 104–105; Simon Sebag Montefiore, *Catherine the Great and Potemkin: Power, Love and the Russian Empire* (London: Hachette UK, 2010), 16–17.

18. Hosking, *Russia and the Russians*, 164–165.

19. Andreas Kappeler, "Mazepintsy, Malorossy, Khokhly: Ukrainians in the Ethnic Hierarchy of the Russian Empire," in *Culture, Nation, and Identity: The Ukrainian-Russian Encounter (1600–1945)*, ed. Andreas Kappeler et al. (Edmonton: Canadian Institute of Ukrainian Studies Press, 2003), 163; Zenon Kohut, "Origins of the Unity Paradigm: Ukraine and the Construction of Russian National History (1620–1860)," *Eighteenth-Century Studies* 35, no. 1 (2001): 71.

20. Alexei Miller, *The Ukrainian Question: Russian Empire and Nationalism in the 19th Century* (Budapest: Central European University Press, 2003), 21.

21. Tolochko, *Kievskaya Rus' i Malorossiya v XIX Veke*, 38.

22. Kelly O'Neill, *Claiming Crimea: A History of Catherine the Great's Southern Empire* (New Haven, CT: Yale University Press, 2017), 1; Orlando Figes, *Crimea: The Last Crusade* (London: Penguin, 2011), 14.

23. King, *Odessa*, 78–89.

24. Montefiore, *Catherine the Great and Potemkin*, 315–317.

25. O'Neill, *Claiming Crimea*, 30, chaps. 1–2.

26. Figes, *Crimea*, 442–452.

27. Rory Finnin, *Blood of Others: Stalin's Crimean Atrocity and the Poetics of Solidarity* (Toronto: University of Toronto Press, 2022), 14.

28. William Taubman, *Khrushchev: The Man and His Era* (New York: Norton, 2003), 24.

29. Charters Wynn, *Workers, Strikes, and Pogroms: The Donbass-Dnepr Bend in Late Imperial Russia, 1870–1905* (Princeton, NJ: Princeton University Press, 2014), 3, 20, 28; Hiroaki Kuromiya, *Freedom and Terror in the Donbas: A Ukrainian-Russian Borderland, 1870s–1990s* (New York: Cambridge University Press, 2003), 28.

30. Olga Andriewsky, "Medved' Iz Berlogi: Vladimir Jabotinsky and the Ukrainian Question, 1904–1914," *Harvard Ukrainian Studies* 14, no. 3/4 (1990): 249–267.

31. Trevor Erlacher, *Ukrainian Nationalism in the Age of Extremes: An Intellectual Biography of Dmytro Dontsov* (Cambridge, MA: Harvard University Press, 2021), 17.

Chapter 2: Of Brothers and Empires

1. Vladimir Putin, "On the Historical Unity of Russians and Ukrainians," President of Russia, July 12, 2021, http://en.kremlin.ru/events/president/news/66181; Owen Matthews, *Overreach: The Inside Story of Putin's War Against Ukraine* (London: HarperCollins, 2022), 33–35.

2. Tolochko, *Kievskaya Rus' i Malorossiya v XIX Veke*.

3. Tolochko, *Kievskaya Rus' i Malorossiya v XIX Veke*, chap. 2.

4. Serhiy Bilenky, *Romantic Nationalism in Eastern Europe: Russian, Polish, and Ukrainian Political Imaginations* (Stanford, CA: Stanford University Press, 2012), 38, 45, 244; Myroslav Shkandrij, *Russia and Ukraine: Literature and the Discourse of Empire from Napoleonic to Postcolonial Times* (Montreal: McGill-Queen's Press, 2001), 63.

5. Bilenky, *Romantic Nationalism in Eastern Europe*, 4–7, 183–189.

6. Bilenky, *Romantic Nationalism in Eastern Europe*, 31, 66; Shkandrij, *Russia and Ukraine*, 7.

7. Miller, *The Ukrainian Question*, chap. 4; Plokhy, *The Gates of Europe*, 166–170.

8. George Liber, *Total Wars and the Making of Modern Ukraine, 1914–1954* (Toronto: University of Toronto Press, 2016), 24.

9. Oleksandr Polianichev, personal communication, August 13, 2023.

10. Fabian Baumann, *Dynasty Divided: A Family History of Russian and Ukrainian Nationalism* (Ithaca, NY: Cornell University Press, 2023), 49–54.

11. Dominic Lieven, *The End of Tsarist Russia: The March to World War I and Revolution* (London: Penguin, 2016), 175.

12. Miller, *The Ukrainian Question*, introduction; Roman Szporluk, *Russia, Ukraine, and the Breakup of the Soviet Union* (Stanford, CA: Hoover Institution Press, 2000), 367.

13. Faith Hillis, *Children of Rus': Right-Bank Ukraine and the Invention of a Russian Nation* (Ithaca, NY: Cornell University Press, 2013), 77; Fabian Baumann, "Nationality as Choice of Path: Iakov Shul'gin, Dmitrii Pikhno, and the Russian-Ukrainian Crossroads," *Kritika: Explorations in Russian and Eurasian History* 23, no. 4 (2022): 743–771.

14. Hillis, *Children of Rus'*, 82–85.

15. Hillis, *Children of Rus'*, 169.

16. David Saunders, "Russia's Ukrainian Policy (1847–1905): A Demographic Approach," *European History Quarterly* 25, no. 2 (1995): 181–208; Andriewsky, "Medved' Iz Berlogi."

17. Hillis, *Children of Rus'*, 175.

18. Sergei Shchegolev, *Istoriia "Ukrainskogo" Separatizma* (Moscow: Imperskaia Traditsia, 2004); "Putin's Declaration of War on Ukraine," *The Spectator*, February 24, 2022, www.spectator.co.uk/article/full-text-putin-s-declaration-of-war-on-ukraine/.

19. Hillis, *Children of Rus'*, 192, 260; Andrey V. Storozhenko, *Proiskhozhdenie i Sushchnost' Ukrainofil'stva* (Kyiv: S. V. Kul'zhenko, 1912), 57; Ivan Sikorsky, *Russkie i Ukraintsy: Glava Iz Etnologicheskogo Katekhizisa. Doklad v Klube Russkikh Natsionalistov v Kieve, 7 Fevralia 1913.* (Kyiv: S. V. Kul'zhenko, 1913).

20. Edmund Levin, *A Child of Christian Blood: Murder and Conspiracy in Tsarist Russia* (New York: Penguin Random House, 2014), 13, 24.

21. Levin, *A Child of Christian Blood*.

22. Hillis, *Children of Rus'*, 263–264.

23. Levin, *A Child of Christian Blood*.

24. Hillis, *Children of Rus'*, 46–47.

25. Hillis, *Children of Rus'*, 260–261, 266–272.

26. Vera Tolz, *Russia: Inventing the Nation* (London: Bloomsbury Academic, 2001), 214.

27. Andriewsky, "Medved' Iz Berlogi," 263–264; Irina Mikhutina, *Ukrainskiy Vopros v Rossii (Konets XIX–Nachalo XX Veka)* (Moscow: Institut Slavianovedeniia RAN, 2003), 127–128.

28. Petr Struve, *Obshcherusskaia Kul'tura i Ukrainskii Partikuliarizm: Otvet Ukraintsu* (Moscow: Russkaia Mysl', 1912), 66.

29. Tolz, *Russia*, 169; Georgii Chernyavskii, *Milyukov* (Moscow: Molodai a Gvardiia, 2015).

Chapter 3: Liberation from Freedom

1. Christopher Clark, *The Sleepwalkers: How Europe Went to War in 1914* (London: Penguin, 2012).

2. Lieven, *The End of Tsarist Russia*, 1.

3. Lieven, *The End of Tsarist Russia*, 58.

4. Christopher Mick, *Lemberg, Lwow, and Lviv, 1914–1947: Violence and Ethnicity in a Contested City* (West Lafayette, IN: Purdue University Press, 2016), 5.

5. John-Paul Himka, *Galician Villagers and the Ukrainian National Movement in the Nineteenth Century* (New York: Macmillan Press, 1988), chap. 2; Mick, *Lemberg, Lwow, and Lviv*, 8; Alexander V. Prusin, *The Lands Between: Conflict in the East European Borderlands, 1870–1992* (New York: Oxford University Press, 2010), 23–32.

6. Yaroslav Hrytsak, "A Strange Case of Antisemitism: Ivan Franko and the Jewish Issue," in *Shatterzone of Empires: Coexistence and Violence in the German, Habsburg, Rus-*

sian, and Ottoman Borderlands, ed. Omer Bartov and Eric Weitz (Bloomington: Indiana University Press, 2013), 228–242; Omer Bartov, *Tales from the Borderlands: Making and Unmaking the Galician Past* (New Haven, CT: Yale University Press, 2022), 172–174.

7. Lieven, *The End of Tsarist Russia*, 175.

8. Bedwin Sands, *The Russians in Galicia* (New York: Ukrainian National Council, 1916), 34.

9. Lieven, *The End of Tsarist Russia*, 7–8, 58, 251; Paul Magocsi, *Roots of Ukrainian Nationalism: Galicia as Ukraine's Piedmont* (Toronto: University of Toronto Press, 2002).

10. Eric Lohr, *Nationalizing the Russian Empire: The Campaign Against Enemy Aliens During World War I* (Cambridge, MA: Harvard University Press, 2003), 25; Mikhutina, *Ukrainskiy Vopros v Rossii*, 188.

11. Peter Holquist, "The Role of Personality in the First (1914–1915) Russian Occupation of Galicia and Bukovina," in *Anti-Jewish Violence: Rethinking the Pogrom in East European History*, ed. Jonathan Dekel-Chen et al. (Bloomington: Indiana University Press, 2010), 52–73; Paul Robinson, *Grand Duke Nikolai Nikolaevich: Supreme Commander of the Russian Army* (DeKalb: Northern Illinois University Press, 2014), 3.

12. Mark von Hagen, *War in a European Borderland: Occupations and Occupation Plans in Galicia and Ukraine, 1914–1918* (Seattle: University of Washington Press, 2007), 20; Alexander Watson, *The Fortress: The Great Siege of Przemysl* (London: Penguin, 2019), 224; Robinson, *Grand Duke Nikolai Nikolaevich*, 139–140, 160–161.

13. Watson, *The Fortress*, 23, 45–46.

14. Włodzimierz Borodziej and Maciej Górny, *Forgotten Wars: Central and Eastern Europe, 1912–1916* (Cambridge: Cambridge University Press, 2021), 248–249, 263; David Stone, *The Russian Army in the Great War: The Eastern Front, 1914–1917* (Lawrence: University Press of Kansas, 2021), 99.

15. Julius Weber, *Rosiiska Okupatsiia Chernivtsiv* (Chernivtsi: Vydavnytstvo 21, 2016), 24.

16. *Otchet Deiatel'nosti Shtaba Vremennogo Voennogo General Gubernatora Galitsii v Period s 29 Avgusta 1914 Goda Po 1 Iulia 1915 Goda* (Kyiv: Tipographiia Shtaba Kievskogo Voennogo Okruga, 1916), app. 14, pp. 12–13.

17. Włodzimierz Borodziej and Maciej Górny, *The Great War in East-Central Europe: Central and Eastern Europe, 1912–1916* (Cambridge: Cambridge University Press, 2021), 245.

18. Weber, *Rosiiska Okupatsiia Chernivtsiv*, 115.

19. S. An-sky, *1915 Diary of S. An-sky: A Russian Jewish Writer at the Eastern Front*, trans. Polly Zavadivker (Bloomington: Indiana University Press, 2016), 51; Vladimir Ie. Grabar', "Zapisi vo vremia prebyvaniia v Stavke Verkhovnogo Glavnokomanduiushchego, 15 avg. 1914–5 maia 1915," 1915 1914, 94, F. 38 D. 50, University of Tartu Library Collections, Tartu, Estonia; Omer Bartov, *Voices on War and Genocide: Three Accounts of the World Wars in a Galician Town* (New York: Berghahn Books, 2020), 39.

20. Watson, *The Fortress*, 279, fn. 38.

21. Grabar', "Zapisi vo vremia prebyvaniia v Stavke Verkhovnogo Glavnokomanduiushchego," 63; Semen Gol'din, *Russkaia Armiia i Evrei 1914–1917* (Moscow: Mosty Kul'tury, 2018), 35, 54; S. An-sky, *The Enemy at His Pleasure: A Journey Through the Jewish Pale of Settlement During World War I* (New York: Macmillan, 2002), 68.

22. William W. Hagen, *Anti-Jewish Violence in Poland, 1914–1920* (New York: Cambridge University Press, 2018), 80; Holquist, "The Role of Personality," 55; An-sky, *1915 Diary*, 90; An-sky, *The Enemy at His Pleasure*, 8.

23. Watson, *The Fortress*, 119; Mick, *Lemberg, Lwow, and Lviv*, 23, 25, 41; Prusin, *The Lands Between*, 54.

24. An-sky, *1915 Diary*, 85–90.

25. Alexander Victor Prusin, *Nationalizing a Borderland: War, Ethnicity, and Anti-Jewish Violence in East Galicia, 1914–1920* (Tuscaloosa: University of Alabama Press, 2016), 33–34.

26. Grabar', "Zapisi vo vremia prebyvaniia v Stavke Verkhovnogo Glavnokomanduiushchego," 42; V. V. Zaitsev, "Politicheskaia Sud'ba Galitsii v Predstavlenii Russkikh Diplomatov (1913–1916)," *Russian History* 32, no. 1 (2005): 86–87; Aleksandra Iu. Bakhturina, *Okrainy Rossiiskoi Imperii: Gosudarstvennoe Upravlenie i Natsional'naia Politika v Gody Pervoi Mirovoi Voiny (1914–1917 gg.)* (Moscow: Rosspen, 2004), 127–129.

27. Grabar', "Zapisi vo vremia prebyvaniia v Stavke Verkhovnogo Glavnokomanduiushchego," 16–17, 80, 95.

28. Himka, *Galician Villagers*, 158; Lohr, *Nationalizing the Russian Empire*, 86.

29. *Otchet Deiatel'nosti*, app. 14, p. 25; Von Hagen, *War in a European Borderland*, 32; Grabar', "Zapisi vo vremia prebyvaniia v Stavke Verkhovnogo Glavnokomanduiushchego," 81.

30. Weber, *Rosiiska Okupatsiia Chernivtsiv*, 101.

31. Mick, *Lemberg, Lwow, and Lviv*, 29, 45; Weber, *Rosiiska Okupatsiia Chernivtsiv*, 120; An-sky, *The Enemy at His Pleasure*, 67.

32. Von Hagen, *War in a European Borderland*, 26.

33. Bartov, *Voices on War and Genocide*, 54; Bakhturina, *Okrainy Rossiiskoi Imperii*, 154. Correspondence in Yiddish was also forbidden.

34. Von Hagen, *War in a European Borderland*, 27; Watson, *The Fortress*, 114; Bakhturina, *Okrainy Rossiiskoi Imperii*, 152.

35. Grabar', "Zapisi vo vremia prebyvaniia v Stavke Verkhovnogo Glavnokomanduiushchego," 23; Von Hagen, *War in a European Borderland*, 24.

36. Georgii Shavel'skii, *Vospominaniia Poslednego Protopresvitera Russkoi Armii* (New York: Izdatel'stvo im. Chekhova, 1954), 124.

37. Mick, *Lemberg, Lwow, and Lviv*, 52.

38. Mitropolit Evlogii (Georgievskii), *Put' Moei Zhizni: Mitropolit Evlogii (Georgievskii)* (Moscow: Khudozhestvennaia Literatura, 2022), 162; Shavel'skii, *Vospominaniia Poslednego Protopresvitera Russkoi Armii*, 123–127.

39. Evlogii, *Put' Moei Zhizni*, 167.

40. Mick, *Lemberg, Lwow, and Lviv*, 56; Bakhturina, *Okrainy Rossiiskoi Imperii*, 194; An-sky, *1915 Diary*, 68.

41. Borodziej and Górny, *Forgotten Wars*, 273; Weber, *Rosiiska Okupatsiia Chernivtsiv*, 88, 92–93.

42. Grabar', "Zapisi vo vremia prebyvaniia v Stavke Verkhovnogo Glavnokomanduiushchego," 95; Von Hagen, *War in a European Borderland*, 34.

43. *Otchet Deiatel'nosti*, app. 14, p. 16.

44. William Fuller, *The Foe Within: Fantasies of Treason and the End of Imperial Russia* (Ithaca, NY: Cornell University Press, 2006), chap. 1; Robinson, *Grand Duke Nikolai Nikolaevich*, 207–208.

45. Gol'din, *Russkaia Armiia i Evrei*, 181; Polly Zavadivker, *A Nation of Refugees: World War I and Russia's Jews* (New York: Oxford University Press, forthcoming), chap. 2; Peter Gatrell, *A Whole Empire Walking: Refugees in Russia During World War I* (Bloomington: Indiana University Press, 2005), 21.

46. Liber, *Total Wars and the Making of Modern Ukraine*, 48; Gatrell, *A Whole Empire Walking*, 23–24, 166–168.

47. Mikhutina, *Ukrainskiy Vopros v Rossii*, 194–205.

Chapter 4: Blood and Chaos

1. Kelly Scott Johnson, "Sholem Schwarzbard: Biography of a Jewish Assassin" (PhD diss., Harvard University, 2012), 148.

2. Gatrell, *A Whole Empire Walking*, 3.

3. Liber, *Total Wars and the Making of Modern Ukraine*, 43.

4. Joshua Sanborn, *Imperial Apocalypse: The Great War and the Destruction of the Russian Empire* (New York: Oxford University Press, 2014), 199–200.

5. Sanborn, *Imperial Apocalypse*, 200–204.

6. Stefan Mashkevych, *Kiev 1917–1920* (Kharkiv: Folio, 2019), 17–18.

7. Sanborn, *Imperial Apocalypse*, 215; Shkandrij, *Russia and Ukraine*, 97.

8. Johannes Remy, "'It Is Unknown Where the Little Russians Are Heading To': The Autonomy Dispute Between the Ukrainian Central Rada and the All-Russian Provisional Government in 1917," *Slavonic and East European Review* 95, no. 4 (October 2017): 696.

9. Mashkevych, *Kiev*, 87.

10. Sanborn, *Imperial Apocalypse*, 214.

11. Mark von Hagen, "The Russian Imperial Army and the Ukrainian National Movement in 1917," *Ukrainian Quarterly* 54, no. 3–4 (1998): 244; Mashkevych, *Kiev*, 160.

12. Mashkevych, *Kiev*, 211, 220–221; Jeffrey Veidlinger, *In the Midst of Civilized Europe: The 1918–1921 Pogroms in Ukraine and the Onset of the Holocaust* (London: Picador, 2022), 58–59, 61.

13. Liber, *Total Wars and the Making of Modern Ukraine*, 65; Veidlinger, *In the Midst of Civilized Europe*, 90.

14. Manuil Margulies, *Letopis' Revoliutsii*, vol. 1 (Berlin: Izdatel'stvo Z. I. Grzhebina, 1923).

15. Anna Procyk, *Russian Nationalism and Ukraine: The Nationality Policy of the Volunteer Army During the Civil War* (Edmonton: Canadian Institute of Ukrainian Studies Press, 1995).

16. Irina Mikhutina, *Ukrainskii Brestskii Mir* (Moscow: Evropa, 2007), 57.

17. Elissa Bemporad, *Legacy of Blood: Jews, Pogroms, and Ritual Murder in the Lands of the Soviets* (New York: Oxford University Press, 2019), 37; Antony Beevor, *Russia: Revolution and Civil War 1917–1921* (London: Weidenfeld & Nicolson, 2022), 141–143.

18. Laura Engelstein, *Russia in Flames: War, Revolution, Civil War, 1914–1921* (New York: Oxford University Press, 2018), 320.

19. Sanborn, *Imperial Apocalypse*, 233.

20. Yekelchyk, *Ukraine*, chap. 4.

21. Chernyavskii, *Milyukov*; Margulies, *Letopis' Revoliutsii*, 1:32–33.

22. Luke Harding, "'Propaganda Literature': Calls to Close Mikhail Bulgakov Museum in Kyiv," *The Guardian*, December 31, 2022, www.theguardian.com/culture/2022/dec/31/mikhail-bulgakov-museum-kyiv-calls-to-close.

23. Liber, *Total Wars and the Making of Modern Ukraine*, 69; Kuromiya, *Freedom and Terror in the Donbas*, 94.

24. Stephen Velychenko, *Life and Death in Revolutionary Ukraine* (Montreal: McGill-Queen's University Press, 2021), 132–138.

25. Vasyl Kuchabsky, *Western Ukraine in Conflict with Poland and Bolshevism, 1918–1923* (Edmonton: Canadian Institute of Ukrainian Studies Press, 2009), 24–25; Von Hagen, *War in a European Borderland*, 12–15.

26. Prusin, *Nationalizing a Borderland*, chaps. 4–6; Mick, *Lemberg, Lwow, and Lviv*, chap. 3.

27. Kuchabsky, *Western Ukraine in Conflict with Poland and Bolshevism*, 263.

28. Procyk, *Russian Nationalism and Ukraine*, 101, 125, 134.

29. Arnold D. Margolin, *From a Political Diary: Russia, the Ukraine, and America, 1905–1945* (New York: Columbia University Press, 1946), 35–48.

30. Kuchabsky, *Western Ukraine in Conflict with Poland and Bolshevism*, 289.

31. Kuchabsky, *Western Ukraine in Conflict with Poland and Bolshevism*, 294–302.

32. Jochen Böhler, *Civil War in Central Europe, 1918–1921: The Reconstruction of Poland* (New York: Oxford University Press, 2018), chap. 3; Norman Davies, *White Eagle, Red Star: The Polish-Soviet War 1919–20 and "The Miracle on the Vistula"* (London: Random House, 2003), 102.

33. Adam Zamoyski, *Warsaw 1920: Lenin's Failed Conquest of Europe* (New York: HarperCollins, 2008), 38.

34. Veidlinger, *In the Midst of Civilized Europe*, 4–5; Thomas Chopard, "Sexual Violence During Pogroms: The Civil War in Ukraine as a Laboratory for Anti-Jewish Violence (1917–22)," *Ukraina Moderna*, no. 29 (2020): 190–220.

35. Henry Abramson, *A Prayer for the Government: Ukrainians and Jews in Revolutionary Times* (Cambridge, MA: Ukrainian Research Institute of Harvard University, 1999).

36. Christopher Gilley, "Beyond Petliura: The Ukrainian National Movement and the 1919 Pogroms," *East European Jewish Affairs* 47, no. 1 (2017): 45–61.

37. Gilley, "Beyond Petliura."

38. Kuromiya, *Freedom and Terror in the Donbas*, 86; Veidlinger, *In the Midst of Civilized Europe*, 67; Bemporad, *Legacy of Blood*, 20–23.

Chapter 5: Making a Model Republic

1. James Earnest Mace and Leonid Heretz, eds., *Investigation of the Ukrainian Famine, 1932–1933: Oral History Project of the Commission on the Ukraine Famine*, vol. 2 (Washington, DC: US Government Printing Office, 1990), 1045–1051.

2. Stephen Kotkin, *Stalin: Paradoxes of Power, 1878–1928* (New York: Penguin Books, 2014), 475–476.

3. Zhores Medvedev, *Soviet Agriculture* (New York: Norton, 1987), 32; Lars Lih, *Bread and Authority in Russia, 1914–1921* (Berkeley: University of California Press, 1990), 126–133; Lynne Viola, *Peasant Rebels Under Stalin: Collectivization and the Culture of Peasant Resistance* (New York: Oxford University Press, 1999), 16.

4. Anne Applebaum, *Red Famine: Stalin's War on Ukraine* (New York: Doubleday, 2017), 24–25, 34.

5. Medvedev, *Soviet Agriculture*, 37–39; George Liber, *Soviet Nationality Policy, Urban Growth, and Identity Change in the Ukrainian SSR, 1923–1934* (New York: Cambridge University Press, 1992), 6; Douglas Smith, *The Russian Job: The Forgotten Story of How America Saved the Soviet Union from Famine* (New York: Farrar, Straus and Giroux, 2019).

6. Benjamin Weissman, *Herbert Hoover and Famine Relief to Soviet Russia, 1921–1923* (Stanford, CA: Hoover Institution Press, 1974), 9.

7. Liber, *Total Wars and the Making of Modern Ukraine*, 78.

8. Kate Brown, *A Biography of No Place* (Cambridge, MA: Harvard University Press, 2009), 20; Terry Dean Martin, *The Affirmative Action Empire: Nations and Nationalism in the Soviet Union, 1923–1939* (Ithaca, NY: Cornell University Press, 2001).

9. Martin, *The Affirmative Action Empire*, 81, 92; Matthew Pauly, *Breaking the Tongue: Language, Education, and Power in Soviet Ukraine, 1923–1934* (Toronto: University of Toronto Press, 2014), 4.

10. Applebaum, *Red Famine*, 92.

11. Martin, *The Affirmative Action Empire*, 9.

12. Liber, *Soviet Nationality Policy*, 87.

13. Pauly, *Breaking the Tongue*; Martin, *The Affirmative Action Empire*, 76, 82.

14. Liber, *Soviet Nationality Policy*.

15. Tolz, *Russia*, 220.

16. Liber, *Total Wars and the Making of Modern Ukraine*, 355–356, fn. 60; Shkandrij, *Russia and Ukraine*, 215–218.

17. Kuromiya, *Freedom and Terror in the Donbas*, 153; Viola, *Peasant Rebels Under Stalin*, 23.

18. Viola, *Peasant Rebels Under Stalin*, 3.

19. Natalya Naumenko, "The Political Economy of Famine: The Ukrainian Famine of 1933," *Journal of Economic History* 81, no. 1 (2021): 7–8.

20. Timothy Snyder, *Bloodlands: Europe Between Hitler and Stalin* (New York: Basic Books, 2010), 25–26.

21. Snyder, *Bloodlands*, 28; Taubman, *Khrushchev*, 76.

22. Yuri Shapoval and Vadim Zolotarev, *Gil'otina Ukrainy: Narkom Vsevolod Balitskiy i Ego Sud'ba* (Moskva: Politicheskaia Entsiklopediia, 2017), 132.

23. Andrei Markevich, Natalya Naumenko, and Nancy Qian, "The Causes of Ukrainian Famine Mortality, 1932–33" (Fairfax, VA: George Mason University, 2022), 7, https://papers.ssrn.com/sol3/Papers.cfm?abstract_id=3894621#; Andrea Graziosi, *The Great Soviet*

Peasant War: Bolsheviks and Peasants, 1917–1933 (Cambridge, MA: Ukrainian Research Institute of Harvard University, 1996).

24. Shapoval and Zolotarev, *Gil'otina Ukrainy*, 8–9, 24, 41.

25. Volodymyr Prystaiko and Yuri Shapoval, *Sprava "Spilky Vyzvolennia Ukrainy": Nevidomi Dokumenty i Fakty* (Kyiv: Intel, 1995), 108, 202.

26. Pauly, *Breaking the Tongue*, 258–268; Prystaiko and Shapoval, *Sprava "Spilky Vyzvolennia Ukrainy"*, 40–141; Martin, *The Affirmative Action Empire*, 249.

27. Myroslav Shkandrij and Olga Bertelsen, "The Soviet Regime's National Operations in Ukraine, 1929–1934," *Canadian Slavonic Papers* 55, no. 3–4 (2013): 417–447.

28. Martin, *The Affirmative Action Empire*, 346–356; Daria Mattingly, "'Idle, Drunk and Good-for-Nothing': The Rank-and-File Perpetrators of 1932–1933 Famine in Ukraine and Their Representation in Cultural Memory" (PhD diss., Cambridge University, 2018), 38, 56.

29. Shapoval and Zolotarev, *Gil'otina Ukrainy*, 228.

30. Bohdan Klid and Alexander Motyl, eds., *The Holodomor Reader: A Sourcebook on the Famine of 1932–1933 in Ukraine* (Edmonton: Canadian Institute of Ukrainian Studies Press, 2012), 277; Kateryna Zarembo, *Skhid Ukrains'koho Sontsia* (Lviv: Choven, 2023), 30–31.

31. David Brandenberger, *National Bolshevism: Stalinist Mass Culture and the Formation of Modern Russian National Identity, 1931–1956* (Cambridge, MA: Harvard University Press, 2002), chap. 3.

32. Serhy Yekelchyk, "The Making of a 'Proletarian Capital': Patterns of Stalinist Social Policy in Kiev in the Mid-1930s," *Europe-Asia Studies* 50, no. 7 (1998): 1229–1230; Serhy Yekelchyk, *Stalin's Empire of Memory: Russian-Ukrainian Relations in the Soviet Historical Imagination* (Toronto: University of Toronto Press, 2004), 17, 19.

33. Anastasiia Lysyvets', *Skazhy pro Shchaslyve Zhyttia. . .* (Kyiv: K.I.S., 2019), 27–38.

34. Markevich, Naumenko, and Qian, "The Causes of Ukrainian Famine Mortality," 25; Applebaum, *Red Famine*, chap. 7.

35. Applebaum, *Red Famine*, 182.

36. O. V. Khlevnyuk et al., eds., *Stalin i Kaganovich: Perepiska, 1931–1936 gg* (Moskva: Rosspen, 2001), 273–274. Underlined in the original.

37. Applebaum, *Red Famine*, chap. 8.

38. Lysyvets', *Skazhy pro Shchaslyve Zhyttia*, 33.

39. Klid and Motyl, *The Holodomor Reader*, 126; Oleh Wolowyna, Nataliia Levchuk, and Alla Kovbasiuk, "Monthly Distribution of 1933 Famine Losses in Soviet Ukraine and the Russian Soviet Republic at the Regional Level," *Nationalities Papers* 48, no. 3 (2020): 530–548; Graziosi, *The Great Soviet Peasant War*.

40. Lev Kopelev, *I Sotvoril Sebe Kumira* (Kharkiv: Prava Liudyny, 2010), 270–271; Mattingly, "Idle, Drunk and Good-for-Nothing," 45.

41. Alexandra Popoff, *Vasily Grossman and the Soviet Century* (New Haven, CT: Yale University Press, 2019), 57; Michael Ellman, "Stalin and the Soviet Famine of 1932–33 Revisited," *Europe-Asia Studies* 59, no. 4 (2007): 672.

42. Carveth Wells, *Kapoot: The Narrative of a Journey from Leningrad to Mount Ararat in Search of Noah's Ark* (New York: McBride and Company, 1933), 113–114; Popoff, *Vasily Grossman and the Soviet Century*, 56–57, 292–295.

43. Stanislav Kul'chyts'kyi, "Pochemu on Nas Unichtozhal? Stalin i Ukrainskii Golodomor," *Kiev: Ukrainskaia Press-Gruppa* 15 (2007): 10.

44. Robert Davies and Stephen Wheatcroft, *The Years of Hunger: Soviet Agriculture, 1931–1933* (Basingstoke, UK: Palgrave Macmillan, 2004); Mark Tauger, "The 1932 Harvest and the Famine of 1933," *Slavic Review* 50, no. 1 (1991): 70–89; Naumenko, "The Political Economy of Famine."

45. Alec Nove, quoted in David R. Marples, "Ethnic Issues in the Famine of 1932–1933 in Ukraine," *Europe-Asia Studies* 61, no. 3 (2009): 508; Markevich, Naumenko, and Qian, "The Causes of Ukrainian Famine Mortality."

46. Hiroaki Kuromiya, *The Voices of the Dead: Stalin's Great Terror in the 1930s* (New Haven, CT: Yale University Press, 2007), 15, 110; Lynne Viola, *Stalinist Perpetrators on Trial: Scenes from the Great Terror in Soviet Ukraine* (New York: Oxford University Press, 2017), 15; John Vsetecka, "The Poetics of Hunger: Responding to Rupture in the Wake of the 1932–1933 Famine (Holodomor) in Soviet Ukraine," *Russian Review* https://onlinelibrary.wiley.com/doi/10.1111/russ.12582.

47. Kuromiya, *The Voices of the Dead*, 16, 218.

48. Taubman, *Khrushchev*, 119–128; Viola, *Stalinist Perpetrators on Trial*, 60.

49. Viola, *Stalinist Perpetrators on Trial*, 21.

50. Arturas Rozenas and Yuri M. Zhukov, "Mass Repression and Political Loyalty: Evidence from Stalin's 'Terror by Hunger,'" *American Political Science Review* 113, no. 2 (2019): 569–583; Vitaliia Yaremko, "The Long-Term Consequences of Blacklisting: Evidence from the Ukrainian Famine of 1932–33" (manuscript, University of California, Berkeley, 2022).

Chapter 6: Unite and Rule

1. Roger Moorhouse, *The Devils' Alliance: Hitler's Pact with Stalin, 1939–1941* (London: Bodley Head, 2014), 1, 25.

2. Yekelchyk, *Stalin's Empire of Memory*, 24–25; Sean McMeekin, *Stalin's War: A New History of World War II* (New York: Basic Books, 2021), 99.

3. Evgeny Finkel, *Ordinary Jews: Choice and Survival During the Holocaust* (Princeton, NJ: Princeton University Press, 2017), 46.

4. Mick, *Lemberg, Lwow, and Lviv*, 262–270.

5. Prusin, *The Lands Between*.

6. Oleksandr Zaitsev, *Ukrainskyi Intehralnyi Natsionalizm (1920–1930-ti roky): Narysy Intelektualnoi Istorii* (Kyiv: Krytyka, 2013); Erlacher, *Ukrainian Nationalism in the Age of Extremes*.

7. Timothy Snyder, *Sketches from a Secret War: A Polish Artist's Mission to Liberate Soviet Ukraine* (New Haven, CT: Yale University Press, 2007); Alexander Motyl, "Ukrainian Nationalist Political Violence in Inter-War Poland, 1921–1939," *East European Quarterly* 19, no. 1 (1985): 45.

8. Timothy Snyder, "The Causes of Ukrainian-Polish Ethnic Cleansing 1943," *Past & Present*, no. 179 (2003): 208.

9. Jacob Mikanowski, *Goodbye Eastern Europe: An Intimate History of a Divided Land* (London: Oneworld Publications, 2023), 235.

10. John-Paul Himka, *Ukrainian Nationalists and the Holocaust* (Stuttgart, Germany: Ibidem, 2021).

11. Jared McBride, "Peasants into Perpetrators: The OUN-UPA and the Ethnic Cleansing of Volhynia, 1943–1944," *Slavic Review* 75, no. 3 (2016): 630–654.

12. Yekelchyk, *Stalin's Empire of Memory*.

13. Alexander Statiev, *The Soviet Counterinsurgency in the Western Borderlands* (Cambridge: Cambridge University Press, 2010), 106.

14. Oksana Kis, *Survival as Victory: Ukrainian Women in the Gulag* (Cambridge, MA: Harvard University Press, 2021), 3; Serhii Plokhy, *The Man with the Poison Gun: A Cold War Spy Story* (New York: Basic Books, 2016), 9.

15. Serhiy Kudelia, "Choosing Violence in Irregular Wars: The Case of Anti-Soviet Insurgency in Western Ukraine," *East European Politics and Societies* 27, no. 1 (2013): 149–181; Statiev, *The Soviet Counterinsurgency in the Western Borderlands*, chaps. 4, 8.

16. Grzegorz Rossolinski-Liebe, *Stepan Bandera: The Life and Afterlife of a Ukrainian Nationalist* (Stuttgart, Germany: Ibidem, 2014).

17. William Jay Risch, *The Ukrainian West: Culture and the Fate of Empire in Soviet Lviv* (Cambridge, MA: Harvard University Press, 2011); Tarik Cyril Amar, *The Paradox of Ukrainian Lviv: A Borderland City Between Stalinists, Nazis, and Nationalists* (Ithaca, NY: Cornell University Press, 2015).

18. Radomyr Mokryk, *Bunt Proty Impreii* (Kyiv: A-ba-ba-ha-la-ma-ha, 2023), part 1.

19. Brian Glyn Williams, *The Crimean Tatars: From Soviet Genocide to Putin's Conquest* (New York: Oxford University Press, 2015), 97.

20. Buta Butaev, *Amet-Khan Sultan* (Moscow: Politizdat, 1990), chap. 2.

21. Williams, *The Crimean Tatars*, 100–109.

22. Finnin, *Blood of Others*; Greta Uehling, "Genocide's Aftermath: Neostalinism in Contemporary Crimea," *Genocide Studies and Prevention* 9, no. 1 (2015): 3.

23. Gwendolyn Sasse, *The Crimea Question: Identity, Transition, and Conflict* (Cambridge, MA: Harvard University Press, 2007), chap. 5.

24. Jonathan Brunstedt, *The Soviet Myth of World War II: Patriotic Memory and the Russian Question in the USSR* (New York: Cambridge University Press, 2021), chaps. 2, 4.

25. Yitzhak Brudny, *Reinventing Russia: Russian Nationalism and the Soviet State, 1953–1991* (Cambridge, MA: Harvard University Press, 1998).

26. Maria Popova and Oxana Shevel, *Russia and Ukraine: Entangled Histories, Diverging States* (Cambridge: Polity, 2023), 32; Zarembo, *Skhid Ukrains'koho Sontsia*.

27. Mokryk, *Bunt Proty Impreii*; Alexei Yurchak, *Everything Was Forever, Until It Was No More: The Last Soviet Generation* (Princeton, NJ: Princeton University Press, 2013).

28. William Taubman, *Gorbachev: His Life and Times* (New York: Simon & Schuster, 2017); Vladislav Zubok, *Collapse: The Fall of the Soviet Union* (London: Yale University Press, 2021).

29. Adam Higginbotham, *Midnight in Chernobyl: The Untold Story of the World's Greatest Nuclear Disaster* (New York: Random House, 2019), 17, 85–88.

30. Higginbotham, *Midnight in Chernobyl*, 182–183.

31. Serhii Plokhy, *Chernobyl: History of a Tragedy* (London: Penguin UK, 2018), 286.

32. Taras Kuzio and Andrew Wilson, *Ukraine: Perestroika to Independence* (London: Macmillan Press, 1994), 101; Plokhy, *Chernobyl*, 306.

33. Leon Aron, *Yeltsin: A Revolutionary Life* (New York: HarperCollins, 2000), 368; Zubok, *Collapse*, 99.

34. Popova and Shevel, *Russia and Ukraine*.

35. Kuzio and Wilson, *Ukraine*, 159; Zubok, *Collapse*, 266.

36. Eugene Fishel, *The Moscow Factor: US Policy Toward Sovereign Ukraine and the Kremlin* (Cambridge, MA: Harvard University Press, 2022), 42, 44; Serhii Plokhy, *The Last Empire: The Final Days of the Soviet Union* (London: Hachette UK, 2015), 49, 63–64.

37. Plokhy, *The Last Empire*, 164.

38. Plokhy, *The Last Empire*, 179.

39. Zubok, *Collapse*, 324–325.

40. Plokhy, *The Last Empire*, 273; Zubok, *Collapse*, 384.

41. Zubok, *Collapse*, 387.

42. Interview with Andrey Kozyrev, July 19, 2023.

Chapter 7: Phantom Pains

1. "Goluboi Ogonek 2014" (Moscow, 2014), YouTube, posted by Schiaccianoci on January 2, 2023, www.youtube.com/watch?v=ckmDB_Ard2w.

2. Yegor Gaidar, *Dni Porazhenii i Pobed* (Moscow: Vagrius, 1996), 153; interview with Kozyrev.

3. Aleksandr Solzhenitsyn, *S Ukrainoi Budet Chrezvychaino Bol'no* (Moscow: AST, 2022).

4. Tolz, *Russia*, 227, 230–231.

5. Geoffrey Hosking, "The Freudian Frontier," *Times Literary Supplement*, March 10, 1995.

6. Timothy Colton, *Yeltsin: A Life* (New York: Basic Books, 2008), 266.

7. Sasse, *The Crimea Question*, 70, 74; Egor Kholmogorov, *Karat' Karatelei: Khroniki Russkoi Vesny* (Moscow: Knizhnyi Mir, 2014), 135.

8. Yurii Luzhkov, *Moskva i Zhizn'* (Moscow: Eksmo, 2017), 313.

9. Egor Kholmogorov, *Russkii Natsionalist* (Moscow: Evropa, 2006).

10. Charles Clover, *Black Wind, White Snow: Russia's New Nationalism* (New Haven, CT: Yale University Press, 2022), 12; Marlene Laruelle, *Is Russia Fascist?: Unraveling Propaganda East and West* (Ithaca, NY: Cornell University Press, 2021), 117.

11. Colton, *Yeltsin*, 266.

12. Paul D'Anieri, *Ukraine and Russia: From Civilized Divorce to Uncivil War* (New York: Cambridge University Press, 2019), 54.

13. Brudny and Finkel, "Why Ukraine Is Not Russia."

14. Tolz, *Russia*, 264–265; Brudny and Finkel, "Why Ukraine Is Not Russia"; Popova and Shevel, *Russia and Ukraine*, 58, 63; Brudny, *Reinventing Russia*, 264.

15. Brudny and Finkel, "Why Ukraine Is Not Russia," 825–826.

16. Lucan Way, *Pluralism by Default: Weak Autocrats and the Rise of Competitive Politics* (Baltimore: Johns Hopkins University Press, 2015).

17. Popova and Shevel, *Russia and Ukraine*; Onuch and Hale, *The Zelensky Effect*.

18. Mariana Budjeryn, *Inheriting the Bomb: The Collapse of the USSR and the Nuclear Disarmament of Ukraine* (Baltimore: Johns Hopkins University Press, 2022), 34.

19. John Mearsheimer, "The Case for a Ukrainian Nuclear Deterrent," *Foreign Affairs*, 1993, 50–66.

20. Andrei Kozyrev, *The Firebird: The Elusive Fate of Russian Democracy* (Pittsburgh: University of Pittsburgh Press, 2019), 77–78; interview with Kozyrev.

21. Fishel, *The Moscow Factor*.

22. Fishel, *The Moscow Factor*, 75; Budjeryn, *Inheriting the Bomb*, 192.

23. Fishel, *The Moscow Factor*, 105–106.

24. George Bogden, "Deceit, Dread, and Disbelief: The Story of How Ukraine Lost Its Nuclear Arsenal," *National Interest*, October 27, 2023, https://nationalinterest.org/feature /deceit-dread-and-disbelief-story-how-ukraine-lost-its-nuclear-arsenal-207076.

25. Budjeryn, *Inheriting the Bomb*.

26. Budjeryn, *Inheriting the Bomb*, 219.

27. Miriam O'Callaghan, "Clinton Regrets Persuading Ukraine to Give up Nuclear Weapons," RTE, April 4, 2023, www.rte.ie/news/primetime/2023/0404/1374162-clinton-ukraine/.

28. Aron, *Yeltsin*, 700.

29. Catherine Belton, *Putin's People: How the KGB Took Back Russia and Then Took on the West* (New York: Farrar, Straus and Giroux, 2020).

30. Steven Lee Myers, *The New Tsar: The Rise and Reign of Vladimir Putin* (New York: Simon & Schuster, 2015); "Putin Says He Discussed Russia's Possible NATO Membership with Bill Clinton," Radio Free Europe/Radio Liberty, June 3, 2017, www.rferl.org/a/russia -putin-says-discussed-joining-nato-with-clinton/28526757.html; Orlando Figes, *The Story of Russia* (London: Bloomsbury, 2022), 286.

31. Mary Elise Sarotte, "A Broken Promise: What the West Really Told Moscow about NATO Expansion," *Foreign Affairs* 93, no. 5 (2014): 90–97.

32. Andrew Wilson, *Ukraine's Orange Revolution* (New Haven, CT: Yale University Press, 2005), 89–91, 94; Myers, *The New Tsar*, 267–273.

33. Wilson, *Ukraine's Orange Revolution*, 1–2, 125.

34. Simon Shuster, *The Showman: The Inside Story of the Invasion That Shook the World and Made a Leader of Volodymyr Zelensky* (London: William Collins, 2024), 52.

35. Mikhail Iur'ev, *The Third Empire: The Russia that Ought to Be* (Moscow: Limbus Press, 2006), chap. 1; Sergei Medvedev, *A War Made in Russia* (Cambridge: Polity, 2023), 11–12.

36. Evgeny Finkel, "In Search of Lost Genocide: Historical Policy and International Politics in Post-1989 Eastern Europe," *Global Society* 24, no. 1 (2010): 51–70.

37. Finkel, "In Search of Lost Genocide," 64–67.

38. Matthews, *Overreach*, 82.

Chapter 8: Ukrainian Winter, Russian Spring

1. Elena Racheva, "Poezd N. 336. 52 chasa s dobrovol'tsami, kotorye edut s voiny," *Novaya Gazeta*, April 28, 2015; interview with Elena Racheva, July 20, 2023.

2. Mychailo Wynnyckyj, *Ukraine's Maidan, Russia's War* (Stuttgart, Germany: Ibidem, 2019), 54.

3. Marci Shore, *The Ukrainian Night: An Intimate History of Revolution* (New Haven, CT: Yale University Press, 2018), 42; Wynnyckyj, *Ukraine's Maidan*, 69.

4. Serhiy Kudelia, "When Numbers Are Not Enough: The Strategic Use of Violence in Ukraine's 2014 Revolution," *Comparative Politics* 50, no. 4 (2018): 501–521.

5. Mikhail Zygar, *War and Punishment: The Story of Russian Oppression and Ukrainian Resistance* (London: Weidenfeld & Nicolson, 2023).

6. John Mearsheimer, "Why the Ukraine Crisis Is the West's Fault: The Liberal Delusions that Provoked Putin," *Foreign Affairs* 93 (September–October 2014): 1–12; Il'ya Zhegulev, "Kak Putin Voznenavidel Ukrainu," *Verstka*, April 25, 2023, https://verstka.media/kak-putin-pridumal-voynu.

7. Dmitry Adamsky, *Russian Nuclear Orthodoxy: Religion, Politics, and Strategy* (Stanford, CA: Stanford University Press, 2020), 184–186; Matthews, *Overreach*, 97; Zygar, *War and Punishment*, 294; Eleanor Knott, "Ethnonationalism or a Financial-Criminal Incentive Structure? Explaining Russia's Annexation of Crimea" (London School of Economics, 2023).

8. Shaun Walker, *The Long Hangover: Putin's New Russia and the Ghosts of the Past* (New York: Oxford University Press, 2018), 144–146.

9. Wynnyckyj, *Ukraine's Maidan*, 150; Noam Lupu and Leonid Peisakhin, "The Legacy of Political Violence Across Generations," *American Journal of Political Science* 61, no. 4 (2017): 836–851.

10. Eleanor Knott, *Kin Majorities: Identity and Citizenship in Crimea and Moldova* (Montreal: McGill-Queen's Press, 2022); Samuel Greene and Graeme Robertson, *Putin v. the People* (London: Yale University Press, 2019); Adamsky, *Russian Nuclear Orthodoxy*, 186.

11. Mark Galeotti, "Hybrid, Ambiguous, and Non-Linear? How New Is Russia's 'New Way of War'?," *Small Wars & Insurgencies* 27, no. 2 (2016): 282–301.

12. Jan Matti Dollbaum, Morvan Lallouet, and Ben Noble, *Navalny: Putin's Nemesis, Russia's Future?* (Oxford: Oxford University Press, 2021), 97; Ilya Yablokov, *Fortress Russia: Conspiracy Theories in the Post-Soviet World* (Cambridge: Polity, 2018), 163.

13. Jade McGlynn, *Memory Makers: The Politics of the Past in Putin's Russia* (London: Bloomsbury, 2023), 89.

14. Arkady Ostrovsky, *The Invention of Russia* (New York: Penguin Books, 2017), 317–318.

15. Anna Arutunyan, *Hybrid Warriors: Proxies, Freelancers and Moscow's Struggle for Ukraine* (London: Hurst Publishers, 2022), chaps. 5–6.

16. Dugin, *Ukraina*, 1–16, 34–38, 233, 237, 251; Kholmogorov, *Karat' Karatelei*.

17. McGlynn, *Memory Makers*, 77.

18. Iryna Voichuk and Alya Shandra, "Victims of 'Donbas Genocide' Were Paid Actors, Prigozhin's Fired Trolls Reveal," *Euromaidan Press*, July 14, 2023, https://euromaidanpress.com/2023/07/14/victims-of-donbas-genocide-were-paid-actors-prigozhins-fired-trolls-reveal/; Eliot Borenstein, *Plots Against Russia: Conspiracy and Fantasy After Socialism* (Ithaca, NY: Cornell University Press, 2019), 232–234.

19. Marat Gabidullin, *V Odnu Reku Dvazhdy* (Yekaterinburg, Russia: Gonzo, 2022).

20. Fishel, *The Moscow Factor*, 176, 187.

21. Stanislav Aseyev, *Svitlyi Shliakh: Istoriia Odnoho Kontstaboru* (Lviv: Vydavnytstvo Staroho Leva, 2020).

22. Matthews, *Overreach*, 183; Sonia Savina, "Pochemu Pri Putine Sokraschaetsia Ukrainskoe Naselenie," *Vazhnye Istorii*, January 23, 2023, https://istories.media/stories /2023/01/24/pochemu-pri-putine-sokrashchaetsya-ukrainskoe-naselenie/.

23. Onuch and Hale, *The Zelensky Effect*.

24. Interview with Ivan Fedorov, October 6, 2022; Popova and Shevel, *Russia and Ukraine*, chap. 6.

25. Volodymyr Kulyk, "National Identity in Ukraine: Impact of Euromaidan and the War," *Europe-Asia Studies* 68, no. 4 (2016): 588–608; Volodymyr Kulyk, "Shedding Russian-ness, Recasting Ukrainianness: The Post-Euromaidan Dynamics of Ethnonational Identifi-cations in Ukraine," *Post-Soviet Affairs* 34, no. 2–3 (2018): 119–138.

26. The anthropologist Jeremy Morris originally introduced the concept of defensive consolidation in the Russian context. See Jeremy Morris, "Russians in Wartime and Defen-sive Consolidation," *Current History* 121, no. 837 (2022): 258–263.

27. Popova and Shevel, *Russia and Ukraine*, 180–185.

28. Valentyna Romanova, *Ukraine's Resilience to Russia's Military Invasion in the Context of the Decentralisation Reform* (Warsaw: Stefan Batory Foundation, 2022), www .batory.org.pl/wp-content/uploads/2022/05/Ukraines-resilience-to-Russias-military -invasion.pdf; Tymofii Brik and Jennifer Brick Murtazashvili, "The Source of Ukraine's Resilience," *Foreign Affairs*, June 28, 2022, www.foreignaffairs.com/articles/ukraine/2022 -06-28/source-ukraines-resilience.

29. Onuch and Hale, *The Zelensky Effect*, 2023, 223.

Chapter 9: To Kill Ukraine

1. Zhegulev, "Kak Putin Voznenavidel Ukrainu."

2. Matthews, *Overreach*, 118.

3. Christopher Miller, Max Seddon, and Felicia Schwartz, "How Putin Blundered into Ukraine—Then Doubled Down," *Financial Times*, February 23, 2023, www.ft.com /content/80002564-33e8-48fb-b734-44810afb7a49.

4. Matthews, *Overreach*, 177–182.

5. United States of America v. Sergey Vladimirovich Cherkasov, A/K/A "Victor Muller Ferreira," March 24, 2023, www.justice.gov/usao-dc/press-release/file/1576151/download.

6. Shane Harris et al., "Road to War: U.S. Struggled to Convince Allies, and Zelen-sky, of Risk of Invasion," *Washington Post*, August 16, 2022, www.washingtonpost.com /national-security/interactive/2022/ukraine-road-to-war/.

7. Harris et al., "Road to War"; Sergei Goriashko, Elizaveta Fokht, and Sofia Samokh-ina, "My Russkie Diplomaty i My Ne Mozhem Oshibat'sia," BBC News Russian Service, August 3, 2023, www.bbc.com/russian/articles/cxrxlwr2q4ro.

8. Onuch and Hale, *The Zelensky Effect*, 8–9.

9. Samuel Charap and Scott Boston, "The West's Weapons Won't Make Any Differ-ence to Ukraine," *Foreign Policy*, January 21, 2022, https://foreignpolicy.com/2022/01/21

/weapons-ukraine-russia-invasion-military/; Jacqui Heinrich and Adam Sabes, "Gen. Milley Says Kyiv Could Fall Within 72 Hours if Russia Decides to Invade Ukraine," Fox News, February 5, 2022, www.foxnews.com/us/gen-milley-says-kyiv-could-fall-within-72-hours-if-russia-decides-to-invade-ukraine-sources.

10. Lorenzo Tondo and Alessio Mamo, "'Some Never Came Back': How Russians Hunted Down Veterans of Donbas Conflict," The Guardian, July 2, 2023, www.the guardian.com/world/2023/jul/02/russians-hunted-down-veterans-of-donbas-conflict -ukraine; Erika Kinetz, "'We Will Find You:' Russians Hunt Down Ukrainians on Lists," AP News, December 21, 2022, https://apnews.com/article/russia-ukraine-europe-3ae1bccfb 0ef34dbe363f7c289ce7934.

11. Finkel, "What's Happening in Ukraine Is Genocide."

12. Alexey Kovalev, "Russia's Ukraine Propaganda Has Turned Fully Genocidal," Foreign Policy, April 9, 2022, https://foreignpolicy.com/2022/04/09/russia-putin-propa ganda-ukraine-war-crimes-atrocities/.

13. "Telekanal RT Ostanovil Sotrudnichestvo s Antonom Krasovskim Iz-za Ego Prizyva 'Topit' Detei v Ukraine," Meduza, October 24, 2022, https://meduza.io/news/2022/10/24 /telekanal-rt-ostanovil-sotrudnichestvo-s-antonom-krasovskim-iz-za-ego-prizyva-topit -ukrainskih-detey-on-otvetil-byvaet-tak-sidish-v-efire-tebya-neset.

14. Liliya Yapparova, "Ni Shagu Nazad, Tovarishchi," Meduza, April 3, 2023, https:// meduza.io/feature/2023/04/03/ni-shagu-nazad-tovarischi.

15. Andrey Pertsev, "'Everything He Does Is Meant to Avoid Suspicion' What the Hell Happened to Dmitry Medvedev?," Meduza, June 28, 2023, https://meduza.io/en /feature/2023/06/28/everything-he-does-is-eant-to-avoid-suspicion; Shaun Walker, "'I Hate Them': Dmitry Medvedev's Journey from Liberal to Anti-Western Hawk," The Guardian, August 1, 2022, www.theguardian.com/world/2022/aug/01/dmitry-medvedev-journey-libe ral-anti-west-hawk-russia.

16. Maria Tsymlianskaia, "Pop menia vyslushal i priamikom v FSB," Mediazona, November 12, 2022, https://zona.media/article/2022/11/11/priest; Timofei Pnin, "Dones na svoiu doch," Mediazona, April 14, 2022, https://zona.media/article/2022/04/14/dsd.

17. Ian Garner, Z Generation: Into the Heart of Russia's Fascist Youth (London: Hurst Publishers, 2023).

18. Jade McGlynn, Russia's War (Cambridge: Polity, 2023).

19. Anna Ryzhkova, "Doch' pered snom molitsia: Gospodi, dai pape klassnyi granato- met," Verstka, May 17, 2023, https://verstka.media/kak-rossiyskie-zhenshiny-obyasniayut -sebe-kuda-zabrali-ih-mobilizovannyh-muzhey-i-kak-zhdut-muzchin-s-voyny.

20. "Putin Zaiavil Chto v Gody Severnoi Voiny Petr I Nichego Ne Ottorgal," TASS, June 9, 2022, https://tass.ru/obschestvo/14870521.

21. Sophia Maksimova, "'I Don't Know What to Do': Taken to the Russian Far East, Refugees from Mariupol Were Promised Housing and Jobs. They Have Yet to Receive Either," Meduza, May 19, 2022, https://meduza.io/en/feature/2022/05/19/i-don-t-know-what-to-do; Dean Kirby, "Mariupol Survivors Sent to Remote Parts of Russia as Investigation Reveals Network of 66 Camps," inews.co.uk, May 7, 2022, https://inews.co.uk/news/putin-mariu pol-survivors-remote-corners-russia-investigation-network-camps-1615516.

22. OHCHR, "Detentions of Civilians in the Context of the Armed Attack by the Russian Federation Against Ukraine, 24 February 2022–23 May 2023," United Nations, June 27, 2023, p. 12, www.ohchr.org/en/statements-and-speeches/2023/06/detentions -civilians-context-armed-attack-russian-federation; "Chamber Used by Russians to Torture Children Found in Kherson," *Kyiv Post*, December 15, 2022, www.kyivpost.com/post /5787; Regina Gimalova, "Grazhdanskie Zalozhniki—Kharakternaia Cherta Voiny Rossii v Ukraine," *Verstka*, February 23, 2023, https://verstka.media/grazhdanskie-zalozhniki -cherta-voiny-rossii-v-ukraine.

23. Liliya Yapparova, "'I Prayed I Wouldn't Be Next': The Secretive Prisons Where Russia Hides and Tortures Ukrainian Civilians," *Meduza*, May 26, 2023, https://meduza.io/en /feature/2023/05/26/they-tortured-people-right-in-their-cells; UN, "Report of the Independent International Commission of Inquiry on Ukraine," October 18, 2022, p. 14, www.ohchr .org/sites/default/files/2022-10/A-77-533-AUV-EN.pdf.

24. Ekaterina Fomina, "Komandir Dal Prikaz: 'V Raskhod Ikh,'" *Vazhnye Istorii*, August 15, 2022, https://istories.media/investigations/2022/08/15/komandir-dal-prikaz-v -raskhod-ikh/; OHCHR, "Detentions of Civilians," 14–15.

25. Olga Tokariuk, "We Have Been Invaded by Fascists," *New Lines Magazine*, May 25, 2022, https://newlinesmag.com/reportage/we-have-been-invaded-by-fascists/; Daria Shulzhenko, "'Torturing People Is Fun for Them.' 16-Year-Old Ukrainian Recalls His 3 Months in Russian Captivity," *Kyiv Independent*, August 5, 2022, https://kyivindependent.com/torturing -people-is-fun-for-them-16-year-old-ukrainian-recalls-his-3-months-in-russian-captivity/.

26. OHCHR, "Detentions of Civilians."

27. Tim Lister, "Ukrainian Cultural Landmarks Suffer Fresh Blows as Another Museum Is Hit," CNN, May 9, 2022, www.cnn.com/style/article/ukraine-culture-destroyed-skovoroda -museum/index.html.

28. Volodymyr Biriukov, "A Blow to History: Ukrainian Literary Works Destroyed in Recent Incidents," *Katapult Ukraine*, February 17, 2023, https://katapult-ukraine.com /artikel/a-blow-to-history-ukrainian-literary-works-destroyed-in-recent-incidents; "Rosiia znyishchyla shchonaimenshe 598 bibliotek v Ukraini," Chytomo.com, July 4, 2023, https:// chytomo.com/rosiia-znyshchyla-prynajmni-598-bibliotek-v-ukraini/; Carol Schaeffer, "A Book Is a Quiet Weapon," *New York Review of Books*, April 21, 2023, www.nybooks.com /online/2023/04/21/derussification-ukraine-libraries/; Richard Ovenden, "Putin's War on Ukrainian Memory," *The Atlantic*, April 23, 2023, www.theatlantic.com/ideas/archive /2023/04/russia-war-ukraine-occupation-libraries-archives/673813/.

29. Jeffrey Gettleman and Oleksandra Mykolyshyn, "As Russians Steal Ukraine's Art, They Attack Its Identity, Too," *New York Times*, January 14, 2023, www.nytimes .com/2023/01/14/world/asia/ukraine-art-russia-steal.html; Tessa Solomon, "Russian Forces Looted More than 2,000 Artworks from Mariupol's Museums, City Council Says," *ARTnews*, May 2, 2022, www.artnews.com/art-news/news/mariupol-museums-russian-looted -artworks-city-council-1234627187/; Yasmine Salam and Dan De Luce, "Russians Are Stealing Art from Ukraine on World War II Scale, Experts Say," NBC News, April 6, 2023, www.nbcnews.com/news/world/russia-stealing-art-ukraine-nazi-level-world-war-2 -rcna77879; Eric Reguly, "Ukrainians Fear Erasure of Their Culture as Russian Bombs

Destroy Heritage Sites," *Globe and Mail*, February 8, 2023, www.theglobeandmail.com
/world/article-as-russian-bombs-destroy-heritage-sites-ukrainians-fear-a-war-against/.

30. Lori Hinnant et al., "Russia Scrubs Mariupol's Ukraine Identity, Builds on Death,"
AP News, December 23, 2022, https://apnews.com/article/russia-ukraine-war-erasing
-mariupol-499dceae43ed77f2ebfe750ea99b9ad9; Vita Chiknaeva, "'Voina zhe ne budet
idti vechno', Kto i zachem pokupaet nedvizhimost' v okkupirovannom Mariupole," *Bum-
aga*, June 28, 2023, https://paperpaper.io/vojna-zhe-ne-budet-idti-vechno-kto-i-za/; Elina
Beketova, "Behind the Lines: Russia's Ethnic Cleansing," Center for European Policy Analysis, July 27, 2023, https://cepa.org/article/behind-the-lines-russias-ethnic-cleansing/;
Robyn Dixon, "Russia Sending Teachers to Ukraine to Control What Students Learn,"
Washington Post, July 18, 2022, www.washingtonpost.com/world/2022/07/18/russia-teach
ers-ukraine-rewrite-history/.

31. "V Melitopole Poiavilis' Ulitsy Dar'i Duginoi i Aleksandra Zakharchenko," RBC.
Ru, April 12, 2023, www.rbc.ru/rbcfreenews/6436f2129a7947259bc8cbbb.

32. Alexander Khrebet, "Ukrainians Under Occupation Face Deportation, Loss of Property After Putin's New Order," *Kyiv Independent*, July 3, 2023, https://kyivindependent.com
/ukrainians-under-occupation-face-deportation-loss-of-property-after-putins-new-order/.

33. Elizaveta Nesterova, "Mentions of Kyiv and Ukraine Removed from Russian Schoolbooks:
'We Have a Task to Make It Look as if Ukraine Simply Does Not Exist,'" *Mediazona*, April 23, 2022,
https://en.zona.media/article/2022/04/23/kyiv_erased; "Publisher Scrubs Mentions of Kyiv from
Kyivan Rus Section of History Textbooks," *Meduza*, April 19, 2023, https://meduza.io/en/news
/2023/04/19/publisher-scrubs-mentions-of-kyiv-from-kyivan-rus-section-of-history
-textbooks; Savina, "Pochemu Pri Putine Sokrashchaetsia Ukrainskoe Naselenie."

34. Yulia Ioffe, "Forcibly Transferring Ukrainian Children to the Russian Federation: A
Genocide?," *Journal of Genocide Research* 25, no. 3-4 (2023).

35. Ioffe, "Forcibly Transferring Ukrainian Children"; Samantha Schmidt and Serhii
Korolchuk, "Near Kherson, Orphanage Staff Hid Ukrainian Children from Russian Occupiers," *Washington Post*, November 20, 2022, www.washingtonpost.com/world/2022/11/20
/kherson-orphans-hidden-mykolaiv-ukraine/.

36. Anna Ryzhkova, "Bol'no smotret' na detei," *Verstka*, August 4, 2022, https://verstka
.media/babushki-ishut-vnuchku-propala-bez-vesti-mariupol; Iryna Lopatina, "'Dad, You
Have to Come—Or We Will Be Adopted!': One Ukrainian Family's Harrowing Wartime
Saga," *Vanity Fair*, October 6, 2022, www.vanityfair.com/news/2022/10/one-ukrainian
-familys-harrowing-wartime-saga; Veronika Melkozerova, "Behind Enemy Lines: Inside
the Operation to Rescue Ukraine's Abducted Children," *Politico*, June 10, 2023, www.poli
tico.eu/article/save-ukraine-children-abduction-russia-war-rescue-operation/.

37. Ioffe, "Forcibly Transferring Ukrainian Children"; "Bili zheleznoi palkoi, derzhali v
podvale. Ukrainskie deti rasskazali kak ikh uderzhivali v rossiiskikh lageriakh," *The Insider*,
March 23, 2023, https://theins.ru/news/260402 .

Chapter 10: Russian Roulette

1. Kate Tsurkan, "How a Celebrated Ukrainian Writer Turned into a War Crimes
Researcher," *Kyiv Independent*, April 27, 2023, https://kyivindependent.com/how-a-celebrated

-ukrainian-writer-turned-into-a-war-crimes-researcher/; Victoria Amelina, "Sirens," trans. Anatoly Kudryavitsky, in *Invasion: Ukrainian Poems About the War* (Dublin: SurVision Books, 2022), www.verseville.org/poems-by-victoria-amelina.html.

2. Anastasiia Chumakova, Damir Nigmatullin, and Liliya Yapparova, "'I Can Do Whatever I Want to You' Russian Soldiers Raped and Murdered Ukrainian Civilians in the Village of Bohdanivka," *Meduza*, July 4, 2023, https://meduza.io/en/feature /2022/04/18/i-can-do-whatever-i-want-to-you.

3. Chumakova, Nigmatullin, and Yapparova, "I Can Do Whatever I Want to You"; Jake Epstein, "Russia's Planting Mines Everywhere, Even Cruelly Hiding Explosives in Everyday Items Like Fridges, Toys, and Children's Books, Ukrainian Military Engineers Say," *Business Insider*, August 5, 2023, www.businessinsider.com/russias-mining-everywhere-ukraine -explosives-fridges-toys-books-military-engineers-2023-8.

4. Erika Kinetz, Oleksandr Stashevskyi, and Vasilisa Stepanenko, "How Russian Soldiers Ran a 'Cleansing' Operation in Bucha," AP News, November 3, 2022, https://apnews.com /article/bucha-ukraine-war-cleansing-investigation-43e5a9538e9ba68a035756b05028b8b4.

5. Daniel Boffey, "'A War Crime': Two Young Boys Among Ukrainians Shot Dead During Attempted Evacuation," *The Guardian*, April 3, 2022, www.theguardian.com/world /2022/apr/02/i-realised-my-husband-was-dead-ukrainians-tell-of-russian-army-atrocities; Anna Myroniuk, "Russian Soldiers Murder Volunteers Helping Starving Animals Near Kyiv," *Kyiv Independent*, March 8, 2022, https://kyivindependent.com/russian-soldiers-murder -volunteers-helping-starving-animals-near-kyiv/; Fergal Keane, "The Sole Survivor of a Russian Shooting—He Lived by Playing Dead," BBC News, July 5, 2022, www.bbc.com/news /world-europe-62011689.

6. Remy Ourdan, "War in Ukraine: In Bucha, the Sheer Hell of Ivana-Franka Street," *Le Monde*, April 10, 2022, www.lemonde.fr/en/international/article/2022/04/10/war-in -ukraine-in-bucha-the-sheer-hell-of-ivana-franka-street_5980141_4.html; Max Bearak and Louisa Loveluck, "In Bucha, the Scope of Russian Barbarity Is Coming into Focus," *Washington Post*, April 7, 2022, www.washingtonpost.com/world/2022/04/06/bucha-barbarism -atrocities-russian-soldiers/; Carlotta Gall and Oleksandr Chubko, "In Bucha, a Final Rampage Served as a Coda to a Month of Atrocities," *New York Times*, January 1, 2023, www .nytimes.com/2022/12/31/world/europe/bucha-ukraine-killings.html; Katie Balevic, "More than a Year after Ukraine Reclaimed Control of a Kyiv Suburb, Its Residents Are Still Identifying Bodies," *Business Insider*, July 9, 2023, www.businessinsider.com/residents-still -identifying-bodies-kyiv-suburb-bucha-year-later-russia-2023-7; Ivana Kottasová, Fred Pleigen, and Claudia Otto, "'There Are Maniacs Who Enjoy Killing,' Russian Defector Says of His Former Unit Accused of War Crimes in Bucha," CNN, December 14, 2022, www.cnn .com/2022/12/13/europe/russian-defector-war-crimes-intl-cmd/index.html.

7. "Russia Sentences Soldier Who Admitted to War Crimes in Ukraine," *Moscow Times*, March 16, 2023, www.themoscowtimes.com/2023/03/16/russia-sentences-soldier -who-admitted-to-war-crimes-in-ukraine-a80494.

8. Svitlana Oslavska, "Inside the Basement Where a Ukrainian Village Spent a Month in Captivity," *Time*, February 15, 2023, https://time.com/6255183/ukraine-basement-yahidne -held-captive/.

9. Chumakova, Nigmatullin, and Yapparova, "I Can Do Whatever I Want to You"; Siobhán O'Grady, Anastacia Galouchka, and Whitney Shefte, "In Russian-Occupied Izyum, She Was Raped and Tortured," *Washington Post*, October 9, 2022, www.washingtonpost.com/world/2022/10/09/izyum-rape-torture-occupation-russia/; UN, "Report of the Independent International Commission of Inquiry on Ukraine," 14–15.

10. UN, "Report of the Independent International Commission of Inquiry on Ukraine," 14–15.

11. Christina Lamb, "She Thought She Was Unshockable, Then Two Castrated Ukrainian Soldiers Arrived," *The Times*, June 17, 2023, www.thetimes.co.uk/article/ukraine-soldiers-castrated-russia-war-0hflzhzlv.

12. "Russian Officer Who Brandished Alleged Ukrainian Skull Dies of Gunshot Wound," Radio Free Europe/Radio Liberty, February 8, 2023, www.rferl.org/a/russia-officer-skull-dead-gunshot-wound-mangushev/32261774.html; Aleksei Sochnev, "On mechtal uvidet' goriashchii Kiev," *RTVI*, March 21, 2023, https://rtvi.com/stories/on-mechtal-uvidet-goryashhij-kiev-vdova-kapitana-igorya-mangusheva-o-ego-zagadochnoj-smerti-bezde jstvii-sledovatelej-i-cherepe-s-azovstali/; interview with Racheva.

13. Mari Saito, "Love Letter, ID Card Point to Russian Units that Terrorised Bucha," Reuters, May 5, 2022, www.reuters.com/investigates/special-report-ukraine-crisis-bucha\-killings-soldiers/.

14. Christopher Browning, *Ordinary Men: Reserve Police Battalion 101 and the Final Solution in Poland* (New York: Harper Perennial, 1993); Scott Straus, *The Order of Genocide: Race, Power, and War in Rwanda* (Ithaca, NY: Cornell University Press, 2006); Daniel Goldhagen, *Hitler's Willing Executioners: Ordinary Germans and the Holocaust* (New York: Knopf, 1996).

15. Scott Straus, "Retreating from the Brink: Theorizing Mass Violence and the Dynamics of Restraint," *Perspectives on Politics* 10, no. 2 (2012): 343–362.

16. Mark Krutov, "Net sil nastupat," Radio Free Europe/Radio Liberty, August 26, 2022, www.svoboda.org/a/tupo-net-sil-natupatj-intervjyu-s-byvshim-voennym-iz-64-y-bri gady/32006060.html.

17. Mark Galeotti, *Putin's Wars: From Chechnya to Ukraine* (London: Bloomsbury, 2022).

18. Pavel Filatyev, *ZOV* (2022), 77, https://gulagu-net.ru/download/2595; "Gulagu.net Rights Group Stops Helping Military Personnel Opposed to War Escape Russia," Radio Free Europe/Radio Liberty, March 29, 2023, www.rferl.org/a/russia-gulagu-stops-helping-soldiers/32340350.html.

19. Irina Dolinina, "Ty Voobshche Ponimaesh', Chto My Fashisty?," *Vazhnye Istorii*, August 18, 2022, https://istories.media/investigations/2022/08/18/ti-voobshche-ponimaesh-chto-mi-fashisti/.

20. Keane, "The Sole Survivor of a Russian Shooting."

21. Browning, *Ordinary Men*; Dara Kay Cohen, "Explaining Rape During Civil War: Cross-National Evidence (1980–2009)," *American Political Science Review* 107, no. 3 (2013): 461–477.

22. Medvedev, *A War Made in Russia*, 16.

23. Fomina, "Komandir Dal Prikaz."

24. "Lavrov Slams Situation in Bucha as Fake Attack Staged by West and Ukraine," TASS, July 12, 2023, https://tass.com/world/1432013; Yousur Al-Hlou et al., "Caught on Camera, Traced by Phone: The Russian Military Unit that Killed Dozens in Bucha," *New York Times*, December 22, 2022, www.nytimes.com/2022/12/22/video/russia-ukraine-bucha -massacre-takeaways.html.

25. Justin Magula, "Exploring Factors and Implications of Violence Against Civilians: A Case Study of the Soviet-Afghan War," *Small Wars & Insurgencies* (2023): 1–26.

26. Ilmari Käihkö, "A Nation-in-the-Making, in Arms: Control of Force, Strategy and the Ukrainian Volunteer Battalions," *Defence Studies* 18, no. 2 (2018): 147–166; Vladislav David-zon, "Azov Battalion—The Defenders of Mariupol," *Tablet*, May 18, 2022, www.tabletmag .com/sections/news/articles/defenders-of-mariupol-azov.

27. Yaroslav Trofimov, *Our Enemies Will Vanish: The Russian Invasion and Ukraine's War of Independence* (New York: Penguin Press, 2024), 83.

28. Yevhen Sosnovsky, "'Ia vyshel vo dvor i uvidel, chto vse doma vokrug sozhzheny'. Istoriia fotografa iz Mariupolia." *Novaya Pol'sha*, May 25, 2022, https://novayapolsha.pl /article/ya-vyshel-vo-dvor-i-uvidel-chto-vse-doma-vokrug-sozhzheny-istoriya-fotografa/.

29. OHCHR, "High Commissioner Updates the Human Rights Council on Mariupol, Ukraine," United Nations, June 16, 2022, www.ohchr.org/en/statements/2022/06/high -commissioner-updates-human-rights-council-mariupol-ukraine; Isobel Koshiw, "Make-shift Graves and Notes on Doors: The Struggle to Find and Bury Mariupol's Dead," *The Guardian*, June 1, 2022, www.theguardian.com/world/2022/jun/01/makeshift-graves-and -notes-on-doors-the-struggle-to-find-and-bury-mariupol-dead-ukraine.

30. Sosnovsky, "'Ia vyshel vo dvor i uvidel, chto vse doma vokrug sozhzheny.'"

31. Sosnovsky, "Ia vyshel vo dvor i uvidel, chto vse doma vokrug sozhzheny."

32. Paul Kirby, "Russian Journalist Maria Ponomarenko Jailed for Highlighting Mariu-pol Killings," BBC News, February 15, 2023, www.bbc.com/news/world-europe-64647267; Lori Hinnant, Vasilisa Stepanenko, and Mstyslav Chernov, "AP Evidence Points to 600 Dead in Mariupol Theater Airstrike," AP News, May 4, 2022, https://apnews.com/article /Russia-ukraine-war-mariupol-theater-c321a196fbd568899841b506afcac7a1.

33. Mick Krever et al., "Mariupol at Risk of Cholera Outbreak as Russia Struggles to Provide Basic Services, Says UK Intelligence," CNN, June 10, 2022, www.cnn.com/2022/06 /10/europe/ukraine-mariupol-potential-cholera-outbreak-intl/index.html; Lexi Lonas, "Don-estk Official: Russia Using Mobile Crematoriums to Dispose of Bodies," *The Hill*, April 12, 2022, https://thehill.com/policy/international/3264666-donestk-official-russia-using-mo bile-crematoriums-to-dispose-of-bodies/.

34. Jason Lyall, "Does Indiscriminate Violence Incite Insurgent Attacks?," *Journal of Conflict Resolution* 53, no. 3 (2009): 331–362.

35. Galeotti, *Putin's Wars*, 95–96, 98; Serhii Plokhy, *The Russo-Ukrainian War* (London: Allen Lane, 2023), 55; Ostap Golubev, Vladimir Malykhin, and Alexander Cherkasov, *A Chain of Wars, a Chain of Crimes, a Chain of Impunity: Russian Wars in Chechnya, Syria and Ukraine* (Moscow: Memorial Human Rights Defence Centre, 2023), 17, https://ruswars .org/report/Report_Memorial.pdf.

Conclusion

1. Tobias Gerhard Schminke, "Ukraine: 92% Want EU Membership by 2030," *Euractiv*, March 3, 2023, www.euractiv.com/section/politics/news/ukraine-92-want-eu-membership -by-2030/; Rating Group, "National Survey of Ukraine (IRI): February 2023," Center for Insights in Survey Research, https://ratinggroup.ua/files/ratinggroup/reg_files/ukr-23-ns -01-ukr_for_public_-_final.pdf.

2. Shelef, *Homelands*, 1.

3. See, for example, Mearsheimer, "Why the Ukraine Crisis Is the West's Fault."

4. Sam Sokol, "Zelenskyy Says Post-War Ukraine Will Emulate Israel, Won't Be 'Liberal, European,'" *Haaretz*, April 5, 2022, www.haaretz.com/world-news/europe/2022-04-05 /ty-article/.highlight/zelenskyy-says-post-war-ukraine-will-emulate-israel-wont-be-liberal -european/00000180-5bc4-d718-afd9-dffcdfdd0000.

5. Martin Kragh, Erik Andermo, and Liliia Makashova, "Conspiracy Theories in Russian Security Thinking," *Journal of Strategic Studies* 45, no. 3 (2022): 334–368.

6. Diana Dumitru and Carter Johnson, "Constructing Interethnic Conflict and Cooperation: Why Some People Harmed Jews and Others Helped Them During the Holocaust in Romania," *World Politics* 63, no. 01 (2011): 1–42.

7. Eugene Finkel, "What the World Learned About Ukraine in a Year of War," *Los Angeles Times*, February 24, 2023, www.latimes.com/opinion/story/2023-02-24/ukraine -war-russia-putin-invasion-one-year-anniversary-history. I thank Luís de Matos Ribeiro for the data on states who have recognized the Holodomor as genocide.

8. Rachel Yehuda and Amy Lehrner, "Intergenerational Transmission of Trauma Effects: Putative Role of Epigenetic Mechanisms," *World Psychiatry* 17, no. 3 (2018): 243–257.

Index

adoption: forced adoption of Ukrainian
  children, 231–233
Afghanistan, war in, 251
agriculture
  history of Kyivan Rus', 20–21
  Soviet collectivization, 105–106, 114–117,
    123–125
  See also Holodomor
aid, international: war in the Donbas, 203
air strikes, 219, 238, 251, 253–254
Aivazovsky, Ivan, 229
Aksenov, Sergey, 193–194
Alexander II (tsar), 30, 41, 44
Alexei (17th-cent tsar), 24–25
Allison, Graham, 172
Alsace-Lorraine, 54–55
Amelina, Victoria, 235–236, 255
American Relief Administration (ARA), 110
Andropov, Yurii, 150
An-sky, S., 65–66, 70, 73
anti-Semitism
  Beilis murder trial, 48–49, 90
  Bolsheviks, 103
  the effect of education on, 267–268
  Jewish blood libels, 47–48
  Russia's anti-Ukrainian rhetoric in
    2023, 222
  See also Jewish communities and individuals;
    pogroms
armed forces (Russian and Soviet)
  bombardment from a distance, 251–252
  Food Supply Army, 109

lack of mental preparation for the war,
    243–246
lack of military discipline, 249–250
massacres in occupied areas, 242–249
Novorossiya fighters, 201–202
rape and murder by Russian troops, 220,
    238–247, 249–251
technological superiority, 217–218
Wall Evidence graffiti project, 247
See also mass murder; plunder and looting;
    Red Army
armed forces (Ukraine), 85–86, 95–96, 98, 200,
    206, 217–218
assassinations, 79–80, 119, 139, 143
Association Agreement (Ukraine and EU),
    185–186, 188
Austro-Hungarian Empire
  alliances and goals of World War I, 55
  collapse and territorial splintering, 95–96
  ethnic and political diversity, 56–60
  partition of Poland, 27–28
  Russian military victory, 61–62
  Russia's Great War objectives, 60–61
  Ukrainophiles migrating to, 42
  See also Galicia; World War I
authoritarianism, 137–138, 143, 170, 175,
    185, 266–267
autocracy
  Putin's relations with the West, 177
  Ukraine challenging the monarchy, 44–45
  Ukraine threatening Russia's, 3–4, 10–11, 162,
    179–181, 185–186

Index

Index

Index

Index

Index